Otto I (the Great) (r.936-973) crowned emperor by the pope (962)
Conversion of Russia to Orthodox church (c.990)

Vikings attempt settlement in Newfoundland (c.986-1025)
Norman invasion of England (1066)
Crusaders capture Jerusalem (1099)

Rise of universities based on law, medicine, theology
Earliest manufacture of paper in Europe by Muslims in Spain
Earliest use of magnetic compass for navigation
Muslims recapture Jerusalem (1187)

Crusaders sack Constantinople (1204)
Latin Empire in Constantinople (1204-1261)
Magna Carta limits power of English kings (1215)
Crusaders recapture Jerusalem (1228)
Mongols conquer China (1234-1279)
Muslims recapture Jerusalem (1244)
Mongols invade Middle East (1256)
Mongols capture Baghdad (1258)
Dante Alighieri (1265-1321)
Marco Polo travels to China and to India (c.1275-1293)
Christian-Mongol army defeated by Muslims (1281)
Muslims capture last crusader castle (1291)

Black Death (bubonic plague) (1347-1351)
Ming dynasty founded, China (1368)
First large-scale production of gunpowder
"Canterbury Tales" by Geoffrey Chaucer (c.1387)

Tamerlane's Mongols sack Baghdad (1401)
Gutenberg Bible printed (1450-1456)
Muslims capture Constantinople; end of Byzantine Empire (1453)
Moscow becomes center of Orthodox church after 1453
Muslims expelled from Spain (1492)
Columbus's first voyage to West Indies (1492)

Balboa sights Pacific Ocean (1513)
"Utopia" by Thomas More (1516)
Martin Luther (1483-1546) posts theses (1517)
William Shakespeare (1564-1616)

A.D. 900   **A.D. 1000**   **A.D. 1100**   **A.D. 1200**   **A.D. 1300**   **A.D. 1400**   **A.D. 1500**

Crusades

Peter Abelard   Francis of Assisi   John Wycliffe

• *Canon Episcopi*

Eudo de Stella

• Leaders of Knights Templar executed

Thomas Müntzer

Michael Servetus

• Final schism between Roman Catholic and Eastern Orthodox churches

Joan of Arc

• *Malleus Maleficarum*

• Orléans heretics

• Knights Templar created

Jan Hus

Paterine heresy

• Alice Kyteler accused of witchcraft

Lollard movement

Berengar of Tours

Waldensian heresy

Giordano Bruno

Joachim of Floris

Tanchelm

Albigensian Crusade

Hussite Wars

Petrobrusian heresy

•*De Heretico Comburendo*

Amalric of Bene   • Inquisition established

Franciscan controversies

Tomás de Torquemada

David of Dinant

Marsilio Ficino

Arnold of Brescia

Witchcraft persecutions

• Dominican order founded

Bogomil heresy

Queens College
Friends of the Library
20th Anniversary Campaign

This book was given by:

John Slater

Encyclopedia
of Heresies and
Heretics

Encyclopedia
of Heresies and
Heretics

Chas S. Clifton

ABC-CLIO

Santa Barbara, California
Denver, Colorado
Oxford, England

Library of Congress Cataloging-in-Publication Data

Clifton, Chas.
    Encyclopedia of heresies and heretics / Chas S. Clifton.
    Includes bibliographical references and index.
    1. Heresies, Christian—Encyclopedias. I. Title.
  BT1315.2.C55 1992   273' . 03—dc20   92-29996

ISBN 0-87436-600-3 (alk. paper)

99 98 97 96 95 94 93 92   10 9 8 7 6 5 4 3 2 1

ABC-CLIO, Inc.
130 Cremona Drive, P.O. Box 1911
Santa Barbara, California 93116-1911

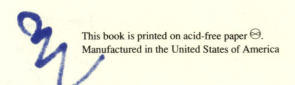

This book is printed on acid-free paper ⊖.
Manufactured in the United States of America

CONTENTS

ACKNOWLEDGMENTS

I am especially grateful to John Sheridan, head librarian at the Colorado College, for opening the college's collection to me. In addition, Bridget Viar of the Cañon City Public Library fielded several dozen interlibrary loan requests as I sought additional sourcebooks.

Heather Cameron, publisher of ABC-CLIO, and Tracey Butler, assistant editor in ABC-CLIO's acquisitions and development department, provided encouragement and put up with some inevitable delays.

Professor Joseph Pickle of the Colorado College religion department and Professor Fred Denny of the University of Colorado religion department provided research suggestions at the beginning of the project.

Michael McNierney, former acquisitions editor at ABC-CLIO, helped develop the project and offered constructive suggestions on entries dealing with Platonic philosophy in particular, an area in which he is far more expert than I.

Mary Currier, my wife, became accustomed to my preoccupations with Montanists and Albigensians as well as to stepping around piles of books in our little house.

Portions of some entries have appeared in articles written for *Gnosis: A Journal of the Western Inner Traditions;* I wish to thank its editors for their support during the preparation of this book.

ACKNOWLEDGMENT
OF SOURCES

Several books furnished most of the original material quoted in translation in this encyclopedia. For Gnostic material of the first and second centuries, I relied largely on Elaine Pagels's *The Gnostic Gospels* (New York: Random House, 1979). Other Gnostic texts quoted were published in *The Nag Hammadi Library in English,* edited by James M. Robinson (San Francisco: HarperCollins, 1990). Another valuable source, particularly for the writings of Epiphanius and the Montanist prophetesses, was *Maenads, Martyrs, Matrons, and Monastics: A Sourcebook of Women's Religions in the Greco-Roman World,* edited by Ross S. Kraemer (Philadelphia: Fortress Press, 1988). Other of Epiphanius's thoughts, such as those on Gnostic sex magic, came from the *The Panarion of St. Epiphanius, Bishop of Salamis,* translated and edited by Philip R. Amidon, S.J. (New York: Oxford University Press, 1990).

Most excerpts from such early churchmen as Tertullian, Irenaeus, and Origen are from *The Early Christian Fathers,* translated and edited by Henry Bettenson (London: Oxford University Press, 1956). Quotations from medieval chronicles and other documents were taken chiefly from the invaluable collection of Walter L. Wakefield and Austin P. Evans, *Heresies of the High Middle Ages* (New York: Columbia University Press, 1969), and, to a lesser extent, from the four-volume work edited by G. G. Coulton, *Life in the Middle Ages* (New York: Macmillan, 1931). Biblical quotations are from the New English Bible (London: Oxford University Press, Cambridge University Press, 1970).

A complete bibliography of works consulted is furnished at the back of this book. Bibliographic notes on individual entries, however, have been omitted in order to keep the text uncluttered and more accessible to the casual or nonspecialized reader. Consequently, many statements that would be footnoted in a more academic publication are not noted or are attributed blandly to "some scholars" or "it has been argued."

INTRODUCTION

To many modern readers, the word *heretic* has an almost noble sound. Influenced perhaps by the persecution of late medieval or Renaissance figures such as Giordano Bruno and Galileo, who suffered for teaching what now seem to be self-evident scientific truths, we tend to think of a heretic as someone who is merely ahead of his or her time. Writers today frequently employ the term that way: A *medical heretic,* for example, might be a doctor who questions his peers' assumptions, but only after his death is he recognized as having identified one of the profession's weaknesses or blind spots. Likewise, some students of religion have viewed heresy as creativity. A typical view was expressed by Robert Ingersoll (1833–1899): "Religion is like a palm tree; it grows at the top. The dead leaves are all orthodox while the new ones are all heretics."

Other explanations for the conflicts between religious orthodoxy and heresy abound. The persecution of participants in the mass heresies of the past—the Bogomils or Albigensian Cathars, for example—is frequently explained in terms of regional rivalries, class struggle, political greed, or lust for power. It is also easy to sympathize with those early female heretics—some of the medieval beguines, for instance, or the earlier Montanist prophetesses—who suffered largely because they assumed spiritual authority outside the male church hierarchies.

Other heretics—the first-century Gnostic Marcion and his followers, or the medieval Waldensians—are seen through modern eyes as reformers and enemies of a wealthy and complacent church. Marcion, for example, has been compared to Martin Luther in his theology. And, of course, there were the witchcraft

trials, for which a variety of explanations has been presented: suppression of a surviving Pagan religion, suppression of female peasant healers in favor of male urban medical professionals, mass delusions, hallucinogenic poisoning, or simply the realization that there was a lot of money to be made in denouncing, trying, and confiscating the property of so-called witches.

Since those times, at least some parts of the world have embraced the idea of freedom of religion and structured their societies to separate church and state. They realize that divergences in religious belief do not automatically threaten secular governments, since most modern governments do not share the imperial Roman concept that worship of the emperor corresponds with worship of a god. From our perspective, the slaughter of the Albigensians at the pope's order or the burning of so-called witches by German Protestants appears equally irrational and abhorrent. But when we look back at the period covered by this book—roughly the first through sixteenth centuries of the Christian era—we have to understand that heresies, heretics, and the religious or secular establishments' responses to them varied over time.

As a "confessional" religion, Christianity not only had to deal with varying interpretations of its core message, but it also had to develop statements or creeds that defined the "correct" interpretation. Only Christianity and Islam, among the world's major religions, have contended with heretics to such an extent, because they are particularly concerned with what their followers *believe* rather than with what they *do*.

In the period covered by this encyclopedia the core concerns of heretics changed on one level but remained the same on another.

At the beginning, all Christians were heretics as far as broad-minded Roman Paganism was concerned. That Paganism was summed up by one classical author who stated that all religions were equally true to the populace, equally false to the philosopher, and equally useful to the magistrate. Within their own ranks, Christians wrangled primarily with questions of who Jesus Christ was and what the essential parts of the gospel message were. But after the fourth and fifth centuries, when Christianity dominated the former Roman Empire, a heretic was often that person who criticized the established church (whether Eastern Orthodox or Western Catholic) on any grounds whatsoever, even if he or she proceeded from an earnest desire to see the church purified or returned to its true ideals. Arching over both types of heresy was the perennial challenge of dualism—a variety of viewpoints that saw the material world as the product of an evil creator who had to be bypassed (even when he came disguised as the Old Testament God) by anyone wishing to find true salvation.

Heresy, Persecution, and the Early Church

During the first three centuries of Christianity's existence, heresy—when it could be defined—could be combated only by moral authority, persuasion, and discourse. And every position later defined as heretical had been held at some time, somewhere, by persons who guilelessly considered themselves to be good Christians. (The orthodox fourth-century writer Epiphanius, bishop of Salamis, despaired: "Even now everyone calls all the sects—Manichaeans, Marcionists, Gnostics, and all the others—'Christians' indifferently, even though they are not Christians.") These Christians circulated gospels and other books attributed to the Twelve Apostles in addition to those now contained in the New Testament. They proposed varied interpretations of the nature of Jesus's incarnation, death, and saving message. They wrestled with issues such as how human sexual drives could best be channeled, whether women could hold positions of religious authority, and to what extent Old Testament law was binding. Indeed, to quote the historian Walter Bauer, "The multiplicity of competing statements of faith regarding the 'saving event' of Jesus Christ

and its theological explanation show ever more clearly that at the beginning of the church's history neither heresy nor orthodoxy was sharply defined or patent: both were concepts developed later."

For example, many early Christians, particularly Gentile converts, refused to believe that Jesus had a mortal body, a position that has come to be known as Docetism, from a Greek word meaning "to show." The Pagan gods, after all, had occasionally appeared in mortal form and vanished when their purposes were accomplished; with them there was no death and resurrection—with the exception of a group including such deities as the Egyptian Osiris and the Norse Baldur, who were slain by other gods and in some cases resurrected, as Osiris was by Isis. To these Christians, who included many of the so-called Gnostics, the crucifixion was only a show, a hallucination projected to its observers. It was unthinkable that a divine being could physically suffer and die.

Other Christians believed that Jesus was indeed a mortal man who, because of his particular virtue, was "adopted" by God and declared to be his son. This heresy is referred to as Adoptionism. Others accepted the notion of the Trinity but could not see how the Father and the Son could both be eternal; the Father, they reasoned, had to have come first in order to beget the Son, and the Holy Spirit could not be equal to and as eternal as the Father. This viewpoint is called Monarchianism. The circulation of these different views prodded church leaders from Paul onwards to define *orthodoxy* in response to centrifugal pressures of different doctrines. When Paul used the Greek word *hairesis* in 1 Corinthians, it was beginning to carry overtones of suspicion; it meant not just another school of thought, but erroneous teaching or false belief. Nevertheless, in some areas, heresy was orthodoxy at different times.

In addition, early Christians who expected the Second Coming within their lifetimes or in the near future had not yet settled on a canon or list of accepted books of Holy Scripture. Gnostic sects and others such as the Montanists continued to produce new prophecies and records of revelations that they treated as equally authoritative, just as today's Church of Jesus Christ of Latter-Day Saints considers the Book of Mormon to be "another gospel." It took some time before the church could decide whether the writings of a later charismatic prophet or influential bishop could be ranked with those of Paul or the author of the Book of Revelation.

Could the Christian message of salvation be reconciled with Greek philosophy? How did the Holy Spirit operate? Could Christians lead a holier life by not eating meat or not having sex? Did Christ come to redeem the entire material world or to take believers away, when they died, from a world that was irrevocably flawed?

During times of persecution and potential martyrdom, these questions became particularly important. If, for example, some Docetist Christians believed that Jesus's crucifixion was an illusion—since no god could be killed by humans—why should they submit to martyrdom in the name of the Christian faith? If Jesus himself had not suffered, the second-century bishop Irenaeus wrote, why did he teach his followers to "turn the other cheek" to their enemies? (Some Gnostics, Irenaeus said, claimed that their magical powers, such as the power of invisibility, made them immune from arrest and trial.)

Early Christians, then, were uniform in neither doctrine nor their response to persecution. Some went ahead and burned incense to the emperor (perhaps with mental reservations); others bribed officials to give them certificates saying that they had performed the ceremony. Around 200, the Christian writer Tertullian mentioned entire congregations that had bribed their way out of persecution. This was wrong, he argued, because God the Father had not permitted Jesus to escape crucifixion; he quoted Romans 8:32: "He did not spare his own Son." Therefore, Tertullian wrote, it was unworthy for Christians to bribe their way out of possible martyrdom. Belief in the incarnation of Jesus and martyrdom were linked, he suggested elsewhere: "When torn and bleeding through your [Romans'] tortures, we shout aloud, 'We worship God through Christ.' Think him a man if you will; through him and in him God wills to be known and worshiped. . . . If [Christ's divinity] is such a belief that the acceptance of it transforms a man, it follows that everything found contrary to it should be renounced."

The peak of Roman persecution lasted from 257 to Constantine's winning control of the Western Empire in 312. Before that, starting in the late first century, Christians had been the subject of slanderous rumors and local persecutions. Besides the charge of atheism equated with treason, other rumors centered on the person and character of Jesus, on alleged sexual orgies among believers during the agape, or communal love feast, and on accusations of baby killing and cannibalism. The emperor Nero's decision to blame this little-known "Oriental" sect for the burning of Rome in 64 is well known. In 94, a number of Christians were martyred in Rome under the emperor Domitian, apparently an outgrowth of an investigation of whether all the city's Jews had paid a special tax levied on them. But in 240 the Christian writer Origen said that only a "few" Christians had been martyred.

The early church fathers taught that martyrs went directly to heaven, and anyone teaching that martyrdom was avoidable or unnecessary threatened the nascent unity of the church. By the second century, the doctrines of apostolic succession and the authority of bishops were gaining; Tertullian, for instance, contrasted hierarchical catholic authority with some heretics' willingness to rotate leadership posts within the group. Under persecution, then, the orthodox leadership viewed variations in doctrine as cracks in Christian solidarity, which their governmental enemies could exploit.

In 249, persecution of Christians increased as the emperor Decius, having won the throne through a coup, attempted to revitalize "orthodox" imperial Paganism and thus fortify and unify the empire itself. Suspect Christians apparently had to produce certificates stating their adherence to Pagan practice; at the same time, many Christians flocked to their imprisoned brethren, or "confessors," who issued certificates—supposedly by power of their imminent martyrdom—promising remission of sin. (Both classes of certificates were widely forged.) Doctrinal divisions among Christians meant little. Followers of Marcion and Montanus, for example, were executed alongside catholics.

During the latter part of the third century, persecutions seemed to follow imperial victories rather than losses. As historian Robin Lane Fox has written, "Victory gave a new force to the ideals of Roman discipline and Roman god-given glory." Consequently, it was at these times that the emperors were likely to enforce religious conformity as they strove to consolidate

Roman laws, morals, and religion in their multiethnic empire.

Persecution intensified in 303 with orders for the destruction of churches and Christian scriptures; this, the so-called Great Persecution, was most intense from 303 to 305. In its periods of ferocity, it convinced many Christians that the world's last days were indeed upon them.

Until Constantine's reign, the only weapon the orthodox could use against heretics was excommunication. But it must be understood that in some areas, the heretics, particularly Gnostic congregations, were more numerous and truly considered themselves to be orthodox. It is interesting to note that no sooner had Constantine seized the western portion of the empire than he was receiving petitions from Roman North Africa urging him to use his authority on one side or the other in a dispute between catholic and Donatist Christians. The latter group, named for their bishop, was at odds with the former over ecclesiastical authority and, ultimately, whether Christians who had backslid during the previous persecution should be readmitted to fellowship without question or should be treated as new converts. (And by extension, whether sacraments conferred by them were valid.)

Under Constantine's successors, Christianity would become increasingly allied with secular authority, and heresy would rapidly return to its status as treason or, in the terms of both ancient and modern writers, an "infection." (For instance, the fourth-century churchman Epiphanius titled his catalog of heresies "The Medicine Box," first describing each heresy like a disease and then "treating" it with arguments from scripture and church tradition.)

Constantine's removal of the seat of government to his new capital of Constantinople (Greek for "Constantine's city"; today's Istanbul, Turkey) left the bishop of Rome positioned to become the sort of combined spiritual and political leader typical of the popes of later centuries—men who took over even the former Roman emperors' title of *pontifex maximus,* or "chief priest." As the imperial government became officially Christian in the fourth century, edicts and persecutions were turned 180 degrees and directed against the last Pagans. Sacrifices to the old gods were forbidden in 391. Former religious holidays were eliminated. Pagan philosophers lost their government-subsidized teaching jobs. Some, such as the Neoplatonist philosopher Hypatia of Alexandria (370?–415), one of antiquity's best-known female thinkers, were even murdered by Christian mobs. (Hypatia was killed and her body burned after she opposed a bishop's campaign of persecution against Jews and Pagans.) Finally, in 529, all Roman subjects were ordered to convert to Christianity. Once more, to reject the imperial religion was to be a traitor and a criminal.

Following Epiphanius, religious writers have frequently employed the "germ theory" of heresy. Orthodox thinking becomes infected with outside ideas, such as Manichaean dualism. It is convenient when actual infection can be seen occurring, such as the passage of Bogomil texts to the Italian Cathars in the eleventh century. Or a cancer model may be employed: some heresies are seen as an overemphasis, an out-of-control growth of some particular part of Christian doctrine or practice, such as the second-century Montanists' New Prophecy movement, or Joachim of Floris's Age of the Holy Spirit. Against that, however, we may set the treason model, which has been employed often enough to justify imprisonment and execution of designated heretics, whereas the response to the infection model might be medicine (proper teaching) or quarantine (excommunication).

Heresy in the Middle Ages

Once Christianity and secular power were aligned, issues of heresies tended to focus on matters of reform or purification of the church, mixed at times with rivalries between classes or ethnic groups. The Bogomil heresy, for example, pitted poor Bulgars, who tended to espouse the heresy in defiance, against their Greek-speaking overlords. French and Italian Cathars, like many medieval heretics in Western Europe, were reacting against the wealthy and politically potent Catholic church, emphasizing a portion of its teaching but repudiating the organized church and much of its tradition.

One scholar, Harold O. J. Brown, identifies three levels in medieval heresy. Dualism was the first heresy, followed by the heresy of poverty—the rejection of wealth and property that motivated the Waldensians, the scholastic philosopher Arnold of Brescia, and eventually Francis of Assisi. Only the last's work survived substantially, and that only barely. The new order of Friars Minor or Franciscans walked a dangerous line, and those who openly taught the heresy of poverty, particularly that Jesus and the apostles had owned no personal property, were persecuted by the church. (A confrontation between such "spiritual" Franciscans and papal representatives forms a backdrop to Umberto Eco's novel *The Name of the Rose*.)

The third and last heretical wave blended into the second, according to Brown. Espoused by Joachim of Floris (circa 1132–1202) and some of the radical Franciscans, it is sometimes referred to as the heresy of the Third Age. Joachim, a monk from southern Italy, taught that history could be divided into three epochs corresponding to the persons of the Trinity. The Age of the Father lasted from Creation until the incarnation of Jesus, which initiated the Age of the Son and replaced Old Testament law with New Testament grace. Around 1260 would come the dawn of the Third Age—the Age of the Holy Spirit—when the inspiration of the Holy Spirit would become more central than the eucharistic commemoration of Jesus's sacrifice. In the Third Age, all believers would be moved to live as purely spiritual lives as nuns and monks did in the Second Age. Although Joachim founded an order of monks and died within the church, some of his followers were condemned for teaching that a believer only had to listen to the Holy Spirit within and for looking for the person of the Antichrist in various secular rulers, most notably the Holy Roman Emperor Frederick II.

As the Middle Ages progressed, heretics raised issues that would later become part of the program of Protestant reformers. For example, the Waldensians' insistence on receiving the sacraments from only godly men—whether consecrated priests or not—flew in the face of the Roman Catholic church's teaching that the sacramental virtue lay in the operation, not in the operant, so that even a sinful priest could celebrate the Mass, hear confessions, pronounce absolution, and so forth. The Waldensians, however, were echoed by Martin Luther when he taught of the priesthood of all believers. The various emphases on mixing worldly poverty (or at least shunning ostentation) with holy living would come up again and again in succeeding centuries.

This book ends roughly with Martin Luther's era, the sixteenth century. At that point the line between heresy and reform grows faint. Why, for example, was Marcion a heretic but Luther, with whom he has been compared for emphasizing faith over good works, was not—at least according to modern Protestants? Although repudiated by the church elders in Rome, Marcion still considered himself to be a true Christian and, unlike some heretics, he wrote no new scriptures but confined himself to the Gospels and Pauline Epistles already known. One explanation is that the two reformers were judged by their political success: Lutheranism lasted; Marcionism did not. Although Catholics and Protestants have hurled the word heretic at each other in subsequent centuries, the temporal success of Luther and the other Protestant reformers in establishing lasting churches shows that once again, the nature of heresy has changed. (Luther himself would put a new spin on heresy when he argued that even church councils could produce error.) Perhaps in today's more pluralistic world some things have come full circle. Different teachings on the nature of Jesus abound, from metaphysical churches that echo Docetism to viewpoints that deny he had a divine nature at all. Some professed Christians have given new books the status of holy scripture, as the second-century Gnostic followers of Valentinus were accused of doing, and elsewhere some small denominations proudly carry the word Gnostic in their churches' names. But as long as religious power and civil authority are not synonymous, accusations of heresy will remain doctrinal disputes only, without the threat of imprisonment, torture, and death. And so let us pray it continues.

HOW THIS BOOK
IS ORGANIZED

Listings for heretics, organized heresies, and schools of thought or key ideas that were judged heretical (e.g., Monarchianism, Iconoclasm) are organized alphabetically. Cross-references are indicated by names in italic capital letters. Short biographies of key early writers on heresy are also provided; in many cases, most of what is known about certain heretics comes from the descriptions of heresy hunters such as Epiphanius or Irenaeus, two early bishops who cataloged their opponents' views at length in order to refute them.

Biographies of key historical figures such as Constantine, the first Christian Roman emperor, and later heresy hunters and inquisitors such as Conrad of Marburg are also included. Some readers may be surprised to find, for example, the Franciscan order included, but in its early days this monastic order walked a fine line between acceptable orthodoxy and the heresy of apostolic poverty—the notion that Jesus and the apostles (in great contrast to the Roman Catholic church) owned no personal property. Indeed, radical Franciscans were periodically rebuked and even executed for promoting these and other disconcerting ideas.

Last, not all conflict arose between catholic and heretical Christianity. Pagan intellectuals also leaped into the fight; therefore, entries are provided on such figures as Celsus, Porphyry, and Iamblichus who, although not Christian, were aware of and in intellectual competition with the first Christian thinkers, whether orthodox or heterodox.

Notes on Dates and Terminology

The conventional B.C. (before Christ) and A.D. (*anno Domini*) designations are used throughout the text. Most dates are A.D., which may be assumed if no designation is given.

Throughout the book the terms *catholic* and *orthodox* without capital letters are used to describe developing mainstream Christianity before the separation into Western and Eastern churches. After the eleventh century, *Catholic* is customarily used for the Roman Catholic church and *Orthodox* for the various Eastern Orthodox churches headed by their archbishops in Antioch, Constantinople, or elsewhere.

Encyclopedia
of Heresies and
Heretics

Abelard, Peter   Although he is better known for his unlucky love affair with Héloïse, teenaged niece of an influential Paris priest, the medieval theologian Peter Abelard was condemned by the Catholic church for his daring theological views. Abelard escaped execution for heresy, but he was denounced by two church councils, ordered by Pope Innocent II to stop teaching and writing, and forced to retire to a monastery.

Peter Abelard was born in 1079 to a noble family in Brittany. As did most intellectually oriented young men of the Middle Ages, he turned toward the Catholic church as the only outlet for his talents. He took minor orders (a term covering the Catholic orders of acolyte, exorcist, reader, and doorkeeper, but not deacon or priest) and studied philosophy and theology in Paris and elsewhere with the leading thinkers of his day.

At age 37, Abelard's personal life took an unexpected turn. Now a leading professor of philosophy, he was invited into the Paris home of Canon Fulbert to tutor the canon's beautiful niece, Héloïse, who was then 17 or 18 years old. Despite his clerical vows, he fell in love with her. At first they tried to keep their relationship secret, but Héloïse became pregnant, and the canon ultimately learned what was going on. As scandal threatened, Abelard sent Héloïse to stay with his relatives in Brittany, where she gave birth to a son.

Héloïse, to judge by her letters (the lovers' correspondence has been preserved to this day), considered love more important than marriage. She wrote, "And if the name wife appears more sacred and more valid, ever sweeter to me is the word friend, or if you are not ashamed, concubine or whore." She desired nothing of Abelard but his pure love and declared that she would follow him to hell itself.

Abelard, however, wanted to marry Héloïse (and thus pacify her angry and politically powerful family), but he also wanted to retain his teaching post, which required him to be—at least officially—single. He persuaded Héloïse to agree to marry him in Paris, with the understanding that she would not live with him and that she would keep the marriage a secret. To guard the secret, he arranged for her to live in a nearby convent.

Although Héloïse was willing to meet his conditions, Canon Fulbert and her other relatives were seething. From their perspective, the scholar had seduced a young woman but refused to acknowledge her publicly. The priest directed a group of men—his servants, hired thugs, or a combination of the two—to ambush Abelard at night in a deserted street. They beat him severely and then castrated him.

Abelard survived and joined the monastery of St. Denis in Paris. Ironically, his castration disqualified him from ever becoming a priest, since the Catholic church would not ordain eunuchs. Héloïse became a nun at age 20 and remained so until her death.

Nudged out of St. Denis for his contentiousness, Abelard created his own institution, a chapel dedicated to the Paraclete (Greek for "the comforter"—in other words, the Holy Spirit), where he stayed and taught until he was elected abbot of another monastery. Meanwhile, he named Héloïse to head a new convent at the Paraclete, where he was able to visit her frequently as the convent's spiritual director. Eventually, gossip that they had somehow renewed their old relationship caused him to stay away. At this point, Abelard wrote one of the Middle Ages' rare autobiographies, *Historia calamitatum* (The story of my calamities). When Héloïse read it, she resumed their correspondence. And though her letters were loving, his were sermons in disguise. The romantic in him was gone, leaving only the intellectual and philosopher.

Abelard lived at one monastery or another until his death in 1142. Héloïse died at the Paraclete in 1164 and was entombed beside him, having already requested that Abelard be buried there. In the early nineteenth century they were reburied together in Paris, where their tomb became a romantic landmark.

Although the story of Abelard and Héloïse captured the imaginations of many persons in subsequent centuries, and their joint tomb in Paris became a perpetual place of pilgrimage, not everyone was impressed by their love story. The nineteenth-century American writer Mark Twain, for example, devoted a section of his European travel book *The Innocents Abroad* to his view that Abelard got exactly the punishment he deserved for using his status as a teacher to take advantage of an innocent girl.

Abelard's heresy, if it may truly be called that, was an intellectual affair—a matter of freethinking in the face of traditional church authority—not a popular movement. At a time when the Catholic church controlled virtually all higher education and universities were just evolving as conglomerations of students attracted to this or that well-known teacher, Abelard was just a professor challenging the administration. Together with such figures as *BERENGAR OF TOURS* and *ARNOLD OF BRESCIA,* Abelard held up the value of the intellect as opposed to the value of dogma.

The philosophical school Abelard helped create was called *SCHOLASTICISM.* In brief, it represented an attempt to justify the Christian faith intellectually, but such free exercise of reason was unsettling to Catholic authorities (as these men's biographies show). For instance, Abelard's first book, written on the nature of the Trinity in an attempt to rationally explain it, was condemned by the Council of Soisins in 1121; he was forced to burn it and was imprisoned for a time. Because he was defeated not philosophically but through church politics, Abelard is also remembered by some as a martyr to free intellectual inquiry, not just as a famous lover. Within the church, the eventual long dominance of Scholasticism owed much to him.

At the instigation of the great abbot Bernard of Clairvaux, he was tried for heresy a second time. A sympathetic contemporary described Abelard's writings being read after supper to an assembly of bishops, most of whom were sleepy after a large meal and several cups of wine and were barely able to rouse themselves to mutter "Damnamus" (We condemn it) when their opinion was asked by the reader. Later, Abelard set out for Rome to make a personal appeal to the pope, fell ill along the way, and died at the monastery of Cluny.

Nevertheless, Abelard shaped the use of dialectic in theological matters: the use of questions, debate, and disputation with the aim of arriving at a rationally satisfying conclusion about the matter under examination. In one of his later works, *Dialogue between a Philosopher, a Jew, and a Christian,* he attempted to show how dialectal methods could be used to convert Jews, Muslims, and others to Christianity.

Adamites　　The term *Adamites* sometimes refers to a radical group of *HUSSITES,* rebels against the German emperor and the authority of the Roman Catholic church during the fifteenth century in what is now the Czech Republic. Confusingly, it is also applied to the brotherhood of the *FREE SPIRIT,* a different movement altogether, and was also applied to a group of second-century heretics. The common thread is the recurrent upwelling of desire to return to the alleged primitive bliss of the Garden of Eden. The Hussite Adamites, for instance, were said to go naked, to believe that they were in a sinless state because their spirits were free, and to attack priests and all manifestations of organized religion. Too radical even for their fellow reformers, these Adamites were massacred by a Hussite force in 1421. Followers of the Free Spirit likewise believed that they had transcended the orthodox idea of sin and were free to do whatever they pleased.

Apocryphal books ascribed to Adam were circulated during the Middle Ages, keeping the myth of his secret magical knowledge alive. It may be said—without stretching the point too far—that the English poet John Milton's epic work *Paradise Lost* (written in 1667) was the last and greatest Adamite work. See also *ANTINOMIANISM; BEGHARDS.*

Adoptionism Adoptionism describes any doctrine held by some Christians (and sympathetic non-Christians) that Jesus was God the Father's "adopted" son. In other words, he was a man of special powers, consciousness, or holiness that God raised to divine status. Adoptionism appeared in Rome in the late second century, a reaction against *GNOSTICISM* or *DOCETISM,* which taught that Christ was a purely spiritual being who, with his divine power, created the illusion of a physical body that ate, drank, and otherwise seemed to be flesh.

The Christian writer *EPIPHANIUS* labeled a man known as Theodotus the Tanner, originally from the eastern part of the empire (hence his Greek name), as the first Adoptionist teacher. Theodotus taught that Jesus was a "mere man" (in Greek, *psilos anthropos)* who received his divine status at his baptism. Theodotus was excommunicated by Victor, the bishop of Rome between 189 and 198. Theodotus the Tanner was succeeded by Theodotus the Money-Changer and Aesclypedotus as Adoptionist teachers in the early third century. Adoptionism, which resembled Unitarianism today in its rationalistic and nonmiraculous emphasis, faded as the orthodox church stressed that Jesus was God incarnate. Palmyra, a Syrian city northeast of Damascus, was an Adoptionist stronghold in the late third century. (See *MONARCHIANISM* and *PAUL OF SAMOSATA*.)

In addition, a number of Spanish clergy in the early Middle Ages held Adoptionist views, and the doctrine was condemned by Emperor Charlemagne in 794. In Spain, Adoptionist ideas may have been influenced by Islam, since much of the Iberian peninsula (present-day Spain and Portugal) was under Muslim rule at that time. Muslims frequently viewed the Christian doctrine of the Trinity (God seen as a unity of three persons) as polytheism, and a counterassertion that Jesus was a uniquely holy individual who was nevertheless human can be viewed as a softening of Trinitarianism in the face of Islam's claims of the prophet Muhammad's status as God's messenger.

Albaneses The Albaneses were various groups of absolute dualists that sprang up during the High Middle Ages, of whom the *ALBIGENSIANS* (Cathars) of southern France are the best known. They earned the term *absolute* for their teaching that the world is a battleground between the forces of the completely good God and his evil adversary. One key text, produced in Italy in the early to mid-1200s, is known today as *The Book of the Two Principles* for its insistence that God cannot be the source of both good and evil but that there must of necessity be two sources. Its author quotes Matthew 7:17–18—"A good tree always yields good fruit, and a poor tree bad fruit. A good tree cannot bear bad fruit, or a poor tree good fruit"—in support of his argument.

The Italian sect of Albaneses squabbled bitterly with their rival dualists, the *CONCOREZZANES,* or Garatenses, who held the mitigated belief that one god of principle had produced both good and evil and that evil, although dominant in this world, would ultimately be defeated. (Compare the teachings of *MANI*.) Such people, the author of *The Book of the Two Principles* wrote, "are wont repeatedly to assert that there is another lord, the evil prince of this world, who was a creature of the most excellent Creator. He, they say, corrupted the four elements of the true Lord God [and created humanity]." To the contrary, the absolute dualists said that an evil god had created this world and all in it—the same view held by numerous *GNOSTICS* a thousand years earlier. The absolute dualist author of *The Book of the Two Principles* further excoriated the Garatenses by saying that since they were ascetics and deliberately did not "go forth and multiply," and since they did not eat eggs, cheese, or milk, the products of animals' sexual intercourse, they were themselves denying the works of the evil god and consequently should accept that there were indeed two principles warring in the universe.

He also challenged his rival heretics to declare whether, if the devil had corrupted the works of God, that action was good or bad. If they said it was good, he argued, then corrupting the work of God was good; and if they said it was evil and against God's will, they would be saying that God was capable of willing evil into being. "It then follows of necessity that there is another principle, one of evil, who forced the true God to permit and suffer the wicked and most vain corruption in His most holy elements, quite against His will." As in the common Gnostic view, this evil creator was equated with Jehovah or Yahweh, God of the

Old Testament, and Christ was the being sent to release humanity from the evil god's material prison.

Albigenses, Albigensians The Albigensians, also referred to as *CATHARS,* were the one heretical group that so threatened medieval Catholicism that an armed invasion of southern France by Catholic armies was authorized by Pope Innocent III in 1209 to suppress them. What the military forces—primarily northern French lords and their followers—began, the *INQUISITION* finished. Nevertheless, only the *KNIGHTS TEMPLAR* equal the Albigensians in their continuing hold on the imagination. Both, for example, are associated with the legend of the Holy Grail—the wine cup used by Jesus and his disciples at the Last Supper, believed to have been taken (in one version of the story) to southern France. In addition, it has been argued that Cathar doctrine underlay the creative surge of song and poetry produced by the region's wandering minstrels, the troubadours, in the twelfth century. Although most Cathar writings were destroyed by their enemies, some scholars have gone so far as to argue that the troubadours' songs, many of which were recorded, can function as texts of Albigensian belief.

The Albigensian hold on the modern imagination is so strong, in fact, that tourists continue to make a circuit of their special sites, including the famed Castle of Montségur, where 200 Cathar "Perfects" died after a lengthy siege (other ordinary believers were merely imprisoned and fined).

Very few Albigensian writings exist: an initiation ritual written in Provençal (the old language of southern France), commentaries on the Gospel of John and the Lord's Prayer, and little more. Therefore, their doctrines have largely been taken from the writings of orthodox inquisitors and commentators. The tone of their conversations with the Cathars is illustrated by a story told by Étienne de Bourbon (circa 1195–1261), a Dominican preacher and inquisitor, about a debate between a Catholic and a Cathar. When the Albigensian argued that

A knight of the 1170s, showing the typical armor worn during the Crusades. (Adapted from Pearcy Dearmer, Everyman's History of the English Church, Oxford: A. R. Mowbray & Co., Ltd., 1909.)

his religion was superior because people changed from Catholics to Cathars but never the other way around, the Catholic replied that this showed their corruption, since wine could change to vinegar but never vinegar to wine.

The heretics called themselves the True Church of God. A Provençal manuscript, "The Vindication of the Church of God," written around 1250, states that the Albigensians refrained from killing, theft, and swearing oaths and otherwise followed Jesus's teachings; consequently, they suffered "persecutions and tribulations and martyrdom in the name of Christ." The "Vindication" continued, "Note how all these words of Christ contradict the wicked Roman Church. For it [the Catholic church] is not persecuted for the goodness or justice which is in it, but on the contrary it persecutes and kills all who refuse to condone its sins and its actions. It flees not from city to city, but rules over cities and towns and provinces and is seated in grandeur in the pomp of this world; it is feared by kings and emperors and other men. . . . And above all does it persecute and kill the Holy Church of Christ, which bears all in patience like the sheep, making no defense against the wolf."

The Albigensian heresy has spiritual, moral, and political roots. The spiritual questions revolved around the basic issue posed by *DUALISM:* How can an all-good god have created a world filled with pain and suffering? The Catholic church taught that God had created the world as good but that it had "fallen" with Adam's disobedience; likewise the medieval Catholic church itself had fallen in many people's eyes as a moral exemplar. The ignoble era of contesting popes arrived in the late eleventh century, but even before then the church's growing opulence and local scandals turned countless pious persons against it. Even Pope Innocent III, who in 1208 would order a military campaign against the Albigensians, denounced some of the Catholic clergy in southern France as "blind, dumb dogs that cannot bark! Simoniacs [see *SIMONY*] who sell justice, absolve the rich and condemn the poor!

They accumulate benefices and entrust the priesthood and ecclesiastical dignities to unworthy priests and illiterate children. Hence the insolence of heretics."

Add to this a political difference. The southern French provinces of Provence, extending inland from the Mediterranean east of the Rhône Valley, and Languedoc west of the Rhône were culturally and linguistically distinct from provinces in the north. Little concerned with their northern neighbors, they looked east toward Italy, south toward the sea for trade, and even west into Spain, and had more in common with Catalonia. Parts of Languedoc were fiefs of the king of Aragon, one of the Christian Spanish kingdoms locked in perpetual conflict with Spain's Muslim-ruled south. This split between north and south was the weapon the pope would use against them when he moved to crush the heretics by military force after preaching and persuasion had failed: northern lords would be promised new southern cities and southern estates to control if they would join this crusade of Christians against Christians.

The French Cathars, who evidently called themselves the True Church or the Church of Christ, may have learned their dualistic teachings from the East; a connection has been postulated between *BOGOMIL* missionaries fleeing Greek Orthodox persecution in the Byzantine Empire and Italian and later French Catharism. In the 1020s and 1030s, isolated instances of heretical teachings with an apparent Italian connection were punished by the bishops in the dioceses of *ORLÉANS* and Arras; several clerics were burned at the king's command at Orléans in 1022 for teaching falsely about the evil of material creation.

Later in the century the First Crusade successfully captured Jerusalem; on Christmas Day in 1100, Baldwin, a French lord, was crowned king of Jerusalem and would spend 17 years holding the borders of Outremer, the crusader enclave in the Middle East. With these events, traffic between Western Europe, Byzantium, and the Middle East increased. This traffic in people and ideas has been offered as a cause of the sudden growth of heretical dualistic ideas in the early twelfth century. At Toulouse in Languedoc, for example, an 1119 papal council anathematized local heretics who claimed that baptism, marriage, and holy communion were not true sacraments; the renunciation of marriage suggests the old *GNOSTIC* notion that procreation merely entrapped more divine sparks in the material world.

A generation later, in 1147, Pope Eugenius III, alarmed at the heretics he found or heard of in the south of France while preaching the Second Crusade, ordered the great reforming abbot Bernard of Clairvaux (later canonized as St. Bernard) to preach against them. The city of Albi appeared to be a center of heresy, hence the name Albigensian. (The heretics were also called Arriani after a village near Toulouse.) Bernard was ultimately unsuccessful in persuading the majority of his heretical hearers to abandon their views, and there the matter rested until further church councils in 1163 to 1165 condemned the heretical rejection of the Old Testament and the sacraments. In fact, in 1167 the heretics held their own open council, summoning their leaders from Italy, other regions of France, Spain, and even Byzantium.

The Byzantine East was represented by a Greek named Niquinta or Nicetas, who claimed to lead the dualist church in Constantinople. Bringing with him both written texts and the prestige of the greatest city in Christendom, he persuaded those present to offer him the leader's chair at this council. In contrast to the Monarchian (see *MONARCHIANISM*) position held by many Italians present, Nicetas was a strict dualist, and his views held sway among the Provençal contingent. (See *ALBANESES* for more on that wing of the movement.)

One reason that the French Cathars were so bold was that their members included the nobility as well as former clerics, artisans, and country people. This was particularly true west of the Rhône River, where the counts of Toulouse and Foix often protected the heretics, and women of noble families frequently took the rigorous vows of the Perfects. In addition, affiliation with the Cathars' True Church may have salved some nobles' consciences as they coveted or sought to take by force some of the Catholic church's extensive holdings in their vicinity.

Albigensian Ritual and Beliefs

The Albigensians and the Italian Cathars adopted some religious texts from the Bogomils as well as producing their own. The former works included *The Ascension of Isaiah,* a compendium of early Gnostic works produced in the first and second centuries. It describes how the Hebrew prophet Isaiah ascended in his spirit body through a series of seven heavens, at the bottom of which good and evil angels battled. In the seventh and highest heaven, Isaiah heard the Father command the Son to descend to earth and into hell. He witnessed Christ's crucifixion at the order of Satan, the prince of this material world, and saw the "harrowing of hell" when Jesus descended there. He learned how he and other righteous people would be united in their spirits with God the Father after death.

The cosmic vision presented in *The Ascension of Isaiah* resonated with Cathar beliefs in several ways: in its picture of the material world ruled by Satan and as the scene of a constant battle between good and evil, in its denial of the Trinity in favor of a Monarchian view of the Son and Holy Spirit subordinate to God the Father, and in its omission of the incarnation of Jesus as a man. In the text, God the Father says, "Go forth and descend from all the heavens and be in the world, and go even to the angel who is in hell, transfiguring thyself into their form. And neither the angels nor the princes of that world shall know thee."

The Albigensians also made use of another Bogomil work, known as the *Interrogatio Johannis* (The questions of John) or sometimes *The Secret Supper.* Brought to Italy in the late twelfth century, it describes the apostle John questioning Christ at a heavenly Last Supper about the origins of the world, the cause of evil, the rebellion of Satan, and the process of human salvation. According to this work, Satan created the world; after his rebellion against God the Father, he could find no peace in heaven, so out of pity God gave him seven days to create what he would. What follows is a version of the Genesis creation story with Satan as creator; he commands a fallen angel of the second heaven to enter a body and animate Adam and an angel of the first (lowest) heaven to animate Eve's body. Directed by the devil, the first couple "were affected by a lust for debauchery, together begetting children of the devil and of the serpent, until the consummation of the world."

In other words, physical creation is the result of Satan's rebellion.

Like some other Gnostic texts, *The Questions of John* teaches that Jesus entered and exited Mary's body through her ear, not by a process of normal birth. Following that text, the Albigensians believed that Christ was created sinless, and they followed the sequence of the Gospel of John: "the Word was made flesh and [subsequently] dwelt among us."

Some sources suggest, however, that the "Virgin Mary" can be interpreted allegorically as the heretics' church, with the "Hail, Mary" prayer understood in that context. This dovetails with the suggestion that the "lady" to whom some troubadour poetry was addressed was also the Cathar church (see below, "The Albigensians and the Troubadours").

Other surviving Albigensian documents, written in Provençal and Latin, describe their ceremonies, primarily the *consolamentum,* a ritual of initiation into what the heretics variously called the True Church, the Church of Christ, or possibly the Church of Love. This ritual, which marked a person's advancement from being a hearer or believer in Cathar teachings to being a Perfect, replaced the orthodox sacraments of baptism and confirmation and, when administered to the dying as it frequently was, the sacrament of extreme unction. But before receiving the *consolamentum,* a Cathar had to undergo at least a year of probation and instruction in the faith. After receiving it, he or she was under strict vows not to eat meat, eggs, or cheese; not to have sexual intercourse; and not to lie, kill, or take an oath. The food restrictions were imposed on the Perfect because meat, cheese, and eggs were directly or indirectly the result of sexual intercourse and procreation. Even the unnecessary procreation of animals was to be avoided because it strengthened Satan's power and—since at least some Cathars apparently believed in a progressive reincarnation of spirits from animals into humans—it further trapped divine or angelic spirits in fleshly bodies, or "tunics" as they were often described in Albigensian terms.

During his or her period of instruction, the candidate was taught, among other things, the Cathar technique of saying the Lord's Prayer, which was frequently said in multiples of two or six accompanied by genuflections. The heretics' wording was identical to the orthodox version except in one place; instead of praying "give us this day our daily bread," they prayed, "give us this day our supersubstantial bread," for they interpreted "bread" in metaphysical terms as divine love. This prayer was used above all others. For example, a Provençal manuscript of the late thirteenth century advises, "if one [Cathar] travels on horseback, let him say a Double [the Lord's Prayer twice]. He should say the Prayer when embarking on a boat, when entering a town, or when crossing a stream by a plank or dangerous bridge." Further, they were advised not to eat or drink after praying in the evening for the last time.

For the *consolamentum* itself, the candidate and his or her instructor stood before one of the Perfects, who asked if he or she wished to receive "the spiritual baptism by which the Holy Spirit is given in the Church of God, together with the Holy Prayer and the imposition of hands by Good Men [Perfects]." After further discourse on the nature of this true, spiritual baptism and receiving an affirmative reply, the Perfect and the candidate exchanged the *meliormentem* (a request for a blessing together with three prostrations or genuflections), and the candidate asked for forgiveness of all sins of thought, word, and deed. Then the Perfects placed a copy of the Gospels on the candidate's head, set their right hands on him or her, and offered various prayers, including a sextuple recitation of the Lord's Prayer.

The obligations laid upon a new Perfect during the ritual included prohibitions against lying, killing, and other acts as mentioned above, plus an obligation of nonviolence and nonretribution against those who might harm him or her. If the *consolamentum* were administered to a sick person, it was repeated in a fuller form if the person regained health. Because of the rigorous life style imposed on Perfects, most Albigensians never received the *consolamentum* until just before death, choosing to remain Believers instead. If a Perfect lapsed from his or her vows, the sacrament was invalidated. Rather than run that risk, new Perfects sometimes chose the path of the *endura*, or "deliberate suicide." Perfects might starve themselves to death or, like the ancient Romans, open a vein while lying in a hot bath and bleed to death. By choosing how and when to end their lives, the Albigensian elite believed that they were defeating Satan and ending the cycle of transmigration and imprisonment in the material world.

The Albigensians also held a monthly worship service (*lo servisi* in Provençal, or *apparellamentum* in Latin) for the confession of sins and absolution by the Perfects of the congregation and vice versa. Their version of Holy Communion excluded the sacramental significance it held in the Catholic church; instead, as in many subsequent Protestant denominations, communion simply commemorated "the most Holy Supper of Jesus Christ and his disciples," to quote the prayer offered at the meal.

Clerical Attacks on the Albigensians

Innocent III, who would later call for a crusade to destroy the heretics of Languedoc, was elected pope in 1198 at the age of 37. His reign was considered the papacy's high point in terms of its temporal power. In 1199, alarmed at the spread of heresy in northern Italy and southern France—a spread encouraged or even abetted by clerical corruption—Pope Innocent ordered a group of Cistercian monks to preach in Languedoc, set up inquiries into the prevalence of heresies, and stiffen and reform the clergy.

This mission had mixed results. Although the authorities in the city of Toulouse promised to seek out and prosecute heretics, and although Count Raymond VI of Toulouse, one of the most powerful aristocrats in the area, returned to the fold for a time, most of the Cathars and their sympathizers ignored the Cistercians' preaching. The pope decided that a stronger weapon was needed after two Spanish clerics—Diego d'Azevedo, bishop of Osma, and Dominic de Guzman—toured the area and declared that only preachers who equaled the Cathar Perfects in their ascetic and pure lives could influence the heretics. But Dominic observed that the papal legates sent by Innocent, headed by Peter de Castelnau and Arnold-Amaury, abbot of Cîteaux, traveled like princes. Dominic (1170–1221) and the bishop of Osma preached against the Albigensians throughout the province and founded an institute for poor girls to secure them from the heretics' influence. Although they were credited with various miracles, they were unable to win back the area and return it to Catholic control. After the subsequent crusade (see below), Dominic would go on to found the Dominican order of monks in Toulouse in 1216, devoted to preaching against heresy and persecuting heretics throughout Western Europe and later the New World.

For their own reasons, many of the southern nobles continued to favor the heretics; Raymond of Toulouse exasperated the papal legates until he was excommunicated in 1207. The following January he summoned Peter de Castelnau under the pretext of agreeing to reject the heretics, but the two parted angrily. On his way eastwards, Peter de Castelnau was murdered beside the Rhône River. Meanwhile, Pope Innocent had lost patience and requested the northern French nobility, including the Duke of Burgundy and many lesser lords, to help him suppress heresy in the south. They would reap the same spiritual benefits as the Crusaders had in Palestine, he promised; they would receive indulgences (the remission of any penance imposed for past sin), and if they died, they would be counted among the martyrs of the church. Some nobles had already agreed, and when news of the papal legate's murder—presumably at Count Raymond's orders—came north, more joined the Albigensian Crusade as the year 1208 progressed.

Although the crusade ultimately crushed the heretics and their sympathizers militarily, the Catholic church's theological response to the Albigensians was more important in the long run. Not only the Dominican order but that of St. Francis of Assisi may be seen as attempts to regain for orthodoxy the moral advantage held by the Cathar Perfects and the spiritual passion of at least some troubadours. In addition, the heretics' challenge to the church forced it to reexamine and restate important doctrines, particularly during the Lateran Council of 1215, called by Innocent III. Opposing Albigensian dualism, the delegates reaffirmed that only one god had created the material world and all spiritual beings, including demons; likewise they affirmed the doctrines of bodily resurrection and transubstantiation, or the presence of the body and blood of Jesus Christ in the bread and wine of Holy Communion. In addition, the Lateran Council ordered that all Catholics must confess their sins in person to their priests, thus providing a check against the spread of heresies. In addition, many historians cite the official encouragement of the cult of the Blessed Virgin Mary from the thirteenth century on as another means by which popular religious feeling was channeled away from heresy.

The Albigensian Crusade

When Pope Innocent III ordered his crusade against the heretics, crusading had been a way of life for Western European knights and their followers for a full century, ever since the First Crusade (1095–1099) had captured Jerusalem. But although the Crusaders' holdings in Palestine and Syria were eventually retaken by Muslim armies, the Albigensian Crusade provided a permanent military victory.

The Crusade entailed more than one campaign. It waxed and waned for 16 years (not counting subsequent short-lived rebellions), with cities and castles changing hands, local lords changing sides, and the full spectrum of senseless cruelties that warfare can produce, especially when motivated by religious dogmas. The Crusade's most infamous anecdote comes from the chronicler Caeserius of Heisterbach (fl. 1220–1235), a Cistercian monk. When the crusaders laid siege to the city of Béziers and later captured it, some of them approached the Crusade's spiritual leader, Arnold-Amaury, abbot of Cîteaux, about how they should deal with the population, a mixture of Catholics and heretics. Arnold, fearing that the Cathars would claim to be Catholics to escape execution, is said to have replied something like, "Kill them all; God will know his own." Whether or not he said those words, Arnold did write to Pope Innocent III describing how the crusaders killed all the men, women, and children found in the city, perhaps 15,000 to 20,000 people. The pope congratulated him, saying that God had permitted the faithful to earn their salvation even though they had been exterminated.

The religious motivation of the war was perhaps most visible in its first years. At the capture of the city of Minerve in 1210, three Perfects returned to the Catholic church, but 140 to 180 were burned, many leaping voluntarily into the flames. "Why preach at us," one of them asked Arnold-Amaury. "We care nothing for your faith. We deny the church of Rome." The same year, during the siege of Termes, the archdeacon of Paris organized a religious confraternity among the camp followers and noncombatants to gather stones for the crusaders' catapults. When the fortified town of Lavaur fell, 90 southern knights were killed, and their leader's Cathar sister was thrown alive into a well. Between 300 and 400 other heretics were burned outside the town walls. Similar tales abounded.

The most notable crusader was Simon de Montfort, who led a small but active army from one corner of Languedoc to another besieging towns; destroying mills, houses, orchards, and vineyards; and keeping a constant pressure on the heretics and their noble patrons and sympathizers. By 1212 he had conquered enough territory to hold a parliament, which formulated procedures by which heretics would be delivered to the church and their property confiscated.

Southern opposition formed around the counts of Toulouse, all of whom bore the name Raymond. It was Raymond VI who apparently ordered or encouraged the murder of the papal legate in

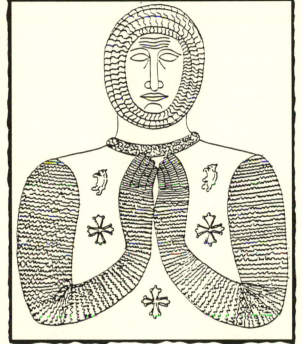

Simon de Montfort. (Portrait adapted from a mural in the St. Nazaire Church in Carcassone, France.)

1208 and stood off Simon de Montfort's army during a nine-month siege in 1216. His son, Raymond VII, was in turn excommunicated in 1220 for persecuting the clergy, but he would live to make peace in 1226 with King Louis VIII of France, who led the crusaders after Simon de Montfort's death during the siege of Toulouse.

By the time the fighting ended, the north of France held political control of the south, which has lasted to this day. The armies of Louis VIII (which included Amaury de Montfort, Simon's son, who continued his father's military campaign) had, in effect, annexed Languedoc. Despite the king's death (probably from dysentery contracted during the war), the exhausted southern nobility could no longer carry on the fight for their independence, nor

were any alliances with outside powers open to them. The feisty quasi-independent cities such as Toulouse and Avignon had seen their walls and towers destroyed by Simon's or the king's armies; the last Perfects were hiding in secret fortresses like that at Montségur.

Montségur, headquarters for two hopeless revolts, was captured by a royal army in 1243, and 200 Perfects were burned. Never again would the True Church have the strength it had entering the thirteenth century, even though it persisted in a small way into the early 1300s when one Autier, a heretic from the town of Ax in southwestern France, returned from a stay among the Italian Cathars and briefly raised a large following until he was captured and burned in 1310. (Persecution of the Italian Cathars continued until mid-century.)

To the historian of religion Mircea Eliade, Albigensianism represented the only successful introduction of an "eastern" religion into Western Europe until the spread of Marxism—which he classified as a millenarian or utopian tradition—in the late nineteenth and early twentieth centuries.

The Albigensians and the Troubadours

A connection between the Albigensian religion and pre-Christian Celtic beliefs has been postulated by many writers who note, for example, that both the Cathars and the ancient Gauls and Irish made a woman into a symbol of the divine. More certainly, the troubadours—the poets and singers who picked up such ancient British tales as those of King Arthur and the lovers Tristram and Isolde and spread them across Europe—developed in the Albigensians' homelands. Because of this connection, some historians, notably the French writer Denis de Rougemont, have examined the troubadours' love poems and songs and claimed to have found evidence of Albigensian doctrine in them. "The troubadours were 'believers' of the Catharist Church and the bards of its heresy," he wrote in *Love in the Western World.* Not all troubadours were openly heretical, he added; some fought alongside the crusaders. Nevertheless, he and others have argued that the "lady" whom troubadours praised was only superficially a mortal woman; underneath, she was the Church of Love.

In the Arthurian story cycle, for example, Lancelot the great knight and lover is, in the end, a physical type, whereas Galahad and Perceval are virtually Cathar Perfects, because they do not "fall" into physical love, but stay on the road of pure, mystic love. To the Cathar elect, profane, physical love is a misfortune. Like Tristram's marriage to Isolde of the White Hands (the second Isolde), it represents a downfall from the pure attachment.

The Albigensian Legacy

Like the Knights Templar, the Albigensian Cathars furnish a screen upon which many people have since projected their particular hopes and outright fantasies. A persistent legend has maintained, for example, that the treasure of Montségur, which most historians think was money and/or sacred writings, was actually the Holy Grail, which traditionally was thought to have miraculous properties. For example, Wolfram von Eschenbach (circa 1170–1220), author of *Parzival,* one of the medieval epics about the Knights of the Round Table and the Holy Grail, refers to the Grail castle as "Munsalvaesche," which has been interpreted as a variation on Montségur. Different versions of this legend have made the treasure out to be the Shroud of Turin (a length of linen cloth that some researchers believe wrapped Jesus's body in the tomb and was mysteriously imprinted with his image).

A 1983 work by Michael Baigent, Richard Leigh, and Henry Lincoln, *Holy Blood, Holy Grail,* caused a sensation by advancing the thesis that the treasure, in addition to being gold or precious stones, was some secret proof or knowledge that Jesus had fathered a child or children (his disciple *MARY MAGDALENE* is usually suggested as the mother) and that certain families in Europe preserved his bloodline. This secret, they suggested, was shared with the leadership of the Knights Templar and a shadowy associated organization, the Priory of Sion.

On other fronts, although the surviving Cathar documents seem almost puritanical, many succeeding esotericists have cherished the belief that Albigensian inner circles may have passed on secret teachings of sex magic, goddess worship (*ISIS* or the Black Madonna in particular), or some aspect of Gnostic Christianity. The Cathars are also special to those in the south of France today who cherish the thought of Languedoc and/or Provence breaking away and regaining independent status as the nation of Occitaine. A twentieth-century plaque commemorating the burning of Albigensian heretics in the city of Minerve reads in translation, "Here on 12 July 1210 some 180 Perfects were burned to death for their faith and for the independence of Occitaine."

Amalric of Bene, Amalricians   A follower of the condemned theologian *JOACHIM OF FLORIS,* Amalric (died circa 1206) and his adherents took Joachim's three-stage theory of history even further than did its founder. Some of the Amalricians were burned along with Amalric's writings in Paris in 1210, and Amalric's body itself was dug up and burned.

In brief, the Amalricians were accused of pantheism, the belief that God and the universe are essentially identical, divinity existing in every part of creation rather than being separate from and "above" it. A frequent outgrowth of mystical contemplation, medieval pantheism sprouted again and again, influenced by the Neoplatonic (see *NEOPLATONISM*) writings of Duns Scotus Erigena and later philosophers such as *DAVID OF DINANT.* In the case of Amalric and his followers, it seems to have been an outgrowth of their anticipation of Joachim's Age of the Holy Spirit and their preaching that the Holy Spirit was, in fact, filling or incarnate in them. One source quoted Amalric's followers as saying, "The Father was incarnate in Abraham, the Son in Mary, the Holy Spirit is daily made incarnate in us." They also said, "All things are one, for whatever is, is God."

Somewhat like the *FREE SPIRIT* movement, which was strongest among pious laypeople who had already separated themselves to some degree from worldly society (such as the *BEGUINES* and *BEGHARDS*), the teachings of Amalric and Joachim tended to affect those already in religious orders but did not spread widely into society.

Amaury of Bennes (or Bene)
See *AMALRIC OF BENE*.

Ammonius Saccus   A teacher of philosophy at Alexandria during the early third century (died circa 242), Ammonius Saccus was apparently raised as a Christian and once worked as an itinerant porter on the city's docks, which gave him the name by which he has been known ever since, Ammonius the Porter. Ammonius's true fame, however, lies in two of his students: the Christian church father *ORIGEN* and the Neoplatonic (see *NEOPLATONISM*) philosopher *PLOTINUS*. He left no writings in his own name, but through his Christian students he helped infuse Neoplatonic ideas into both catholic and *GNOSTIC* Christianity, primarily the emphasis on the radically different origins of the body and the soul.

Like many of the early Christians, Ammonius saw the soul as able to leave the body and experience other realms of existence, "leaving the body as if it were inanimate, with only a breath of life, to keep it from dying entirely—and using her own activity only in dreams, to foresee the future, and to live in the intelligible world [in other words, the world of pure ideas]."

Anabaptists   The term *Anabaptist* means simply "rebaptizer." During the Protestant Reformation, it was applied to a number of groups that opposed infant baptism, particularly the sixteenth-century churches that produced such modern denominations as the Mennonites, Schwenckfelders, Amish, and Hutterites. Many of these were also pacifists. Earlier in church history, however, the term was applied to anyone who advocated rebaptizing persons who had originally been baptized by heretics or by clergy who had wavered under persecution. (See *DONATISM*.)

Not all Anabaptists focused on spiritual concerns. During the early sixteenth century, however, one group of Anabaptists, whose leaders included Thomas *MÜNTZER*, helped spark the Peasant War that raged during the 1520s in Germany.

Antinomianism   Derived from the Greek words meaning "against law," antinomianism may refer to any position that argues that salvation comes from faith alone. More specifically, in a discussion of heresy, such medieval groups as the various *APOSTLES,* the brethren of the *FREE SPIRIT,* and the *LUCIFERANS*—not to mention earlier *GNOSTICS*—were considered antinomian because they held that all the church's moral teaching could be set aside by someone who was "filled with the Holy Spirit." Their critics were more than eager to accuse such sectarians of sexual promiscuity, *HOMOSEXUALITY,* sacrilege, and worse crimes such as cannibalism or making pacts with Satan.

Antinomian behavior could also result from *DUALISM*. The belief that earthly bodies were part of the evil creation of Satan or the *DEMIURGE* often produced the attitude that all morality was a sham. Only the spirit was real; consequently, whatever one did in the body—particularly sexual activity—was of no importance. However, it was important to some dualist heretics to avoid engendering more children, thus trapping additional pure spirits in fleshly prisons.

Apollonius of Tyana   A contemporary of the apostle Paul, Apollonius was born to well-off Greek parents in Anatolia, then part of Asia Minor but now part of Turkey. As a young man he was attracted to the teachings of the Pythagoreans, the most severely ascetic of all the Greek philosophical schools. The Pythagoreans were simple-living vegetarians who resembled—and may have been influenced by—the yogis of India. Indeed, Apollonius himself is credited with traveling all the way to India to study with Brahman scholars. He claimed to have rid several cities in the eastern Mediterranean region of plagues and insect pests—for instance, expelling scorpions from Antioch through magical ceremonies involving the burial of a bronze scorpion. In Rome he enjoyed great celebrity before running afoul of the emperor Severus; the circumstances of his death are unknown. The second-century philosopher Philostratus II wrote a flattering biography of Apollonius, which educated Pagans later drew on when comparing Apollonius favorably with Christ.

Apostles   In the thirteenth and fourteenth centuries, the term *apostle* was applied, often in a negative sense, to wandering *BEGUINES, BEGHARDS,* and the brothers and sisters of the *FREE SPIRIT,* who claimed to follow an apostolic life of wandering, preaching, and begging food, shelter, and the other necessities of life without belonging to any established monastic order or obtaining the permission of the church authorities.

One of the most widely known apostolic (or pseudo-apostolic) in the eyes of the church, groups originated in the 1260s in the Italian city of Parma. Its members are often referred to in Italian as *apostolici.* Like the *FRANCIS-CANS,* its members were wandering preachers who begged for their needs; unlike St. Francis, however, founder Gerard Segarelli did

Apollonius of Tyana. (From Jacques Boissard, De Divinatione et Magicis.)

not receive papal permission to found a permanent order—nor, apparently, did he seek it. Members of his group were described as wearing long robes, beards, long hair, and sandals—not the normal appearance of thirteenth-century Italians, but fitting the traditional picture of Jesus and his followers.

The group was officially condemned by Pope Honorius IV in 1284. Segarelli was burned, and several of his followers were imprisoned by the bishop of Parma. He was replaced as leader by a more dynamic man named Dolcino, who spread the sect throughout Italy, claiming that he was doing God's will and that his followers needed no other religious leaders. He preached the coming return of Christ and the end of the current age somewhat in the style of *JOACHIM OF FLORIS.* He went so far as to say that Francis of Assisi, not long deceased,

had fallen from truth and that he, Dolcino, was Francis's spiritual heir. Dolcino created such an uproar in northern Italy that a new pope, Clement V, ordered a crusade against him in 1307. Dolcino and forty-odd followers were surrounded on a mountain in Novara and eventually captured; he and two assistants were burned. Some surviving followers held to his teachings for several decades.

Dolcino's contemporary, the Florentine poet Dante Alighieri, places him in hell in his epic poem *The Divine Comedy.*

Another leader who claimed to fulfill Joachim's prophecies was *GUGLIEMA,* leader of an apostolic sect in and around Milan circa 1270.

Arianism, Arians
In 326, the Christianizing Roman emperor Constantine set out to destroy so-called heretical books. His edict began: "Constantine, Victor, Greatest Augustus, to bishops and laity: [The heretic] Arius, having imitated wicked and impious men, deserves to suffer the same loss of privileges as they. . . . we now order that Arius and those who agree with him shall be called Porphyrians [referring to the Neoplatonic philosopher *PORPHYRY*] . . . and besides this, if any book written by Arius be found, it is to be consigned to the fire, so that not only his corrupt teachings may vanish, but no memory of him at all may remain."

Arius, who lived from about 250 to 336, emerged from the religious foment of Alexandria, second city of the Roman Empire, where he was both a poet and an ascetic priest. Around 319 he became embroiled in a dispute with the bishop of Alexandria over the nature of Christ—how he could be the begotten Son of the Father and yet have been in existence before the creation of the world and time. Arius was excommunicated; the bishop declared him to be a heretic equal to *SIMON MAGUS* and *MARCION*. Arius, gathering adherents among the clergy and laypeople, taught a form of what is now called *MONARCHIANISM*—the belief that God the Father is primary and the Son and Holy Spirit are subordinate to the Father.

To Arius—whose work is known only through the writings of his theological opponents such as Athanasius, a subsequent bishop of Alexandria—God the Father was "uncreated" and was the first principle from which all else, including the Son and the Holy Ghost, was derived. Arius taught that although the Father is eternal, the Son was created at some point and thus is not eternal.

His teachings were officially condemned by a theological conclave convened by Constantine in 325, the Council of Nicaea. The emperor himself had not been baptized, but his sponsorship of the council, held only two decades after the last great imperial persecution of Christianity by the emperor Diocletian, was a political triumph. It was also a political convention in a sense, with Arian bishops canvassing for votes against the opposition, which was led by Athanasius, the current bishop of Alexandria. The Arians lost, and the council voted that Christ was "one in essence with the Father."

When Arius refused to agree to the new Nicene creed, he was declared a heretic and banished. Constantine, backing the council's vote with the power of his government, turned Arianism into a crime. However, Constantine relented and lifted Arius's banishment in 330, because the Arian controversy was splitting the church and developing political overtones. Arians had become well-established in many eastern dioceses, and the theological fracas between Arians and Nicenes continued with exchanges of episcopal letters, theological pamphlets, and sometimes open violence. In 335, the Arian bishops gained the upper hand; this time Bishop Athanasius was banished. Returning to Alexandria, Arius fell ill and died suddenly. His followers assumed that he had been poisoned.

Besides being supported by a portion of the hierarchy, Arian views were upheld by two of Constantine's successors, Constantius II (337–361) and Valens (364–378). The intervening emperor, *JULIAN THE APOSTATE*, who was raised a Christian but returned to Paganism as an adult, refused to favor either party.

Arianism was most congenial to the Goths, people from eastern Europe who spoke a Germanic language and who alternately were allies and enemies of the Roman Empire. Some of these tribespeople had sought Roman protection in the fourth century from the marauding Huns. (The Huns [Tatars] themselves were raiding westward from central Asia because their earlier victims, the Chinese, had built the Great Wall to keep them out.) Ulfilias (circa 311–381), a famous missionary to the Goths, was himself an Arian, and Arian Christianity spread among these people as they settled along the borders of the empire and enlisted in its armies.

Later, various independent-minded Gothic kings broke away from the alliance and attacked Constantinople, captured Rome (in A.D. 410), and established kingdoms in Spain and North Africa. Arian Christianity went with them. Among these northerners, God the Father could conceivably be equated with Odin or Wotan, who had gradually become chief of their pantheon; the Son, a lesser, created being in the Arian view, was more like their semidivine racial ancestor Mann (man). Arianism in the Gothic kingdoms was eventually eradicted by the Muslim conquest of North Africa and most of present-day Spain and Portugal, as well as by ecclesiastical pressure from the catholic church. See also *NICAEA, COUNCILS OF*.

Arius See *ARIANISM*.

Arnold of Brescia Although not as well remembered today as later heretics such as Giordano *BRUNO*, during the High Middle Ages Arnold of Brescia was the prototype of the questioning intellectual who becomes a charismatic spiritual leader.

He was born in Lombardy in northern Italy to noble parents. Since he was not in line to inherit the family lands and title, he was sent to a monastery to study, then encouraged by his teachers to study theology at the University of Paris. His idealism clashed with his clerical training, however. He grew disgusted at the corruption of the church and on his return home began to preach apostolic poverty—the idea that the clergy should emulate Jesus and the apostles and own nothing. This teaching was particularly offensive to the medieval Catholic church, which was also a wealthy landlord, but Arnold's preaching found ready hearers in Milan, where the *PATARINI* had challenged the city's clerical landlords a century earlier. Forces led by Arnold seized control of the city and attempted to make it a self-ruling commune. Forced out by papal authority, Arnold returned to Paris and continued preaching; he was again banished and moved to Zurich and later Bohemia.

He was persuaded to apologize for his actions and beg pardon of Pope Eugenius III, who ordered him to come to Rome where he might be better watched. Once in Rome, Arnold was again disgusted by clerical opulence and corruption. His preaching found support among the people, who rose up, temporarily drove out the pope and his entourage, and declared a commune with Arnold as its leader in 1146. Two years later Eugenius, having gathered sufficient mercenary troops, recaptured Rome, but the rebellion flared up again in 1150. Once more in control of the government, Arnold moved to impose his ideas of apostolic poverty and perfection on the local ecclesiastical establishment, but his puritanism alienated his supporters among the nobility, and a succeeding pope, Hadrian IV, regained control of Rome and had Arnold arrested, imprisoned, and garroted. Despite Arnold's support of Holy Roman Emperor Frederick Barbarossa (head of an empire that was neither holy nor Roman except in name) over the popes, the emperor never supported Arnold. Arnold's personal asceticism and his insistence that the church give up its landholdings and temporal powers were too much of a threat to the political establishment of the day. His followers did not attempt to carry on with his program after his execution.

The idea that Christians and the Catholic church itself should follow the example of Jesus and the apostles, spurn privilege and riches, and follow the leading of the Holy Spirit cropped up again and again in the Middle Ages, centuries before the Protestant Reformation. It did not die with Arnold but was continued by other reformers such as *FRANCIS OF ASSISI* and the *WALDENSIANS*.

Arriani   See *ALBIGENSES*.

Augustine of Hippo   After the apostle Paul, Augustine of Hippo influenced the development of Christianity more than anyone else for centuries. Born in 354 in the town of Tagaste in the Roman North African colony of Numidia (now Soukh-Ahras, Algeria), he is referred to as Augustine of Hippo, a city where he later served as bishop, to distinguish him from another sainted Augustine, the sixth-century missionary to Britain and first archbishop of Canterbury.

Augustine's father, Patricius, was a Pagan for most of his life; his mother, Monica, was a Christian who prayed steadily for her son's conversion (she was later canonized herself). The young Augustine received Greek and Latin schooling from the local schoolmaster and also studied in the nearby town of Madaura. His father struggled to save enough money to send Augustine for further studies in the colonial metropolis of Carthage (destroyed by Muslim conquerors in 698, it was located near present-day Tunis). Augustine later wrote, "He [Patricius] cared only that I should have a fertile tongue [as a lawyer and teacher of public speaking], leaving my heart to bear none of your fruits, my God, though you are the only Master, true and good, of its husbandry."

We know a great deal about Augustine's inner life because of his autobiography, *Confessions,* which focuses on his intellectual and spiritual development and his eventual conversion from *MANICHAEISM,* the religion of his young adulthood, to Christianity. From age 17 or 18 until his conversion to Christianity, he lived with a Carthaginian woman who bore him one son, Adeodatus (Latin for "God's gift"). He described her as "a mistress who I had chosen for no special reason but that my restless passions had alighted on her. But she was the only one and I was faithful to her." When after 13 years Augustine decided to contract a formal marriage with a woman of higher social status, Adeodatus's mother left him. Their separation was apparently engineered by Monica, who wanted her son to be respectably married to a woman of his own class. Adeodatus died at about age 17, having been baptized together with his father in 387. Augustine wrote of his son that at 15, "there were many learned and respected men who were not his equals in intelligence."

In about 383, Augustine moved to Rome and then Milan, where he was a state-supported teacher of rhetoric and literature. There he continued to study Greek philosophy, particularly *NEOPLATONISM,* but also was influenced by an educated Christian bishop and former provincial governor, Ambrosius, whose character he greatly admired. Another older man, Simplicianus, drew Augustine into a circle of Christian intellectuals who studied works of such philosophers as *PORPHYRY* and *PLOTINUS* in an attempt to reconcile Neoplatonic philosophy with Christianity. Eventually, as the historian Henry Chadwick wrote, Augustine became convinced that "from Plato to Christ was hardly more than a short and simple step, and that the teaching of the Church was in effect 'Platonism for the multitude.'"

As he spent more time with Christians such as Simplicianus, who had been able to reconcile their intellectual training with their devotion to Christ, Augustine underwent more inner torment. In one of *Confessions'* best-known passages, he describes lying in mental torment in the garden of his house in Milan, struggling with the decision to give himself to Christ, when over the garden wall he hears a child saying to someone, "Take it and read, take it and read." He stood up, interpreting the remark as a command to take up the Christian scriptures, and went to where he had laid a copy of Paul's Epistles. Opening the book at random, he read from Romans 13 a passage containing the words: "no reveling or drunkenness, no debauchery or vice, no quarrels or jealousies! Let Christ Jesus himself be the armor that you wear; give no more thought to satisfying the bodily appetites."

At that moment his doubts fell away. He had already chided himself for indulging in bodily desires instead of living as a model of philosophical detachment. Now he dropped the pride that had held him back from converting and immediately announced to a close friend and then to his mother, Monica, his desire to be baptized. He finished the current school term and then resigned his teaching post. At age 33, he was baptized together with Adeodatus. Monica, aged 56, died soon after, having seen her longest-held wish granted.

Augustine returned to North Africa. Four years later, in 391, he was made a presbyter (priest). In 395 he was consecrated bishop of the city of Hippo, an office he held until his death in 430.

During those 35 years, Augustine wrote a large number of books, producing works that subsequent generations of Christian thinkers have turned to again and again. His subject matter ranged from the nature of Christian government to effective prayer, from the nature of the Trinity to how Revelation should be read allegorically, not literally. The Protestant reformers such as Martin Luther and John Calvin drew on Augustine's explanation of predestination, the doctrine that God selected a group who would be saved and that humans could not know his plans. Catholic and Protestant theologians alike turned repeatedly to his ideas on how there could be no salvation outside the church, his writings on original sin (transmitted, Augustine believed, through male semen), and his views on the relationships between Father, Son, and Holy Spirit.

Believing that humanity needed an orderly, lawful government to counteract its natural turn toward sin, Augustine proceeded to the concept of a "just war," departing further from the pacifism adopted by many earlier Christians. Force was justifiable when used in self-defense or in the recovery of stolen property, he wrote. Although fully aware of the weakness and corruption likely to afflict any earthly government, he saw in earthly rulers a shadow of the heavenly ruler.

Augustine's writings on government, which make up part of his largest work, the multivolume *City of God,* were undoubtedly influenced by current events. During the second half of his life, the Western Roman Empire was disintegrating, left to fend more and more for itself after *CONSTANTINE'*s founding of his new eastern capital, Constantinople. By Augustine's day, no emperor ruled from Rome itself; the emperors and their regional commanders moved from Paris to Milan to the cities of the Danube, wherever the threat from barbarian tribes compelled them. In 410, one of these tribal armies, that of the Visigoths, former Roman allies, sacked Rome and then moved west to conquer much of Roman-controlled Spain. Augustine himself would die as an army of Vandals—who, like the Visigoths, were originally from eastern Europe and spoke a Germanic language—was besieging his city of Hippo.

Of greater concern to the bishop of Hippo, however, was warfare within the church. Augustine's conflict with the heretic *PELAGIUS* was noteworthy, but at home in North Africa he was in the middle of the long-standing battle between the catholic church and the Donatists (see *DONATISM*). The Donatist party originated among strict believers in the early 300s who denounced other Christians for backsliding during imperial persecutions. By the time of Augustine's consecration as bishop of Hippo, Donatists outnumbered catholics in the city. From their perspective, Augustine was the heretic, and theirs was the pure, uncontaminated faith. By this time, the dispute had become a self-renewing feud, complete with church burnings, beatings, and occasionally worse.

The catholic party, however, had the government on its side. A combination of secular force, Augustine's liberal terms toward his opponents (he accepted their sacraments and ordinations, although the reverse was not true), and his political leadership of the catholic clergy helped his co-religionists considerably. Donatism, however, translated into ethnic (Berber or Punic people versus Roman colonists) and regional (country versus city) conflicts, and it persisted in some form until Muslim armies swept the area in the early 700s, making Christian controversies moot.

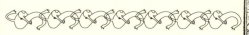

Barbeliotes   See *BARBELOS*.

Barbelos   In some *GNOSTIC* cosmologies, a divine being called Barbelos (or Barbelo) held a similar place to *SOPHIA*, the feminine aspect of the godhead (or a female emanation of the godhead) that embodies divine wisdom. The situation is confused, however, because in some Gnostic writings Barbelos is seen as male; in others she is the daughter of the first Sophia; in others Barbelos is male-female.

Barbelos is sometimes described as the mother of Ialdabaoth, the *DEMIURGE*, or creator of the visible, material world. Through her the other Aeons—personified abstract qualities such as Foreknowledge, Incorruption, or Eternal Life—are created until the Pleroma, or plenitude—the total array of divine emanations—is completed.

IRENAEUS, in his catalog of heresies, speaks of a sect of Barbeliotes or Borborians, Gnostics who saw creation as proceeding from the Aeon Barbelos. The *Apocryphon of John*, one of the Gnostic texts Irenaeus knew about but was only rediscovered for modern readers in the *NAG HAMMADI* collection, speaks first of "the Monad" as "the invisible one who is above everything," existing before time and indescribable in human terms, "the immeasurable light which is pure, holy, and immaculate." In this book, Barbelos is the first emanation from the perfect Monad; he is "the first power . . . the perfect glory in the aeons. . . . the invisible, virginal Spirit," who in turn produces Ennoia (or Pronoia), the First Thought. Pronoia and subsequent Aeons glorify Barbelos for creating them and granting them eternal life. In the *Apocryphon*'s creation story, Sophia is created at a lower level; she desires to make her own creation, but cannot manage perfection and so creates Ialdabaoth (or Yaltabaoth), the first archon or ruler of the world.

Although the *Apocryphon of John* is classified as a Christian Gnostic text, insofar as it places Christ among the eternal Aeons, another of the Nag Hammadi tractates, *Zostrianos,* has no Christian references, but similarly places Barbelos among the inhabitants of the heavenly world.

Several other Nag Hammadi tractates also include Barbelos, among them the *Trimorphic Protennoia,* composed around 200 and believed by scholars to be contemporary with the *Apocryphon of John*. In it, the First Thought makes three descents into the world (hence the title) to redeem and free humankind. Identified with Barbelos, she appears as three "permanences," Father, Mother, and Son. In the third appearance, she says, "I put on Jesus. I bore him from the cursed wood, and established him in the dwelling places of his Father. And those who watch over their dwelling places did not recognize me. For I, I am unrestrained together with my seed, and my seed, which is mine, I shall place into the Holy Light within an intangible Silence."

Basilides   Considered the first great theologian of *GNOSTICISM,* Basilides, who died around 140, developed an elaborate scheme of how God and the material world are related, which was later carried on by *VALENTINUS*.

EPIPHANIUS, a later cataloger of heresies, considered Basilides to be a direct spiritual descendent of *SIMON MAGUS*; whether or not that is true, his teachings went far beyond what we know of the first-century Simon.

Basilides's description of the cosmos 2began with one unknowable god—called Abrasax, the father of all—whose emanations

were Mind, Logos, Prudence, Power, and Wisdom. From these emanated assorted other spiritual beings, arranged in descending hierarchies and inhabiting 365 lower heavens. The angels in one particular heaven produced this visible world. One of these angels was Yahweh, God of the Jews, who was "brasher than all the other angels," according to Epiphanius's account. Because this angel was so warlike and haughty, "the other nations too waged war on this people [the Jews] and afflicted it with many evils: because of the other angels' jealousy."

Basilides also taught *DOCETISM*— that Jesus did not suffer at the crucifixion but only appeared to. In Basilides's version, Jesus magically switched places with Simon of Cyrene, the man forced to help carry his cross.

He was also hated by the orthodox for disparaging martyrdom. As Gnostics, possessors of the secret wisdom, his followers were under no obligation to die for their faith and should reveal it only to those capable of understanding, which was justified by Jesus's remark about not casting pearls before swine.

A wandering beghard. "Bread for God's Sake" was the characteristic appeal of the beghards. (Woodcut by Felix Hemmerling, circa 1500.)

Beghards Less organized than their female counterparts the *BEGUINES,* beghards were pious men who attempted to live their lives in imitation of Jesus's disciples without entering formal religious orders. The term covers a variety of pious and not-so-pious wanderers, particularly in what is now Germany and Belgium. They were always regarded with mistrust by church authorities because they had no secular or ecclesiastical masters. They were seen rather as enticing hardworking blacksmiths, shepherds, artisans, and farm workers away from their jobs and into a life of beggary on the roads. Their open-air preaching and interpretation of holy scripture frequently varied from orthodoxy, particularly when flavored with attacks on corrupt clergy in the manner of many medieval reformers labeled heretics by the Catholic church. Other beghards offered the usual variety of anticlerical teachings shared by many heretics: that the Bible should be translated from Latin into other languages; that sinful priests should not celebrate the Eucharist or, variously, that any believer could; that other sacraments had no value; and so on. The fact that some beghards offered a return to the perceived simplicity and purity of the early church is illustrated by the various other things they were called: good men, good lads, good Christians.

The first recorded use of the term *beghard* in the Low Countries comes from the mid-thirteenth century, although such brotherhoods were undoubtedly active sooner. In some cases they received similar protection and exemption from taxation as beguine establishments, but records of the time show that beghard houses in towns were far less common than beguine houses. As with the beguines, those beghards who organized to live a common religious life supported themselves through their work and performed acts of charity received more civil protection than those who became wandering preachers. Beghard communities sometimes chose to live under the Third Order (or tertiary) of St. *FRANCIS OF ASSISI,* which was designed for laypeople who had families and jobs but who wanted to combine them with religious practices similar to the Franciscan monks'. (Franciscan tertiaries are more associated with France and Italy; beghards with Germany, Switzerland, and the

Low Countries.) Others drew up their own rules; one communal house required that each brother remain chaste, receive communion at least seven times yearly, keep the secrets of the community from outsiders, and remain within the house at night. After the Black Death (bubonic plague) swept through Western Europe in the 1340s, some beghard communities adopted burial of the dead as their charitable function.

Throughout the thirteenth and fourteenth centuries, church authorities cautioned against beghards and other wandering preachers who delivered sermons without proper authority, particularly if they also preached that a priest in a state of mortal sin could not celebrate the Mass or absolve the sins of his parishioners, which contradicted the Catholic position that the efficacy of the sacrament did not depend on the priest's personal purity. The Dominican monk Johannes Nider, who lived in the late fourteenth century, denounced beghards who "use subtle, sublime, spiritual and metaphysical words, such as the German tongue can hardly express, so that scarcely any man, even an educated man, can fully understand them; and in these they wrap up lofty sentences about spirit, abstraction, various lights, divine persons, and the degrees of contemplation." See also *FREE SPIRIT; JOACHIM OF FLORIS; LOLLARDS.*

Beguines   The term *beguine* is of unknown origin, but it describes an unmarried woman who followed a religious life without formally becoming a nun. Some beguines were approved of by the church; others were considered heretics, and the distinction between the two was a vague one.

The beguine movement arose from a desire among certain twelfth-century women to follow the *vita apostolica*—the apostolic life of a wandering poor preacher supported by the charity of his or her hearers. (Men who took a similar vocation were called *BEGHARDS.*) After the apostles themselves, the ideal practitioner of this life was the eleventh-century saint, *FRANCIS OF ASSISI.* The beguines, however, endured an ambiguous relationship with the Catholic church and were not completely compatible with secular society either.

The first beguine community (in French, *beguináge*; in Flemish, *begijnhof*) was founded at

Liége in Belgium in the 1170s, and Belgium remained the center of organized, large-scale beguine activity. According to some sources, many members were widows of crusaders. The beguine movement has been interpreted as one outcome of the medieval *Frauenfrage* (woman problem) caused by the imbalance in the sexes due to men's deaths in war and the guild system's encouragement of late marriage among craftsmen. These women planned a life organized around prayer and works of charity. They supported themselves by weaving, spinning, and other crafts. Like the nuns who had earlier joined the Second Order of Franciscans (the Poor Clares) or the Third Order (tertiary), made up of religious laymen and laywomen, the beguines sought to give up their worldly lives and be truer Christians. Unlike nuns, however, they were not required to surrender private property and they were free to leave if they chose.

In many cases, beguines had a spiritual director, a male cleric who guided their religious lives and provided some legitimacy to their efforts. Franciscan friars frequently filled that role, which is why in some cases "beguine" became synonymous with a woman who had joined the Third Order. Beguines also worked with cloistered nuns, whose vows kept them from having any dealings with the outside world except conversations through a grill in the convent gate. Beguines could deal with tradespeople, the convent's tenant farmers, and others without breaking their less strict vows.

For both the nuns and the beguines, the life they chose offered an alternative to marriage and childbirth as well as a secure refuge when they got older. Both young girls and widows who controlled property were moved to become beguines. For example, Blessed Christina von Stommeln (b. 1242), a teenaged mystic, joined a beguine community in Cologne at age 13 and stayed there until she was 18. She then lived as a beguine in her hometown of Stommeln. The beguine communal houses were also refuges for aristocratic women who wished to extricate themselves from tangles of succession and inheritance or from marriage with men who wanted to control them and their estates—along the lines of Eleanor of Aquitane, King Henry II's widow, who retired to a convent.

Throughout the Middle Ages, orders of nuns frequently expected novices to bring with them into the order sizable financial contributions, since the nuns did not engage in economic activity. As a document from Flanders, the Ghent memorial of 1328, indicated, many women of different social classes who were unable to make suitable marriages and who lacked money had nowhere to go. Beguine communities permitted these women to be self-supporting and "to preserve their chastity by vow or without vow and to provide themselves with food and clothing without embarrassment to themselves or the convenient conniving of their friends."

In addition, such a life could be an intellectually stimulating one. Except for those few aristocratic women who had private tutors, it was often the only way for a woman to live in an environment where she could read and study. Some beguines, such as Hadewijch of Flanders and Beatrijs van Tienen, wrote poems, letters, and accounts of religious visions that circulated among other beguine communities. This intellectual life did not escape criticism: beguines in Germany and the Low Countries were denounced by fourteenth-century Dominicans for having religious books in their native language. (The morally severe Dominicans were frequently scandalized by the beguines and frequently considered them all to be in a state of damnation.)

The life of Marie d'Oignies, a beguine from Liége, exemplifies many of these women's concerns and motives. Born around 1177 to well-to-do parents, she was married at age 14. She and her husband evidently shared a desire to lead the apostolic life; they took vows of chastity and worked in a leper colony. Seeking to lead an even more religious life, Marie at about age 30 moved into a quasi-monastic cenobitic community of men and women that was directed by secular priests but not affiliated directly with any monastic order. One of the priests, Jacques de Vitry, later wrote her biography. By the time Marie died six years later, the women, aided by Jacques, had formed a self-supporting and self-regulating community.

From what is today Belgium, the beguine movement spread into France, Germany, and other countries. Many of their contemporaries saw the beguines as pious women whose holy lives were a reproach to the established church and even to the Franciscan order, which had

begun to love its air of poverty even before St. Francis's death in 1226. Jacques de Vitry described some of the Liége beguines as ecstatic mystics; "others were drawn with such intoxication of spirit that in sacred silence they would remain quiet a whole day, with no sense of feeling for things about them, so that they could not be roused by clamor or feel a blow." A German poet of the late Middle Ages praised the beguines not only for their holy life and self-denial, but also because they endured abuse and rejection for the sake of God.

Although some beguines lived almost cloistered lives and, like St. Douceline, even practiced physical austerities, others moved in secular society. These vagabond beguines, or holy women (*mulieres sanctae*), whether living alone in towns or wandering from place to place, especially irritated ecclesiastical authorities. Some became companions and counselors to the nobility. At times their advice was based on visions and professed psychic abilities: King Philip III of France, who reigned from 1270 to 1285, consulted a beguine to learn whether his queen was guilty of poisoning and conspiracy. The court chronicler who recorded the incident disapproved, referring to all beguines as "pseudo-prophetesses." This incident again indicates the split between some beguines and the church, since spiritual authority based on personal visions was bound to come into conflict with papal authority.

Opposition from secular society was undoubtedly based in part on a perception that beguines were unfeminine. They had given up the status conferred by marriage and replaced it with a somewhat lower status than that enjoyed by a nun. Although some beguines enjoyed the protection of a male confessor or spiritual director, others relied on their own authority and sought their own spiritual truth. When society turned on beguines, it was to accuse them of being pious hypocrites, women who did not know their place, and, occasionally, lesbians. By the 1400s, the earliest Protestant reformers would sometimes include beguines along with the Catholic clergy in their condemnations.

The increased persecution of beguines in the late Middle Ages was tied to a popular disenchantment with the Franciscan friars who, in many people's eyes, had lost their original purity and zeal. Increasingly insecure, the Franciscans themselves often turned on the beguines and beghards, their unofficial imitators. One Franciscan, Gilbert of Tournai, accused them of translating the Bible from Latin into French without permission, thus creating errors and heresies. Gilbert did not specify what the errors were; it was horrifying enough that laywomen might be translating and discussing the Bible on their own. The secular clergy, meanwhile, denounced beguines for not submitting to the authority of parish priests and bishops.

In the early fourteenth century the church hierarchy's hatred for beguines mounted. A council in 1311 and 1312 produced a decree condemning women "commonly known as beguines" who wore nunlike clothing but took no vow of obedience, did not give up private ownership of property, and did not follow an approved rule of religious life. According to the council, beguines taught erroneous doctrines about the Trinity and the sacraments. The decree forbade women to live as beguines, yet contradictorily said that pious women could live communally, which some scholars suggest showed the churchmen's inability to distinguish between "good" and "bad" beguines. Earlier church councils had also legislated against beguines and beghards for preaching to the people with authority and "leading simple souls into error."

About this time church authorities began to excommunicate beguines and in some cases to try them for heresy. Some were executed, including Marguerite of Poret, burned in Paris in 1310. (Some scholars place Marguerite more with the *FREE SPIRIT* movement, a radical mystic movement to the left of the beguines and beghards, but shading into them.)

John XXII, pope from 1316 to 1334, persecuted both beguines and the more radical Franciscans (known as spirituals), who continued to advocate holy poverty even as other clergy and monastic orders grew richer and richer. He abolished many beguináges, although some, such as the house in Marseilles founded by St. Douceline (b. 1214), survived— in that particular case, until 1407.

As the fourteenth century moved toward its rendezvous with the Black Death (periodic, severe outbreaks of bubonic plague), beguine communities were more frequently condemned. Yet the movement persisted through the Refor-

mation (where it was in turn denounced by some Protestant authorities). Some groups lasted into the twentieth century as communities of women in Belgium, the Netherlands, and Germany who did charitable work among the poor.

The beguines have also been considered heretics because of their name, which some have considered to be an abbreviation for *ALBIGENSES*, a term synonymous with heresy since the bloody suppression of the Albigensian heretics (see *CATHARISM*) in the early 1200s. In addition, one churchman, Philip the Chancellor, denounced them as heretics in a sermon from the 1230s, describing the "fruits of heresy" as including the "fruits of the belly." In other words, the beguines, although supposedly chaste, became pregnant after consorting with male heretics. (The idea that heretical religious discussions led to illicit sexual intercourse was a common clerical theme in the Middle Ages.) And as indicated above, the beguines were denounced for owning religious books in languages other than Latin; at times, even owning a Latin Old Testament or New Testament was suspect.

But the accusations against the beguines were not made because they preached heretical doctrines or offered sacraments outside the church. Rather, the basic accusation was one of having too much pious zeal outside "the system." The threat posed by the beguines was that their personal piety would cause people to treat them as religious authorities equal to and in competition with orthodox priests and monks. The fact that they were women heightened the danger, since the medieval church by and large regarded women in the terms set out by St. Jerome centuries earlier: "the gate of the devil, the path of wickedness, the sting of the serpent, in a word a perilous object."

Berengar of Tours　Born in the early eleventh century (he died in 1088), Berengar of Tours was one of a line of Catholic intellectuals who helped form the intellectual movement known as *SCHOLASTICISM,* which dominated the church's intellectual life in the later Middle Ages. But like his follower Peter *ABELARD,* Berengar was condemned as a heretic in his own time.

His name is associated with the controversy over whether the body and blood of Christ were truly present in the Eucharistic elements of bread and wine. Some theologians argued that they were only mystically present, and others declared in favor of their real presence—now a traditional Catholic dogma, but at that time an innovation. The real presence was important to the latter group because without it they could not explain the benefits of the sacrament of Holy Communion.

Berengar argued that the bread and wine did not contain the literal body and blood of Jesus (however mystically disguised), for, if they were consumed by a nonbeliever, there was no benefit. Only a faithful Christian *really*—but not physically—consumed them. Thus the transformation of the everyday bread and wine took place in the consciousness of the believer.

Berengar's distinction was not well received, however. In 1050 and 1059 he was tried and condemned for heresy. Ultimately he was forced to sign a confession in support of what would become the official Catholic position on the transubstantiation of the Eucharist, affirming that the bread and wine, once consecrated by a priest, "are not only a sacrament, but the very body and blood of our Lord Jesus Christ and are sensually, not only as a sacrament but in truth, handled and broken by the hands of the priest and crushed by the teeth of the faithful." He later argued that his signing of the confession was coerced and hence not binding.

Not only Berengar's position on transubstantiation but, more importantly, the intellectual method by which he had arrived at it influenced many of the more intellectual clergy, although he created no popular movement. Theologically, however, Berengarism was defeated by the more absolute doctrine of transubstantiation outlined in Berengar's confession and elaborated by subsequent Catholic theologians. In that doctrine, Christ was declared to be present both symbolically and in reality.

Bloemardinne of Brussels
See *MEN OF INTELLIGENCE.*

Bogomil
The Bogomil heresy, which began in the Balkans around 930, was the first large-scale medieval dualist movement. Not only did it persist in the Byzantine Empire for some time, but Bogomil missionaries traveled to Italy and

Provence (southern France) and perhaps other parts of Western Europe, seeding their doctrines and contributing to the later rise of the *ALBIGENSIAN* heresy.

Its founder was Bogomil (meaning "beloved of God" or "worthy of God's pity" in the Slavonic language, a precursor of modern Bulgarian), a village priest. Possibly influenced by the *PAULICIANS,* Bogomil began to teach a dualist doctrine that God had two sons, Christ and Satanael (i.e., Satan). Satanael, identified in typical dualist fashion with the God of the Old Testament, had created the material world. The Eastern Orthodox church together with its icons, sacraments, and hierarchy were under Satanael's control, Bogomil taught. Unlike the Iconoclast (see *ICONOCLASM*) party within the Orthodox church, Bogomil did not reverence the cross, because Christ had been killed on it by Satanael's agents.

Further, Bogomil taught that the only valid prayer was the Lord's Prayer (a prayer also retained by the Albigensians), that true believers should not eat meat or drink wine, and that marriage and procreation were to be avoided. In these teachings he resembles many *GNOSTIC* teachers of seven or eight centuries earlier. Bogomil congregations had no priesthood or hierarchy; men and women confessed their sins to one another and gave one another absolution.

The spread of Bogomil's teachings has been explained by historians as a peasant religious uprising masking the Slavonic-speaking Balkan peasants' resentment of their Byzantine Greek rulers in Constantinople (modern Istanbul) and of Constantinople's local agents. The Bogomil heresy pitted a Slavic peasantry and their Bulgarian overlords, who were of Tatar stock and had been converted by Byzantine missionaries, against one another, as well as pitting a Greek-speaking church hierarchy against Slavic village priests.

Certainly this gave the heresy an additional dimension, and parallels are frequently drawn between the tenth-century Balkan situation and the subsequent events in southern France in which the Albigensian heresy had its own political dimension. But we must realize that much of Bogomil doctrine had early precedents in Paulicianism, *MANICHAEISM,* and Gnosticism, and the fact that it was received in the West indicates that it also spoke to the current of ascetic dualism that always flows within conventional Christianity. Scholars remain divided about whether there might be a secret doctrine passed on from century to century or whether certain ideas reoccur over and over because of Christianity's own internal tensions over the world and the degree to which believers must be separated from it.

By the early ninth century, antidualistic works were being translated from Greek into Bulgarian, evidence of the Eastern church's campaign against the heresy. Nevertheless, Bogomil ideas spread into the capital of Constantinople itself after the conquest of Bulgaria in 1018 by the Byzantine emperor Basil III; chroniclers reported the ideas among both monks and the nobility. They reportedly met in secret while openly pretending to be Orthodox believers.

Anna Comena, an imperial princess and noted Byzantine historian, described Bogomil ascetics as gloomy-looking men, covered up to the nose and walking with a stoop.

Bogomil believers were divided into two groups: the Church of Dragovitsa (after a village in Macedonia), whose members were absolute dualists, maintaining that Satan was a cosmic power equal to God; and the Bulgars, or old Bogomils, who as mitigated dualists considered Satan to be God's fallen brother. The two tolerated each other, but the absolutists naturally drifted further away from Christianity. The absolute dualists also carried their ideas West, influencing the spread of Cathar ideas in Italy and France.

When areas of the Balkans where Bogomilism was widespread were conquered by the Ottoman Turks in the fifteenth century,

Characteristic tombs of the Bogomils. (Courtesy of Judith Mann.)

many Bogomils embraced Islam. The capture of Constantinople by the Turks in 1453 sealed the end of organized Bogomilism in the East, although traces of Bogomil ideas persisted in Balkan folktales about how God and the devil created the universe together.

Borborians   See *BARBELOS*.

Brothers and Sisters of the Free Spirit
See *FREE SPIRIT*.

Bruno, Giordano   Perhaps the best-known Renaissance heretic executed by the Catholic church, Bruno typifies the idea of a heretic as a freethinking intellectual ahead of his time. Subsequent generations have used him as—somewhat contradictorily—a symbol of scientific inquiry, occult explorations, and romantic individualism. Frances Yates, historian of Western occultism, for example, suggested that Bruno provided William Shakespeare with a model for the characters of the magician Prospero in *The Tempest* and of Berowne (Biron), the nimble-tongued discourser on love in *Love's Labor Lost*.

Born in 1548 at Nola near the Italian city of Naples, son of a retired soldier, Bruno's intellectual promise led him to the Dominican order. As a Dominican priest, he studied theology, philosophy, and science, becoming particularly adept at feats of memory. Soon, however, he began to overstep doctrinal bounds, arguing that through philosophy all religious doctrines and secular learning could be comprehended. Ultimately, his elevation of human reason over church authority led to his being accused of heresy, and in 1576 he fled Naples and became an intellectual wanderer.

Bruno combined lecturing and writing in Geneva, Paris, Oxford, and London but usually ended up in disputes with academic, ecclesiastical, or governmental authorities. While in London, he produced a work, *On the Infinite Universe,* influenced by Copernicus's insistence that the planets revolved around the sun rather than around the earth. For the first time in postclassical thought, the physical universe was described as infinite and filled with innumerable stars; Bruno went on to describe the stars themselves as ecstatic, living beings. His book *On Heroic Rages,* published in London in 1585, provided a Neoplatonic picture of the philosophical soul's ascension to God.

During the late 1580s and early 1590s, Bruno lived in Protestant parts of Germany—Marburg, Wittenberg, Helmstadt, Frankfurt am Main—and also in Prague, where he felt safer from ecclesiastical persecution. His independent conduct and outspoken views sometimes alienated Protestant leaders, whose intolerance at times approached the late medieval Roman Catholic standard. In 1592, invited to Venice by a Venetian nobleman who wished to learn the art of memory, he was betrayed to the *INQUISITION,* accused of heresy, imprisoned, and eventually burned alive in Rome on 17 February 1600. After his death, Bruno was regarded in progressive circles as a martyr of science and enlightenment, and his trial and execution were held up by anticlericalists as evidence of the Catholic church's corruption.

Cainites Like some modern so-called Satanists, the Cainites described by *EPIPHANIUS* worshiped the "stronger power" in the universe and claimed to honor Adam's son Cain because he killed his weaker brother Abel. Likewise they honored Jacob's brother Esau as well as Judas. Of the latter, Epiphanius said, "they consider him their kinsman and count him among those possessing the highest knowledge, so that they carry about a short writing in his name which they call the Gospel of Judas. . . . No one can be saved, they say, except by making the journey through everything, as *CARPOCRATES* also says."

Although Epiphanius, writing in the 370s, did not give any dates or places for his Cainites, he described them as consecrating their lustful or illegal acts to various heavenly beings, saying "O such-and-such angel, I am practicing your deed; O such-and-such authority, I am performing your action." This is similar to the way some *GNOSTICS* were said to perform sacramental sexual intercourse as an offering to one of the heavenly powers. Having claimed to have examined some of the Cainites' scriptures, Epiphanius dismissed them with a quotation from Genesis on how Cain was cursed by God.

Calixtines See Jan *HUS*.

Canon Episcopi An ecclesiastical legal document of unknown origin, the *Canon Episcopi* was an obstacle to the late medieval inquisitors who treated *WITCHCRAFT* as heresy. It has also been cited as evidence that pre-Christian Paganism coexisted with Christianity into at least the early Middle Ages.

The *Canon Episcopi* was first publicized in about 906 by Regino of Prüm, the abbot of Treves (or Trier, a city in western Germany), who claimed

that it had originated in the fourth century. It then passed into the body of religious law.

In essence, the canon stated that witchcraft as commonly imagined was a delusion. What constituted heresy was the belief in the reality of witchcraft, not witchcraft itself. At the same time, as the following excerpt shows, the canon's author accepted the reality of sorcery and traffic with the devil.

> Bishops and their officials must labor with all their strength to uproot thoroughly from their parishes the pernicious art of sorcery and malefice invented by the Devil, and if they find a man or woman follower of this wickedness to eject them foully disgraced from their parishes. . . . Those are held captive by the Devil who, leaving their creator, seek the aid of the Devil. And so Holy Church must be cleansed of this pest. It is also not to be omitted that some wicked women, perverted by the Devil, seduced by illusions and phantasms of demons, believe and profess themselves in the hours of the night to ride upon certain beasts with Diana, the goddess of Pagans, and an innumerable multitude of women, and in the silence of the dead of the night to traverse great spaces of earth, and to obey her commands as of their mistress, and to be summoned to her service on certain nights. . . . For an innumerable multitude, deceived by this false opinion [of those women], believe this to be true, and so believing, wander from the right faith and are involved in the error of the Pagans when they think that there is anything of divinity or power except the one God. . . .

Who is there that is not led out of himself in dreams and nocturnal visions and sees much when sleeping that he has never seen waking? Who is so stupid and foolish as to think that all these things which are only done in spirit happen to the body, when the Prophet Ezekiel saw visions of the Lord in spirit and not in the body, and the Apostle John saw and heard the mysteries of the Apocalypse in the spirit and not in the body, as he himself says, 'I was in the spirit.' . . . Whoever therefore believes that anything can be made, or that any creature can be changed to better or to worse or be transformed into another species or similitude except by the Creator himself who made everything and through whom all things were made, is beyond doubt an infidel.

Thus the *Canon Episcopi* denied the reality of transvection, or witches flying through the air from place to place, as well as denying the common tales of witches transforming themselves into cats, horses, beetles, and other creatures.

In the 1400s, however, spurred perhaps by a scarcity of other sorts of heretics, various inquisitors and prosecutors sought to find a way around this time-honored piece of church law. Some accepted part of the canon's points; for instance, around 1435, Johannes Nider, a Dominican professor of theology at the University of Vienna and later a prior, held that transvection was only a dream and that witches could not change their bodily shapes. He nevertheless believed that witches existed and had evil powers. His contemporary, Alphonus de Spina, a converted Spanish Jew who became a *FRAN-CISCAN,* wrote a book entitled *Fortalicium Fidei* (Fortress of the faith) that discussed witches along with other heretics, Jews, Muslims, and demons as enemies of true Christianity. Written about 1459, it was published in 1467. Other theological writers in France and Germany began to develop similar ideas.

Nicholas Jacquier, a Dominican inquisitor and persecutor of the *WALDENSIANS* and *HUSSITES,* produced in 1458 the *Flagellum Haereticorum Fascinariorum* (A flail against the heresy of witchcraft), arguing that the so-called witchcraft of his day was a new heresy,

a deliberate renunciation of Christianity rather than lingering Paganism, and hence not covered by the canon's prohibition of belief in witchcraft. His logic would be expanded shortly thereafter by the authors of the *MALLEUS MALEFICARUM* (Hammer of witches), the most complete and infamous handbook of demonology and alleged witchcraft that the *INQUISITION* produced, as well as by various Protestant witch-hunters.

Carpocrates   Known as the licentious Gnostic, the third-century teacher Carpocrates preached—whether or not he practiced—a freewheeling, everything-is-permitted form of *GNOSTICISM.* His teachings followed the basic Gnostic pattern that the true God is outside creation, the world having been created by, variously, evil angels or a lying, deluded, lesser god. Enclosed in each person is a spark of divinity that must be awakened so that it can return to God.

Although some Gnostics separated themselves as much as possible from worldly processes (for example, sexual intercourse), Carpocrates took the opposite course. He advocated doing and trying everything within the realm of human experience to escape the cycle of reincarnation.

In his doctrine, the spiritual part of a person could not be corrupted, and the physical part could not be saved. Moral codes and laws, such as rules governing sexual behavior or private property, were created by the lesser god, the lord of this world (also called the *DEMIURGE* or Ialdabaoth), as part of his plan to keep the "light" trapped in matter. To this Carpocrates added his version of reincarnation (a concept already promulgated in the Greco-Roman world by the followers of the Greek thinker Pythagoras): Before souls could return to God, they had to live in many bodies and experience all kinds of action, "lest they must again be sent into another body because there is still something lacking in their freedom," as the catholic writer *IRENAEUS* summarized it. Only when a soul had done everything could it be freed from reincarnation. This secret was concealed, Carpocrates taught, in Luke 12:57–59: "When you are going with your opponent to court, make an effort to settle with him on the way; otherwise he may drag you before the judge, and the judge hand you over to the constable, and the constable put you in jail. I tell you, you will not come out till you have paid the last farthing." The true meaning of this parable, he said, was that the "opponent" was the creator and ruler of the world, and that "jail" was the human body. Therefore, no one could escape reincarnation until the last worldly action had been experienced. Carpocratian Gnostics merely meant to speed up the process that all people must go through.

By committing what the unenlightened saw as sins or crimes, therefore, the Carpocratian Gnostic was paying the price of salvation. Jesus, however, had escaped this process because he had not lost the true knowledge (in Greek, *gnosis)* of how the universe was made and who the true unbegotten God was. Although in Carpocrates's view Jesus was the mortal son of Joseph, this true knowledge gave him the power to violate Jewish law. Irenaeus wrote, "The soul, therefore, which is like that of Christ can despise these rulers who were the creators of the world, and, in like manner, receives power for accomplishing the same results."

It is likely, however, that Carpocrates talked a more radical game than he played; according to Irenaeus, a lot of the rule breaking involved sex rather than murder, mayhem, riot, and insurrection. The Carpocratians, he wrote, "lead licentious lives," and they practiced various magical arts, prepared love potions for money, and so forth. To have truly carried out Carpocrates's teachings would have put a horrible burden on his followers: Instead of "if it feels good, do it," it would have been a case of "nothing is forbidden, so everything is compulsory."

According to Irenaeus, the Carpocratians had a secret mark, a brand inside the right earlobe. One of Carpocrates's disciples was a woman named Marcellina, who brought his teachings to Rome in the mid-second century, during the episcopate of Anicetas (155–166).

"[Carpocratians] style themselves Gnostics," Irenaeus wrote. "They also possess images, some of them painted . . . while they maintain that a likeness of Christ was made by Pilate at that time when Jesus lived among men. They crown these images and set them up along with the images of the philosophers of the world, that is to say, with the images of Pythagoras and Plato and Aristotle and the rest.

They have other modes of honoring these images after the same manner as the Gentiles."

According to some sources, Carpocrates's son Epiphanes wrote a sex manual at the age of 17, but some scholars question whether Epiphanes was a person or a ceremony.

Gnostics, possibly the Carpocratian variety, were probably the target of the brief epistle attributed to Jude, which says, "These men are a blot on your love-feasts, where they eat and drink without reverence. . . . They are a set of grumblers and malcontents. They follow their lusts. Big words come rolling from their lips, and they court favor to gain their ends. . . . These men draw a line between spiritual and unspiritual persons although they are themselves wholly unspiritual."

EPIPHANIUS, cataloging heresies two centuries after Irenaeus and relying on the latter for much of his material, repeated most of Irenaeus's denunciations of the Carpocratians' frenzied search of physical experience. See also *CHASTITY; DUALISM.*

Cathari, Catharism, Cathars   Derived from *katharos,* the Greek word for "pure," the term *Cathars* or *Carthari* was used by the church to describe a variety of heretical movements between the third and thirteenth centuries. Most were dualistic, influenced by *MANICHAEISM* or *GNOSTICISM,* and saw the universe as the battleground of a good god and an evil god, the latter often considered equivalent to the Old Testament creator of this world.

Among the sects lumped under the term *Cathari* were the *PAULICIANS, NOVATIANS, BOGOMILS, ALBANESES, CONCOREZANES, PATARINI, ALBIGENSIANS,* and *WALDENSIANS* (see individual entries for more information). These groups generally repudiated the church hierarchy, having their own bishops and deacons, and advocated an ascetic life style that might include celibacy, vegetarianism, and even ritual suicide. Usually adherents were divided into two groups, an inner group of "perfects" who took the strictest vows and an outer group of "believers" or "hearers" who lived more worldly lives but followed the perfects' teachings otherwise.

Catharism arose in the eastern Mediterranean region and spread slowly westward, but since the term was a generic one, it cannot be used to prove organizational connections between groups. For instance, *EPIPHANIUS,* a Palestinian-born bishop writing in the late fourth century, described a sect of Cathari begun by a bishop named Novatus in Rome during the time of the persecuting emperor Decius, whose reign began in 549. The Novatians considered themselves to be purer Christians than their fellows; Novatus fell out with his fellow bishops over, among other things, whether individuals who had sinned after baptism—particularly by making an offering to the emperor in order to avoid martyrdom—could be readmitted to the church. Novatus held that they could not unless they underwent severe penance. "Swollen with arrogance on account of those who had lapsed under the persecution, he and his followers would have nothing to do with those who had repented after the persecution, and went over to the heresy of saying there was no salvation [for them], but that there was only one repentance, and after baptism there could be no further mercy for one who had lapsed."

Subsequently, Epiphanius continued, the Novatians went on to shun anyone who married a second time (Epiphanius himself believed that the clergy should marry only once, if at all).

Some of these concerns resurfaced during the Middle Ages among various heretical groups, including the best-known Cathars, those of northern Italy and southern France. The Albigensian heretics brought Catharism to its greatest period of influence in the twelfth and thirteenth centuries before being militarily destroyed in the early 1200s by what, ironically, was the only permanently successful medieval Crusade, which began in 1209.

The word *Cathar* also provided medieval Germans with a generic term for heretic, *Ketzer.* Berthold von Regensburg, a thirteenth-century Franciscan preacher, used the term in a sermon, making a pun on *Katze* (cat) and comparing the insidious heretic to a stealthy cat

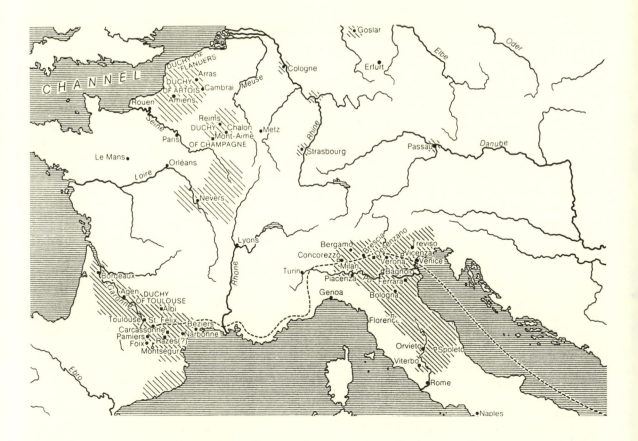

Expansion of Cathar doctrines in Europe from the late twelfth century into the thirteenth century. (Reprinted, by permission of the publisher, from Erbstösser, Heretics in the Middle Ages, *Edition Leipzig, 1984.)*

30

whose breath "is most unwholesome and dangerous. . . . Therefore is the heretic called Ketzer, because he is like no beast so much as the cat herself; and even so swiftly hath he defiled a man's body."

Celestines
See *FRANCISCANS; FRATICELLI.*

Celsus   A Pagan philosopher who lived from 125 to 175, Celsus wrote a blistering attack on the early Christians. It was rebutted by the Christian theologian *ORIGEN* in a book called *Against Celsus.*

Among Celsus's objections to the Christian gospels: Why did Jesus not know that Judas Iscariot would betray him? The author of Mark said that Jesus had foreknowledge but that the prophecy had to be fulfilled; the author of John had Jesus arrange the betrayal by giving the piece of bread to Judas. On the other hand, Celsus was favorably impressed by the mutual help individual Christians and congregations offered to one another.

A satirical view of a monk and nun about to break their vows of chastity. (From an anonymous woodcut.)

Celsus (quoted by Origen) gave a picture of prophet-ridden Palestine that helps us understand the milieu of both the gospels and other religious figures of the time such as *SIMON MAGUS* and *APOLLONIUS OF TYANA*. Around temples, Roman military camps, and cities it was common to find self-proclaimed prophets, he said. "Each has the convenient and customary spiel, 'I am the god,' or 'a son of god' or 'a divine spirit,' and 'I have come, for the world is about to be destroyed, and you, men, because of our injustice, will go with it. But I wish to save you, and you shall see me again coming back with heavenly power. Blessed is he who worships me now! On all others, both cities and countrysides, I shall cast eternal fire.'" Celsus

placed Jesus among these wandering healers and professed miracle workers, and Origen, in attempting to refute him, had to argue that Jesus's miracles were more lasting, more real, and performed without the aid of demons.

Cerdo   A Syrian *GNOSTIC* of the first century, Cerdo is credited with influencing the teachings of *MARCION,* whose radical reinterpretation of Jesus's teachings was considered heretical by the early church. From Cerdo, Marcion is said to have acquired the typical Gnostic idea that the creator of the world, or the *DEMIURGE* (from a Greek word meaning "public craftsman"), is not the true God. The Demiurge was Yahweh, the wrathful and warlike Old Testament God, but "behind" or "above" him was the true, good, loving, spiritual Father, who sent Christ to tell humanity how to escape the evil material world and its self-deluded creator. Cerdo, like many Gnostics, taught that since the physical world is evil, Christ only appeared to have a physical body and to suffer—a heresy known as *DOCETISM*. Likewise he rejected the doctrine of the resurrection of the flesh.

Cerinthus   Little is known about the early *GNOSTIC* teacher Cerinthus except that his teachings have been compared to those of *CARPOCRATES*. He was apparently a contemporary of the apostle Paul, lived in Asia Minor, and advocated a type of *DOCETISM*, saying that at the crucifixion the divine part of Jesus escaped and flew up rather than suffered.

Chastity   Too much emphasis on avoiding sexual relations and procreation was actually a sign of potential heresy to the medieval Catholic church. This was so not only because the medieval church was notorious for its priests who had common-law wives and cardinals who had mistresses, but because dualist groups such as the *CATHARS* frequently preached against marriage and against conceiving children. The heretics' teaching was based on the idea that each of us carries a divine spark that is imprisoned in the evil material world. To create more children allows more divine particles of the true God (or his angels, depending on the variety of dualist teaching) to be made subject to Satan, ruler of the physical universe.

Chastity was, of course, valued by early Christians; some married couples who converted to the new religion agreed to stop having sexual relations and to "live like angels," expecting the imminent return of Christ in their lifetimes. Both divorce and remarriage after a spouse's death were considered undesirable. Many of the noncanonical "acts" of various apostles went to extremes in praising virginity over marriage. Jesus, after all, praised those who made themselves "eunuchs for the sake of the kingdom of heaven" (Matthew 19:12), and some Christian men such as *ORIGEN* the theologian took the words literally and castrated themselves. These chaste orthodox Christians saw themselves as being free to listen to God instead of being bound to spouses and families; by overcoming the lusts of the flesh they outdid even angels in holiness, since angels had no physical bodies to deal with. (For one conflict in particular see *JOVINIAN*.)

As time passed, church leaders downplayed the importance of chastity in favor of a sacramental view of marriage and procreation. But the desire of some people to live a more perfect life and to take the words of Jesus and St. Paul literally never disappeared. Soon, chastity outside of official channels—especially when contrasted with the corruption and licentiousness among the clergy—became a sign of heresy. In 1176 in the French city of Rheims, a peasant girl was accused of *CATHARISM* after rejecting a sexual proposition by a handsome young priest; after accusation and imprisonment, the girl confessed to belonging to a dualist sect and was duly burned at the stake.

If, however, the heretic was a radical dualist, he or she might accept the teaching that, once the true nature of the dual material/spiritual cosmos had been comprehended, sex was not evil as long as no children were engendered. Birth-control methods being primitive back then, heretics who clung to this view were frequently accused of practicing unnatural acts. The corruption of the term *Bulgar* (as a synonym for *Bogomil*) into *bugger* as a slang term meaning "to have anal intercourse" reflects this accusation. See also *BOGOMIL; DUALISM; GNOSTICISM*.

Chenoboskion Library
See *NAG HAMMADI*.

Collyridians This was the name given by *EPIPHANIUS,* a fourth-century bishop, in his encyclopedia of heresies to a group of Arabian women who performed a special worship in honor of Mary, the mother of Jesus. Although not describing these women in detail, other than to say that their practice had originated in Thrace (an area now subdivided among Greece, Bulgaria, and Turkey), Epiphanius described how they decorated a chair or square stool, spread a cloth on it, and on one day a year put out an offering of bread in Mary's name. He described the sect as "quite ridiculous," using his brief description chiefly as a launching point for his attack on the ordination of women. About the Collyridians, he continued: "Which of the prophets ever bade us worship a man, to say nothing of a woman? For she [Mary] is a chosen vessel, but a woman, and in no way different in nature, highly honored though she is in her will and her senses, as are the bodies of the saints."

Concorezanes Named after Gorzia, a town in Albania, the Concorezanes were one branch of the twelfth-century *BOGOMIL* heresy. They were also known as Garatenses. Both they and the *ALBANESES* represent Italian manifestations of *DUALISM*, the idea that the world is a battleground between cosmic forces of good and evil. Medieval dualism in southern France produced the famous heresy of the *ALBIGENSES*.

Conrad of Marburg One of the most notorious early officers of the *INQUISITION*, Conrad was a secular priest who had been involved in the military crusade against the *ALBIGENSIAN* heretics in the early thirteenth century, a campaign that included the mass burnings of large groups of real or suspected heretics. Later, in

1225, he joined the household of Elizabeth of Thuringia (a German principality), wife of Landgrave (Prince) Louis IV of Thuringia.

After the landgrave's death in 1227, Elizabeth, then only 20 years old and of highly religious character, joined the *FRANCISCAN* Third Order. With Conrad as her spiritual director, she spent her remaining four years undergoing physical austerities and ministering to the sick; subsequently, Conrad has been accused of contributing to her early death by urging her to greater and greater denial of bodily needs.

After Pope Gregory IX's promulgation of the constitution for the new, centralized Inquisition in 1231, Conrad was put in charge of destroying heresy (particularly *WALDENSIANISM*) in Germany, along with reforming monasteries and denouncing corrupt priests. According to records of his time, Conrad caused the execution of so many suspected heretics with so little formality that he frightened the German clergy and nobility. When one rich German count, Henry of Sayn, was accused of heresy in 1233, he managed to summon a council of bishops and priests to hear the charges Conrad laid against him. Conrad refused to accept the council's verdict of innocent; five days later he was murdered along with a Franciscan monk by persons unknown.

Constantine   The reign of the Roman emperor Constantine the Great from 312 to 337 was a turning point for Christianity. It marked the effective end of governmental persecution of Christians (and, ultimately, the beginning of Christian persecution of Jews), except during the brief reign of the emperor *JULIAN THE APOSTATE* from 361 to 363.

Before he won the throne during a period of civil war, Constantine, as caesar (regional ruler) of the West in 306, restored property that had been seized from Christians in Britain and Gaul during the great persecution of 303–305. Confiscated Christian properties were restored in the eastern empire in 312. After 320 he began to promote Christianity more vigorously, giving congregations government money to build or rebuild churches and preferring Christians for government jobs. He influenced church leaders to call the councils of Arles (314) and *NICAEA* (325).

Constantinople (present-day Istanbul), the new "Christian Rome," was founded in 330 as capital of the Roman Empire. It remained the capital of the Eastern (Byzantine) Empire until it fell to the Turks in 1453.

Traditionally, Constantine's favoritism toward the Christian religion began in 312 as he prepared for battle with a rival emperor outside Rome. Raised in the imperial cult of *SOL INVICTUS* and officially a Pagan who had once seen a vision of the sun god Apollo, Constantine now had a dream in which Christ appeared to him, telling the future emperor to place the chi-rho monogram (a combination of the Greek letters *X* and *P*—the first two letters in the Greek spelling of Christ) on his soldiers' shields. Later pious legend improved the story, changing the dream into a vision in which Constantine and the army saw a chi-rho in the sky, accompanied by the Latin words *In hoc signo vinces* (In this sign, conquer).

His victory the following day convinced Constantine that Christianity was the true religion, but he delayed his baptism until he was on his death bed, perhaps because formal conversion would have interfered with the necessities of imperial rulership, such as having his second wife and one son executed as alleged plotters against him. See also *DONATISM*.

David of Dinant   A scholar accused of promoting pantheistic materialism, David of Dinant (or Dinan) was probably born in Belgium around 1160. In about 1200 he was teaching philosophy at the University of Paris, where he followed Duns Scotus Erigena's interpretation of Aristotle, identifying the ancient Greek philosopher's "primary matter" with God and dividing reality into three categories: matter (bodies), intellect (souls), and spirit (eternal substance). Ultimately, according to later medieval philosophers such as Thomas Aquinas, David taught that these three categories were the same, manifestations of a single principle of being.

This teaching, in the church's view, displayed the heresy of pantheism, seeing God embodied in all things rather than as a separate creator of all. David died around 1206; in 1210 a church council at Paris condemned his work and ordered copies burned. Anyone possessing David's writings after 25 December 1210 was a heretic, the council declared. As a result, his teachings can only be reconstructed from the comments and paraphrases of other scholars. See also *AMALRIC OF BENE; SCHOLASTICISM*.

De Heretico Comburendo   This act, whose title translates as "On the burning of a heretic," was passed by the English Parliament in 1401 against the *LOLLARDS*. It followed the general pattern set out by the papal decrees establishing the *INQUISITION:* Heretics were to be arrested and tried before ecclesiastical courts, and if they refused to repent, they were to be handed over to the secular authorities to be burned. It was modified in 1414 to decrease church authority and provide more secular control over the process.

Demiurge   Based on a Greek word meaning "craftsman," Demiurge was a title applied by many *GNOSTICS* to the creator of the material world. Although used by the philosopher Plato 400 years before the Christian era as a name for the creator, the title must be understood in Gnostic terms as referring to a mere craftsman as opposed to the true God, whose realm was entirely spiritual.

Although Gnostic explanations of the universe were many and varied, a common theme was that through cosmic conflicts or through the misadventures of divine beings such as *SOPHIA,* human souls became trapped in gross, physical bodies in the Demiurge's world. Not only were most people unaware of their true origin, but the Demiurge himself—frequently equated with the God of the Hebrews—acted under a misconception that he was the true God, whereas in fact he was a lesser being produced by the true God. Another title for him was Cosmocrator, or "world ruler." Since the Gnostics saw orthodox Jewish and Christian religious leaders as part of the Demiurge's retinue, they saw no purpose in obeying these leaders' instructions.

Both Gnostic Christians and the Neoplatonist (see *NEOPLATONISM*) philosophers who influenced them tended to see the physical world as a separate and inferior creation. Mainstream Christianity, as defined by such theologians as *AUGUSTINE OF HIPPO,* saw it as being created by God out of nothing, without the intervening figure of the Demiurge. See also *ALBIGENSIANS; BARBELOS; MANICHAEISM; SOPHIA*.

Dionysius the Areopagite   An Athenian Greek who lived in the first century, this Dionysius is said to have been a member of the Court of Areopagus, an Athenian legal body consisting of a council of nobles, hence his common title. He is briefly mentioned in Acts 17:34 as being converted to Christianity by the preaching of Paul, who had been hauled before the Court of Areopagus and ordered to explain the new doctrines he was preaching both in the Jewish synagogue and in the marketplace.

During the sixth century, however, Dionysius's name was plucked from the New Testament and attached to a body of Neoplatonic (see *NEOPLATONISM*) writings in order to give a Christian gloss to a work of essentially non-Christian philosophy. As a presumably educated Greek converted to Christianity, Dionysius was a plausible candidate, and medieval writers and readers were accustomed to seeing works attributed to famous ancient figures—Moses, King Solomon, and so forth. (The tendency to attribute more recent writings to ancient authorities has been common among literate religious communities around the world.) The actual author (or authors) of these writings is now usually referred to as "pseudo-Dionysius" and may have lived in Egypt or Syria. The sixteenth-century scholar Desiderius Erasmus was among the first to suggest that the biblical Dionysius was not the actual author.

As a conduit for introducing Neoplatonic thought into Christianity, the works of pseudo-Dionysius were very influential in both the Eastern and Western churches. They were translated into Latin in the ninth century by the Irish theologian Duns (Johannes) Scotus Erigena and helped influence the medieval theologians' view of heaven as a realm filled with "light"—an emanation from God that was not material but a force that filled material objects to a greater or lesser degree.

Docetism   From a Greek word meaning "to appear," Docetism represents a persistent attempt within Christianity to solve the logical paradox of how God could suffer and die as a man. The term has been used in different eras to describe any teaching that says that Jesus did not physically suffer and die on the cross, but only appeared to do so, producing through his divine power a collective hallucination on the part of onlookers. The first Docetist on record is *SIMON MAGUS,* whose activities were mentioned in the book of Acts. There was no one sect of Docetists; the teaching appeared at various times and places as non-Jewish Christians in particular attempted to cope with the

unheard-of notion that a divine being could suffer death at the hands of humans. The reverse of Docetism might be said to be those explanations of the crucifixion that claim that Jesus himself was not crucified but died a normal death at some other time and place.

Parts of the New Testament appear to have been written to counter Docetic teachings. For example, the first letter of John 4:2–3, dealing with false prophets, says, "This is how we may recognize the Spirit of God: every spirit which acknowledges that Jesus Christ has come in the flesh is from God, and every spirit which does not thus acknowledge Jesus is not from God." Likewise, the brief second letter of John says, "Many deceivers have gone out into the world, who do not acknowledge Jesus Christ as coming in the flesh. . . . If anyone comes to you who does not bring this doctrine, do not welcome him into your house or give him a greeting; for anyone who gives him a greeting is an accomplice in his wicked deeds."

The spread of Docetic teachings by Gnostic Christians provoked the first formal orthodox Christian creed, that of Ignatius of Antioch (martyred during the reign of the Emperor Trajan between 98 and 117). This creed affirmed that Jesus "truly, and not in appearance" did and suffered all the events recorded in the Gospels. See also *GNOSTICISM.*

Donatism   Caused by a dispute within the churches of Roman North Africa (primarily present-day coastal Libya), the Donatist schism was the first in which imperial authority was asked to uphold one Christian group and suppress another. On the surface, the Donatists (named for Donatus of Casae Nigrae, later bishop of Carthage) were opposed to the consecration of another man, Caecilian, to that post in 311; underneath, however, lay a simmering dispute over the character of the priesthood.

Like some of the strict medieval reformers who were also often considered heretical, the Donatists held the clergy to a strict moral standard. A sinful priest, they believed, could not validly administer the sacraments such as baptism, marriage, or the Eucharist. In this particular case, the issue involved the behavior of some priests and bishops during the persecution of Christians ordered by the emperor Diocletian, at its peak between 302 and 305. Although a number had been martyred, others were accused of collaborating with the imperial authorities. Caecilian, in particular, was accused of being a *traditor,* one who handed over his Bible to be destroyed. Holding that no *traditor* should be consecrated, a group of 70 dissident bishops— nucleus of what would become the Donatist faction—met and declared his consecration to be invalid. They declared Caecilian to be excommunicated and replaced him with another man, who was followed in turn by Donatus himself four years later.

In 312, meanwhile, *CONSTANTINE* the Great, who favored Christianity, had risen to the throne. Caecilian's party begged the new emperor to intervene on its behalf and uphold the mainline North African church. After first attempting to delegate the problem to Pope Miltiades, the emperor by his own authority summoned a church council in 314. The council voted to uphold Caecilian's consecration, but the schismatics, now led by Donatus, refused to accept its decision.

Between 317 and 321, Constantine actively persecuted the Donatists; his son Constans did the same, exiling Donatus in 347. The Donatists, however, grew to include the majority of North African Christians. In the 360s, under the Pagan emperor *JULIAN THE APOSTATE,* who refused to take sides in Christian disputes, their power increased and they moved toward becoming an independent regional church, in some cases becoming allied with an antilandlord group of social revolutionaries called Circumcellions.

During the early fifth century, the prominent theologian *AUGUSTINE OF HIPPO* was involved in numerous disputes with the Donatists and himself sought aid from the Christian emperor Honorius to get them suppressed by force of imperial law. The open power of the Donatist church was effectively broken by an imperial decree in 412 that banned the heretics, confiscated their property, and exiled their bishops.

Some Donatists may have regrouped after Roman North Africa was invaded by the Vandal tribes in 429. After armies of what was now the Byzantine Empire reconquered the area in the 530s, church authorities continued to be concerned about the Donatist presence. In the subsequent century, however, the movement seems to have vanished beneath resurgent catholic power and the subsequent Muslim invasions.

Dualism   Generally speaking, dualism refers to any of several religious or philosophical positions that see the universe as made up of two incompatible principles, such as spirit (or ideas) and matter, or good and evil. To such groups as the *GNOSTICS, BOGOMILS, MANICHAEANS,* and *ALBIGENSIANS,* a dualistic conflict underlay the way they interpreted scriptures and conducted their lives.

Within the Mediterranean and Near Eastern worlds, Greek religion and philosophy were perceived as more concerned with the fundamental gap between the spiritual and material worlds, whereas the notion of the universe as the battleground of good and evil cosmic principles was usually seen as Persian. Inevitably, however, the two forms of dualism became commingled. Several centuries before Plato, the Orphic mystery cult of Greece taught that humanity's goodness lay in its spiritual component, which was imprisoned in a material body and had to be liberated, as the mythical musician Orpheus had liberated his beloved Eurydice from the Underworld. Again and again through subsequent centuries, this doctrine would be extended as a justification for various ascetic doctrines. For example, dualists judged vegetarianism to be superior to eating meat because animals were a product of sexual intercourse, and by eating meat people perpetuated the evil cycle of material reproduction. Likewise, dualistic beliefs would lead Gnostics and others to avoid all forms of sexual intercourse or at least to avoid conceiving children. In either case, the fundamental idea was to keep souls from being imprisoned in new bodies. Less extreme dualists, such as numerous Greek philosophers in the Platonic tradition, would advocate disciplining the body and subordinating its wants while focusing the mind on higher goals.

Within such long-lived heretical sects as the Bogomils and Albigensians, both mitigated and absolute or radical dualists could be found. Mitigated dualists tended to see Satan or the principle of evil as having sprung from God or being permitted by God to exist until some future date. In one Bogomil story, for example, God permitted his younger brother Satan to create the material world. Mitigated dualism tended over time to be replaced by a more absolute or Manichaean form, probably influenced ultimately by Persian religion, which saw the universe as permanently divided into good and evil realms forever at war with each other. Manichaeans divided the history of the cosmos into three epochs: In the first, light (good) and darkness (evil) were completely separated; in the second (present) epoch, they were intermingled and in conflict; and in the third epoch, all lost particles of light imprisoned in matter would be reunited with their source and the original separation would be restored.

Dualistic tendencies have always posed a problem for Christianity, particularly when Christians have sought to reform what they saw as a lax or corrupt church. As the historian Jeffrey Burton Russell wrote, "In all Christian puritanism there is a touch of dualism." The ideas that the body is the temple—rather than the prison—of the spirit and that God approves of creation can easily be shifted into dualist oppositions between spirit and flesh and between God's kingdom and the kingdom of this world. Because gentile Christianity grew up in an environment influenced by both Greek and Persian dualism (not to mention the dualistic tendencies of radical Jewish sects such as the Essenes), dualistic thinking has frequently crept into it, particularly in the area of gender and sexuality, but also in the concept of renunciation generally. This thinking may also underlie the significance placed on such dichotomies as settled land/wilderness and Christians/heathens.

Ebionites The term *Ebionitism* is used to refer to a Palestinian and Syrian form of Christianity practiced by Jews and emphasizing Jesus's Jewish nature. Scholars believed that the Ebionite communities used a gospel or gospels similar to the Gospel of Matthew (considered the most Jewish of the four canonical gospels), but that their version left out the virgin birth and resurrection of Jesus. Instead, the Ebionites considered Jesus to have been an exceptional prophet who upheld Jewish law.

In his work *Against Heresies,* the catholic writer *IRENAEUS* upheld the church's position against the Ebionites thus: "How can they be saved unless he was God who wrought their salvation on the earth? And how shall man pass to God unless God has passed into [or, in some translations, has been contained in/received into] man? How shall man be freed from the generation of death, except he pass into a new birth, wonderfully and unexpectedly given by God, for a token of salvation, a birth from a virgin, receiving a rebirth through faith?"

The term *Ebionite* comes from a Hebrew word meaning "a poor person"; whether it refers to the Ebionites' actual poverty and whether that poverty was voluntary or not are difficult to say. In Romans, St. Paul does mention sending aid to the needy Jewish Christians in Jerusalem. On the other hand, the term was used over the first four centuries of the Christian era to denote various Jewish converts to Christianity who also maintained links with the Jewish community. Beyond that, it also came to be used generically to signify anyone who denied Jesus's divinity and considered him to be only an outstanding religious teacher.

Elchaisai See *MANI.*

Elkesai, Elkesaite Mughtasilism See *MANI.*

Encratites See *MARCION.*

Epiphanius Born about 315 in Palestine, Epiphanius studied in Egypt and entered a desert monastery there. Later he returned to Palestine and founded another monastery around 335. In approximately 366 he became bishop of Constantia (modern Salamis) in Cyprus. He died during a sea voyage in May 402.

Epiphanius is best known for a work called the *Panarion* (Greek for The medicine chest), which offered antidotes to a variety of heresies. It was written between 374 and 376 and was dedicated to two Syrian abbots. Epiphanius described his book as "a medicine chest for those bitten by wild animals"—that is, those infected by false teachings.

His encyclopedic treatment covered not only the controversies of his time but also Greek philosophical schools such as Epicureanism, Stoicism, and Platonism, plus Jewish sects. In all, 80 heresies were described, some from first-hand knowledge and others from hearsay or legend. Four sects were given as the mothers of the rest: barbarism or primitive religion, Scythism or the religion of people from the time of Noah onwards, Hellenism or classical Paganism, and Judaism.

As a former monk, Epiphanius was particularly concerned with sexual issues and the problem of women's religious behavior, and many of his diagnoses of heresies and their remedies focus on women. He opposed women becoming religious leaders, which happened in a number of heretical groups. "The female sex is easily mistaken, fallible, and poor in judgment," he wrote. Starting, for example, with a description of women in Arabia who on certain days baked little breads or cakes and offered them in honor of the Virgin Mary (the *COLLYRIDIANS*), he produced an argument against women ever holding priestly office. "Never in any way did a woman function as a priest toward God, not even Eve herself who had indeed fallen into transgression." Had Christian women been intended to hold such offices, he continued, Mary would have done so, but since she did not, that established a negative precedent. "Lest some [like the heretics mentioned] think that the holy Virgin is something special, [Jesus] called her woman, as if prophesying that there would in the future be schisms on earth and heresies, lest any be too much in awe of the holy Virgin and therefore fall prey to this ridiculous heresy."

Likewise, Epiphanius denounced the *MONTANISTS* for appointing women clergy: "Even if women among them are ordained to the episcopacy and presbyterate because of Eve, they hear the Lord saying, 'Your orientation will be toward your husband and he will rule over you.'"

But of all heresies, that of *GNOSTICISM* touched him most deeply, for he wrote, "I myself, dearly beloved, fell in with this sect and was indoctrinated into it from the mouth of its practitioners." He claimed that Gnostic women had tried to seduce him in his youth and that upon his complaint to the local Christian bishop, some 80 Gnostics were harried from his hometown. The Gnostic elite were all homosexuals, however, in his view.

Living during the growth of the heresy of *ARIANISM,* Epiphanius was particularly devoted to combating it, and he upheld the theological party of Athanasius over the followers of the theologian *ORIGEN,* whom he accused of false teaching about the preexistence of souls and the relation of God the Son to God the Father. He also opposed what he saw as the excessive veneration of holy images (see *ICONOCLASM*). In the early 390s he is said to have destroyed a painting in a Jerusalem church.

Epiphanius's concern with correctness and orthodoxy extended to his other writings: He is also known for two treatises, *On Gems* and *On Measures and Weights*. He died in 403 and was later declared to be a saint, his feast day being 12 May.

Eudo de Stella   A hermit from Brittany whose name means "Eudo of the Star" (also referred to in French as Eudes de l'Etoile), this charismatic wandering preacher probably carried a Breton name such as Eon or Eun. Around 1145 he is recorded to have begun preaching wherever crowds gathered. In the words of one outraged chronicler, "Although he was uneducated and scarcely knew even the letters of the alphabet, he discoursed and preached from Holy Writ with a filthy mouth. Although not in holy orders, with impious boldness he disgracefully celebrated Mass, to the error and the destruction of the corrupted people."

The number of "corrupted people" grew so large that Eudo organized his own church with himself at its head, a second Christ. He gave his closest disciples titles such as Wisdom and Judgment. According to ecclesiastical chroniclers, he declared that the phrase used in Latin-language prayers—*Per eundem Dominum nostrum Jesum Christum*—did not mean "through the same Jesus Christ our Lord" but rather "through Eun Jesus Christ our Lord."

Eudo's self-proclaimed messianic mission apparently coincided with a period of harsh winters and bad harvests in Brittany, so many people with no resources left joined his wandering band. At some point their leader moved from peacefully preaching to violently taking what the group needed, and his followers began attacking churches and monasteries, undoubtedly with the rationale that their inhabitants were not preaching the truth anyway.

The chronicler William of Newburgh wrote of Eudo that he seemed to have "a remarkable luster about him, a royal sumptuousness and arrogance; those who attended him, free from care and labor, expensively garbed, feasting ostentatiously, seemed to live in the greatest joyousness, so much so that many who came to attack him were beguiled, not by his true aspect but by his illusion of splendor." (William then advances the argument that Eudo and his followers banqueted not on stolen or donated food, but on delicacies furnished by demons.)

Their outlawry reached the attention of the Archbishop of Rouen, who sent soldiers to capture Eudo. In 1148 the prophet was imprisoned and examined by a church council meeting in the city of Rheims. There he declared that his name also lay concealed in the words *Per eum qui venturus est judicare vivos et mortuos et seculum per ignem*; in other words, Eun was the one who would "come to judge the living and the dead and the world by fire."

Furthermore, he carried a staff with one forked end and explained it by saying, "This is a matter of sublime mystery. For as long as it looks to heaven with its two prongs, as you now see it, God has two parts of the world and the third part he yields to me. On the other hand, if I turn these two topmost points of the staff downward toward earth and raise the lower end, which is single, to point toward heaven, keeping two thirds of the world for myself, I relinquish only the third portion to God." This heresy brought Eun/Eudo imprisonment on bread and water at Rouen, where he died. His leading disciples were convicted and executed by burning; according to the chroniclers, they remained steadfast in their heresy until their deaths.

Eutyches   Head of a monastery near Constantinople (modern Istanbul), Eutyches lived circa 378–454. He was the originator of the *MONOPHYSITE* heresy, the idea that Christ had one nature that mingled human and divine elements.

Fedeli d'Amore   This group, whose name translates roughly as love's faithful, was apparently a quasi-Gnostic, initiatory assembly of persons holding to an esoteric religion disguised as the cult of the Unique Lady. During the twelfth century, when the troubadours were spreading the cult of courtly love and the knight's devotion to his idealized lover throughout Western Europe, some used the figure of this woman as a symbol of the transcendent Wisdom accessible to the spiritually discerning. According to one text of the time, the Fedeli played on the Latin word for "love," *amor,* breaking it into "a," meaning "without," and "mor(t)," French for "death."

Although little is known about the Fedeli d'Amore, their outlook appears to have been similar to Dante's a century later, when the Florentine poet took a mortal woman whom he loved, Beatrice, and elevated her in his epic poem on Purgatory to a saintly figure comparable to the Blessed Virgin herself, casting Beatrice as one who could lead him closer to God.

Ficino, Marsilio   An Italian scholar working for the Florentine ruler Cosimo de Medici, Ficino (1433–1499) was no heretic himself—in fact, he entered holy orders later in life. But his patron had set up an academy of learned men and acquired a number of philosophical manuscripts that he desired translated from Greek into Latin. At Cosimo's request, Ficino translated the *Corpus hermeticum,* an important group of esoteric texts, as well as various works of Hellenistic philosophy—all part of Cosimo's desire to revive ancient learning.

When Cosimo acquired the *Corpus hermeticum* around 1460, he told Ficino to make its translation his priority. As it happened, this collection of 17 works ascribed to the legendary philosopher Hermes Trismegistus (thrice-greatest Hermes)—who, according to some accounts, was the grandson of Thoth, Egyptian god of wisdom—would revive *NEOPLATONISM* in its original, un-Christianized form in an intellectual climate ready to receive it. The most famous of these works, the *Poimandres,* is a moderate dualist (see *DUALISM*) dialog describing the origin of the world. In it, the world is the result of the fall of Anthropos, the celestial man, who, entranced by the world of the *DEMIURGE*, mates with Nature and produces humanity: celestial sparks in physical bodies.

Hermes Trismegistus, in fact, would lend his name to this new, magically oriented combination of religion and philosophy: hermeticism. The hermetic manuscripts were greeted by their new readers as containing the wisdom of ancient Egypt, although they were in fact much more recent. They combined erudite speculation with magical ways of understanding and manipulating the physical world. Embraced by many readers because they seemed to show how a unified perennial philosophy began in ancient Egypt and anticipated Christianity (a theme later developed by Rosicrucians and Masons), the manuscripts also engendered a revival of ceremonial magic, alchemy, and astrology—all attempts to find the links between religious knowledge and knowledge of nature.

Flagellant Sects   Medieval flagellants—persons who whipped themselves and one another in penance for their or a community's sins—occasionally formed groups that attracted the church's condemnation, even though flagellation was a permitted form of monastic discipline, either self-imposed or as punishment.

Occasional outbreaks of group flagellation occurred among medieval laypeople during times of high social stress. One began in the mid-thirteenth century in Italy, following the plague of 1259; the Umbrian hermit Raniero Fasani has been credited with organizing processions of *disciplinati* who whipped themselves in public. The practice of self-flagellation spread to other countries, but was prohibited by the church in 1261. (The anticipated world changes prophesied by *JOACHIM OF FLORIS* also contributed to the flagellants' activities.) Processions led by priests marched from town to town; when they arrived at a town, they would stand in the street or square in front of a church flogging themselves for hours. Invariably, some townspeople would join the procession and swell its size as it moved on.

Although the Italian flagellation movement died away after two years, some of its members moved north into Germany and spread the same message: God was angry with humanity for its misdeeds and had decided to wipe it out as he had in the time of Noah's flood. Moved by the pleas of the Virgin Mary, he had relented, but on the condition that people abandon their adultery, blasphemy, usury, and other sins. And, according to a miraculous letter that carried the text of a marble tablet supposedly found on the altar of the Church of the Holy Sepulcher in crusader-controlled Jerusalem, believers should join a flagellant procession for 33 1/2 days, equivalent to the years of Jesus's life on earth.

Although the flagellation mania was short-lived, the idea lived on in religious brotherhoods and became part of European religious consciousness, occurring again and again in times of social crisis. For example, a second large-scale outbreak of flagellation began in the mid-fourteenth century after the Black Death (bubonic plague) swept through Europe. Faced with the rapid and unexplainable death of a sizable percentage of the population—in some areas, perhaps a fourth to more than half of the people died—the survivors frequently decided

A procession of flagellants whipping themselves in public. (From Book of Hours. *Courtesy of the Bodleian Library, University of Oxford. MS. Douce 144, fol. 110R.)*

that they were being punished by God. Led by renegade priests, monks, *BEGHARDS,* or other self-appointed masters, they formed processions and marched from town to town, assembling before churches to sing hymns and whip themselves raw. By now flagellants wore uniforms similar to the crusaders' surcoats: a white robe with red crosses on the front and back. The masters, whether ordained or not, took the status and roles of priests, hearing the flagellants' confessions, imposing penances, and absolving their sins. When the flagellants stripped to the waist and whipped themselves in their public demonstrations, the master would also beat them, saying afterwards, "Arise, by the honor of pure martyrdom."

The flagellants' displays of whipping, hymn singing, and praying drew huge numbers of spectators, some of whom were inevitably recruited. Realizing that the flagellants were, in effect, substituting their practices for the normal church sacraments, Pope Clement VI forbade the demonstrations in 1349, but they continued to reappear, spurred by later outbreaks of the plague as the century continued.

The church's objection was based on two positions: (1) the penitential practices were inappropriately turned into public displays instead of being performed alone and privately, and (2) flagellant groups frequently turned to heretical thoughts, for example, preaching the onset of the millennium when Christ would return to rule for 1,000 years. Particularly in Germany, flagellant spokesmen began to condemn the Catholic church as corrupt and its sacraments as worthless. Some flagellants also incited hatred toward the Jews, accusing them of having caused the plague—although Jews, of course, suffered from it too. This resulted in mob actions such as the massacre of most of Frankfort's Jewish population in July 1349. (Similar massacres happened in the German cities of Cologne and Mainz.)

Later flagellant groups arose in Spain in the fifteenth century, encouraged by the apocalyptic preaching of St. Vincent Ferrer (circa 1350–1419, canonized 1455). These groups were connected with the Spanish and Portuguese lay brotherhoods (*confradías*) that were chartered by clerical or secular authorities under patronage of a particular saint. They grew to the point where their public processions and whippings during Holy Week were eventually banned in the eighteenth century, although the ban took decades to become effective. Their practices were transferred to the Western Hemisphere, where the tradition (also influenced by the Third Order of *FRANCISCANS*) was continued in New Mexico and southern Colorado by the Penitentes (La Fraternidad Piadosa de Nuestro Padre Jesús Nazareno), another group of laymen frequently condemned by Catholic authorities, into the twentieth century.

A Franciscan monk. (Adapted from Percy Dearmer, Everyman's History of the English Church, Ox- *ford: A.R. Mowbray & Co., Ltd., 1909.)*

Francis of Assisi, Franciscans

The order of monks founded by St. Francis of Assisi in the early thirteenth century survives today and is not considered heretical. But even before Francis died in 1226, some of his followers went beyond his teachings and took positions that caused them to be theologically condemned and in a few instances executed. At the root of most Franciscan controversies lay the issue of holy or apostolic poverty, a condition personified by Francis himself as Dame Poverty.

Although he was born to relatively well-off parents, flirted with a military career in the perennial wars between northern Italian city-states, and had other youthful adventures, Francis abruptly changed his life in his early twenties. He lived as a hermit and devoted himself to charitable works, aiding lepers and other social outcasts, and restoring abandoned churches. His actions were based largely on the directions given by Jesus to the 12 disciples in Matthew 10:7–10: "And as you go [out to preach], proclaim the message: 'The kingdom of Heaven is upon you.' Heal the sick, raise the dead, cleanse lepers, cast out devils. You received without cost; give without charge. Provide no gold, silver, or copper to fill your purse, no pack for the road, no second coat, no shoes, no stick; the worker earns his keep." The mendicant Franciscan friars were to take their orders from that passage, down to the blessing "Peace be upon this house" when entering a dwelling. They were to own only one garment and always walk on their journeys, never ride horses.

Although his actions led his family to disinherit him, Francis gathered his own disciples and in 1210 received papal permission to form a monastic order, the Friars Minor (lesser friars). Like the Dominican order, formed at about the same time (see *ALBIGENSIANS*), the Franciscans were devoted primarily to wandering and preaching, although with less emphasis on combating heresy. With Francis's blessing, a female follower named Clare formed an order of nuns called the Poor Clares (also referred to as the Second Order). Toward the end of his arduous life, Francis also laid the groundwork for a Third Order (or tertiary) of pious laypeople who would take less stringent vows than the Franciscan monks or Poor Clares. (Some female tertiaries, particularly in southern France and Italy, were also referred to as *BEGUINES*.)

Although many Franciscans became known as preachers, missionaries, and teachers, the order also attracted men who saw it as a vehicle to return to a type of primitive Christianity. The original Franciscans lived in crude huts built near their chapel, but after their founder's death, more elaborate buildings were constructed at Assisi, and the order's organizational structure was expanded and formalized. These and other developments perturbed one group of monks, referred to as Observants (the most radical of whom were called Spirituals), who felt that the saint's example and precepts were no longer being followed. Another group, known as Conventuals, supported the changes and, unlike Francis himself, held that it was proper for their order and for the larger Roman Catholic church itself to gather money and real estate. During his lifetime, however, Francis had urged the monks not to accept gifts of churches or other property, for they were to "sojourn always as guests, strangers, and pilgrims," living only on what was given to them. "The Lord called me by the way of simplicity and showed me the way of simplicity. I do not want you to mention to me any [monastic] rule, either of St. *AUGUSTINE* or St. Benedict or St. Bernard,"

Francis had told those friars who wanted a more ordered life.

As the Franciscan order became more settled and bureaucratic, the Spiritual faction began to see Francis as a key figure of the Third Age, prophesied by *JOACHIM OF FLORIS* to begin around 1260. The ongoing dispute between the Spirituals and ecclesiastical authorities intensified. The Spirituals argued that Jesus and the apostles had owned nothing during the Savior's lifetime, and their opponents held that the issue was not "possession" but "usage." In 1229, however, Pope Gregory IX issued a bull in response to Franciscans' questions that, in effect, laid aside some of the founder's wishes for the order on the ground that the monks had not formally accepted them. The bull also gave the friars permission to accumulate money and to buy what they needed rather than to depend on gifts, although an agent, not a monk, was to handle the funds.

The radical faction continued to cling to Francis's own original ideas even when their action meant defying the pope, and some began to be censured for it. (This dispute between Franciscans and papal authorities forms part of the setting of Umberto Eco's novel *The Name of the Rose*.) Authorities on the other side pointed to the common purse held by Judas in which Jesus and the apostles placed money they were given; this, they argued, set a precedent by which the church could own buildings and other material goods. Inevitably the issue of Franciscan poverty became a critique of ecclesiastical corruption in general, with the Spirituals accusing the pope, bishops, and abbots of other orders of having strayed too far from the apostolic ideals by owning not just churches but castles, palaces, towns, and farmlands. (The same criticisms were being made by other heretical groups such as *WALDENSIANS* and Albigensians.)

Increasing persecution led to the fragmentation of the Spirituals by the 1320s. Heads of Franciscan houses who identified with the Spiritual faction were removed from office. In 1318, four Spirituals were burned in Marseilles for refusing to submit to the Franciscan order's new structure. This execution, ordered by Pope John XXII, hardened the feeling of the Provençal (southern French) beguines and their sympathizers against him, building no doubt on the Provençal resentment of the papacy dating from the Albigensian Crusade of the previous century. As some Spiritual friars were demoted, split up among different monasteries, or in extreme cases executed, others left the order on their own but retained what they believed was the true Franciscan way of life, becoming known as *FRATICELLI.*

Fraticelli   The Fraticelli, whose Italian name means "little brothers," were radical members of the *FRANCISCAN* monastic order, some of whom split from it in disgust during the thirteenth and fourteenth centuries. These Franciscan "irregulars" were most numerous in Italy and Sicily. In 1318, Pope John XXII issued a bull, *Gloriosan ecclesiam,* accusing them of saying that there were in fact two churches: the "carnal" Roman Catholic church and the "spiritual" church consisting of them and their followers—one decadent and one following the way of the apostles. Along with condemning the Fraticelli for their attacks on the clergy, the pope accused them of spreading unfounded prophecies about the coming end of the world, based on the apocalyptic writings of *JOACHIM OF FLORIS* and his interpreters.

One monk, Angelo del Clareno, established several communities of Fraticelli in parts of Italy, where the populace and local rulers supported them. Another group, known as *MICHAELISTS* for their leader, Michael of Cesena, eventually found refuge in Naples. Michael of Cesena carried on a battle of tracts with the Catholic hierarchy and was ultimately excommunicated in 1328 for his attacks on papal authority.

The Fraticelli faded from view in the following century, but their ideals were in a sense continued by other radical church reformers such as the *LOLLARDS* as well as by reformers within the Franciscan order itself.

Free Spirit   More an intellectual current than an organized movement, the name Free Spirit is applied to beliefs and actions of the most radical *BEGUINES* and *BEGHARDS,* who rejected ecclesiastical governance and claimed to perceive God everywhere (the doctrine of pantheism). Furthermore, adherents of the Free Spirit claimed to have united their individual wills with God's, which left them free to do whatever they pleased.

Because the Free Spirit was not a distinct heretical sect, the brothers and sisters were persecuted only as individuals or if an entire house or community of beguines or beghards shifted into the Free Spirit camp.

Scholars have traced one key Free Spirit idea—the soul's oneness with God—to a renewed spread of Neoplatonic (see *NEOPLATONISM*) ideas in Western Europe during the thirteenth century. Contrary to orthodox ideas of God as the creator and the world as his creation, Neoplatonic thinkers saw the world as emanating or proceeding from God in a series of stages from the more spiritual to the more physical. Humans, by identifying with the spiritual parts of themselves, could become more attuned to the divine and ultimately be reabsorbed by it. As an intellectual proposition, this restated ideas of *GNOSTICISM* and *DOCETISM* and, from a catholic Christian viewpoint, denied the importance of Christ's incarnation.

The adherents of the Free Spirit were criticized in their own time, however, for making such ideas the basis for a libertine life style, for indulging themselves however they wanted, and for denying that they had thereby sinned. They proclaimed that they could listen to the promptings of the spirit without needing priests, that they were beyond the need to confess their sins or keep other medieval church rules about fasting, and that their children were free from original sin. (These statements have been echoed many times in centuries since, for example, in the proclamations of Moses David Berg, leader of the Children of God sect in the 1960s and 1970s.)

The Roman Catholic church, meanwhile, issued its summary of Free Spirit beliefs in order to condemn them. A bull of Pope Clement V, issued in 1311, listed eight core beliefs, here summarized:

1. That someone in this life could reach a state of perfection and be beyond sinning.
2. That such a person had such control over his senses that he no longer had to fast or pray.
3. That he is free from all obedience to the church.

4. That the free in spirit can obtain full blessedness in this life.
5. That every man so blessed does not need the divine light of glory to love God.
6. That only imperfect people need to perform virtuous actions.
7. That sexual intercourse is not a sin when desired.
8. That there is no need to respect Christ's body in the Eucharistic host (thus denying the Catholic doctrine of transubstantiation or the physical presence of Christ in the communion bread and wine).

At about the same time, Clement also issued decrees against the beghards and beguines, primarily in northern Europe, thus forever linking them with the charge of heresy. These groups of laymen and laywomen seeking to live the apostolic life sometimes lived in communal houses, but others wandered from place to place and supported themselves by contributions in the manner, they said, of Jesus and his disciples on the roads of Palestine. Their wandering (as opposed to the authorized wandering, preaching, and begging of the Franciscan friars) and their cry in German-speaking lands of *Brod durch Got* (bread for God's sake) now brought upon them an enduring charge of heresy. Judging from the records of heresy trials, the Free Spirit was most common in Germany, the Netherlands, and parts of present-day Switzerland and the Czech Republic.

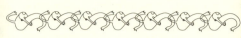

Garatenses
See *ALBANESES; CONCOREZANES.*

Gioacchino da Fiore
See *JOACHIM OF FLORIS.*

Gnosticism, Gnostics A movement influenced by Greek philosophy, Asian and Middle Eastern mysticism, and alternative interpretations of Jewish and Christian teachings, Gnosticism early on became the chief rival to orthodox Eastern and Western Christianity. On the one hand, Gnosticism merged with speculative Greek philosophy; on the other hand, it permitted the expression of personal revelations. Its ascetic side also appealed to world-weary souls who felt that their true origins lay outside the messy material world. Many Gnostic ideas remain current today in metaphysical Christian and New Age groups.

Before the discovery in late 1945 of the *NAG HAMMADI* collection of Gnostic texts and their subsequent translation and interpretation, most of what was known about Gnosticism—including even the use of the word gnostic as a descriptive term—came from the writings of heresy-hunting churchmen, such as *IRENAEUS, HIPPOLYTUS,* and *EPIPHANIUS.* Some Gnostic teachers, such as *MARCION,* apparently organized separate congregations, but other Gnostic Christians were most likely part of orthodox congregations, possibly forming a separate clique within them, or else formed shifting groups.

Like persons undergoing psychoanalysis, Gnostics were on an inward quest for the illumination or knowledge that would set them free from the world's bondage. Some completely rejected church organizations, but others considered themselves to be a more advanced, more spiritual group within the larger Christian community of more ignorant believers. According to Irenaeus, Gnostic Christians held that a secret tradition, passed down by word of mouth, had more authority than the inconsistent scriptures. He wrote how they quoted 1 Corinthians 2:6–8 to support their view: "And yet I do speak words of wisdom to those who are ripe for it, not a wisdom belonging to this passing age, nor to any of its governing powers, which are declining to their end; I speak God's hidden wisdom, his secret purpose framed from the very beginning to bring us to our full glory." Because of the individual nature of Gnosticism, it is unlikely that most Gnostic Christians cared to concentrate on forming lasting organizations.

Despite the proliferation of Gnostic texts, the knowledge had to be experienced personally, not learned from books. The aftereffect of the Gnostic experience might have resembled what psychologist Carl Jung wrote about a blissful vision he experienced while convalescing from illness in 1944, when he was in his late sixties: "[The visions] were the most tremendous things I have ever experienced. And what a contrast the day was: I was tormented and on edge; everything irritated me; everything was too material, too crude and clumsy, terribly limited both spatially and spiritually. It was all an imprisonment, for reasons impossible to divine, and yet it had a kind of hypnotic power, a cogency, as if it were reality itself, for all that I had clearly perceived its emptiness. Although my belief in the world returned to me, I have never since entirely freed myself of the impression that this life is a segment of existence which is enacted in a three-dimensional boxlike universe especially set up for it."

Gnostics divided humanity into three classes: the spiritually advanced pneumatics (from Greek for "air," "spirit"); the less-aware psychics (from the Greek *psyche),* who were motivated by the mental and emotional tides of their souls; and the totally materialistic somatics (Greek for "sleepers") or hylics (from a Greek word meaning "wooden"). "He who hears, let him get up from the deep sleep," wrote the author of the *Apocalypse of John,* one of the Nag Hammadi texts; in other words, awaken to the spiritual realities. St. Paul's use of the "psychic man" who is inferior to the "spiritual man" reflects a partially shared outlook.

Various persons and groups have been labeled Gnostic over the centuries, and most have shared several ideas. The most basic of these is that all people carry within them a spark of divinity, but that they have lost knowledge of this divinity and of their true spiritual origin outside the material world. Rather than seeing a spiritual struggle between God and the devil taking place, Gnostics described a conflict between the true, unknowable high God and a lesser god who rules this world. This lesser god, often called the *DEMIURGE* (from a Greek term meaning "public craftsman"), was identified with the angry, rule-giving god of the Hebrew Scriptures. (The Greek philosopher Plato had used the term *Demiurge* to describe the creator of the material world in the fourth century B.C.) Jesus, in contrast, had been sent by the high God to teach people how to free themselves from the Demiurge's control and return to their spiritual home upon death. His role was more like that of a supreme guide rather than a king or judge.

Allied with this view of Jesus's role was a teaching called *DOCETISM* (from a Greek word meaning "to appear"). Docetism taught that Jesus only appeared to be a flesh-and-blood human being who was born and crucified. In reality, what his family, disciples, and audiences saw was only an illusion created by his divine power. It was impossible, many Gnostics believed, for a true emissary of the high God to have been conquered even temporarily by the Demiurge and allowed to suffer and die. This teaching infuriated the nascent orthodox establishment because it devalued martyrdom. During the 200s, when persecution of Christians mounted, the willingness to confess one's allegiance to Jesus Christ and accept martyrdom rather than acknowledge the Roman gods

(not acknowledging the deified emperors and the gods was equivalent to treason and a capital offense) was seen by Christian leaders as a unifying principle as well as a spiritually blessed act. Anyone who suggested that martyrdom might not be necessary since Jesus only appeared to suffer undermined the health of the Christian community, the orthodox bishops thundered. Although not all Gnostic Christians were, strictly speaking, Docetists, virtually all separated Jesus the man from Christ the redeemer, believing it impossible for a representative of the true, high God to incarnate in the corrupt material world.

For the Gnostics, life's chief spiritual issue was not sin and separation from God as in orthodox Christianity but ignorance about the true nature of the false Demiurge's traps and how to surmount them. They believed that Jesus and other teachers offered a way out for those who were sufficiently discerning to understand them—that percentage of the population who could profit by the knowledge or *gnosis* that was opaque to the orthodox Jewish or Christian religious leaders. That was their interpretation of the Gospel message, "Many are called, but few are chosen."

VALENTINUS, an important Gnostic teacher of the second century, quoted Jesus as saying, "I became very small, so that through my humility I might take you up to the great height whence you had fallen." Valentinus or one of his followers wrote in a book called the *Gospel of Truth,* "Ignorance . . . brought about anguish and terror. And the anguish grew solid like a fog, so that no one was able to see. For this reason error is powerful." In other words, most people, being ignorant of Gnostic truth, live like sleepwalkers or like sleepers suffering nightmares. In modern psychoanalytical terms, a Gnostic would say that the average person does not realize that the unconscious has within it the paths to both destruction and liberation from the nightmare of meaningless existence. "Whoever has not known himself has known nothing, but he who has known himself has at the same time already achieved knowledge about the depths of all things," wrote the author of *The Book of Thomas the Contender,* one of the fourth-century collections of Gnostic writings buried near Nag Hammadi in Egypt and discovered by accident in December 1945.

Gnostics generally accepted that the kingdom of God was an interior state, a transformed consciousness, rather than a future event. Consequently, they rejected the idea that God's will was revealed in history because history, together with the material world's rewards, its governments, and its aspirations, were part of the Demiurge's plot to keep people ignorant of their true spiritual natures. Marcion, for example, argued that the world was created by a barbaric god; otherwise, why would he have afflicted women with the pains of childbirth and directed the massacres and wars of the Old Testament?

Likewise, as the early orthodox church grew in complexity and influence, Gnosticism provided a radical critique of its power and bureaucracy. Valuing their individual understanding of spiritual truth, producing their own books of revelations, teachings, and prophecies, Gnostics were certain to be at odds with the bishops, creeds, and rituals of the mainstream churches in Christianity's first centuries. Each Gnostic was his or her own ultimate authority, and they rejected apostolic succession—the teaching that bishops' spiritual authority derived in direct man-to-man succession from the original Twelve Apostles of Jesus.

Many Gnostic teachings depicted Jesus having close women disciples as well as men, and key Gnostic texts were written by or attributed to women (see *MARY MAGDALENE*). Because some Gnostic texts used feminine images for the divine, scholars have argued that women played a more prominent role in Gnostic groups than in orthodox congregations. Little is known, however, about how and to what extent Gnostic groups were structured.

Gnostic Rituals:
The Bridal Chamber and Sacred Sex

Unlike mainstream Christianity or Judaism, Gnosticism tended to take extreme positions on human sexuality. Many Gnostics were ascetics and rejected all sexual contacts. Others, such as the notorious *CARPOCRATES,* preached freedom through excess. Judging from their writings, some Gnostics attempted to make sexual union sacramental, possibly seeing it as a way of raising the individual's spiritual powers. Although many Gnostics advocated chastity in order to halt the further imprisonment of divin-

ity, others apparently saw sexual activity as one road to ecstasy and the soul's true knowledge of its condition. At the same time, many Gnostics (and subsequent dualists like the *MANICHAEANS* and *ALBIGENSIANS*) attempted to stop further creation by not conceiving children and in some cases by not eating meat or even, in the most radical instance, harvesting crops by their own hands. They saw sexual desire leading to procreation as one of the Demiurge's subtlest traps.

Nevertheless, sex and cosmology overlapped in some Gnostics' notions, even as the concepts of *spirit, light,* and *seed* were related, as pointed out by the historian of religion Mircea Eliade. (*AUGUSTINE OF HIPPO,* however, would identify semen as the physical medium for the transmission of original sin. Only Christ, he argued, was born without sexual intercourse and hence without original sin or lustful feelings.) In addition, sexual offerings apparently could be made to the Archons (or Aeons), the guardians of the different heavens interposed between this earth and the heaven of the true God, who barred the passage of inferior souls. Epiphanius, a disapproving catholic bishop, cites several instances of Gnostic leaders who taught the practice of making sexual offerings, claiming that sexual intercourse could become, for example, an offering to *BARBELOS,* a divine being described in some Gnostic texts as the mother of Ialdabaoth the Demiurge. (Barbelos was sometimes seen as female and equated with *SOPHIA*; in other instances, Barbelos was male, the first emanation from the godhead and the perfect spirit.)

Writing in the 370s, Epiphanius described how male and female Gnostic Christians would perform a special ritual after sexual intercourse. At that point, he writes, they would "hold up their blasphemy to heaven, the woman and the man taking the secretion from the male into their own hands." Gazing reverently upwards, they would pray, "We offer you this gift, the body of Christ." Then, Epiphanius continued, "they consume it, partaking of their shamefulness, and they say, 'This is the body of Christ and this is the Pasch for which our bodies suffer and are forced to confess the passion of Christ.' They do the same with what is of the woman when she has the flow of blood: collecting the monthly blood of impurity from her, they take it and consume it together in the same way. This they say is the blood of Christ." Such libertine Gnostics, he wrote in his antiheretical encyclopedia *Panarion,* also would pray naked at other times, believing that the power in the semen and menstrual blood was soul, which they would consume and collect after both intercourse and male masturbation. (For a similar sexual ritual see *MARCUS.*)

One intriguing but sketchy Gnostic rite recorded in several sources is that of the bridal chamber. Underlying the bridal chamber ritual may have been the idea that the limitations of gender had to be overcome before the Gnostic Christian could rise to the highest heaven of the true God. The enigmatic *Gospel of Philip* may hold a key to the actions of Marcus or the Gnostic sexual rituals described by Epiphanius. Many of the texts recovered at Nag Hammadi are fiercely ascetic: For example, the *Testimony of Truth,* a puritanical denunciation of both catholic Christians and other, less radical Gnostics, suggests that no one who has married and yielded to fleshly passions can ever rise to "the light." Philip, however, appears to describe a five-stage Gnostic initiation (the various verses may have become jumbled in copying, thus further baffling the modern reader). According to translator Wesley W. Isenberg, the stages appear to be baptism (by total immersion), an anointing with chrism (oil), the sacrament of bread and wine, the ransom or redemption, and the bridal chamber. (The last term may also cover the entire initiation, Isenberg suggests.) Like most of the Nag Hammadi books, the *Gospel of Philip* was written in Coptic, the language of Egypt before the Muslim conquest, but Isenberg believes that the original text was composed in Greek as late as the late third century, possibly in Syria. Isenberg suggests that the *Gospel of Philip* is a teaching document, a catechesis, rather than a gospel in the usual sense.

Several possible interpretations of the bridal chamber suggest themselves, particularly as the author of the *Gospel of Philip* uses marriage and sexual intercourse as spiritual metaphors in various places. One interpretation is that some type of ritualized sexual intercourse was performed, which symbolized the union of the soul with God or the union of God with his primary emanation, seen variously as Sophia, the Pronoia

(First Thought), or the Holy Spirit. This would certainly fall within the Western tradition, and indeed some later medieval cabalists would describe a parallel between marital intercourse and the union of God the Father with the Shekinah—the glory of God and the feminine aspect of divinity—often described as being in exile after Adam and Eve's expulsion from Eden. In addition, Irenaeus's description of Marcus's sexual rites, if we may take it at face value, suggests that at least some Gnostics performed a type of sacramental sexual rite. But lacking the testimony of Gnostic insiders themselves, this interpretation as applied to the *Gospel of Philip* remains conjectural.

The other obvious interpretation is that the numerous references to sexual intercourse are metaphorical. In support of this view, we find a passage advocating the customary Gnostic view that not all people are capable of *gnosis*: "If [the Gnostic initiate] is a sensible fellow, he understands what discipleship is all about. The bodily forms will not deceive him, but he will look at the condition of the soul of each one and speak with him. There are many animals in the world which are in human form. When he identifies them, to the swine he will throw acorns, to the cattle he will throw barley and chaff and grass, to the dogs he will throw bones. To the slaves he will give only the elementary lessons, to the children he will give the complete instruction."

From there, the author moves to comparing *gnosis* to sexual intercourse. "No one can know when the husband and the wife have intercourse with one another except the two of them. . . . If there is a hidden quality to the marriage of defilement [in other words, ordinary marriage], how much more is the undefiled marriage a true mystery! It is not fleshly but pure. It belongs not to desire but to the will."

In a following passage, the writer suggests that only a deserving person may enter the bridal chamber; lesser humanity may "yearn just to hear [the bride's] voice and to enjoy her ointment, and let them feed on the crumbs that fall from the table, like the dogs." This passage suggests two things. One is that the *Gospel of Philip*'s author probably represented ascetic Gnosticism with his reference to the "marriage of defilement." It is hard to imagine using such language and then turning around and carrying out a sacramental sexual ritual—hard but not impossible. The other insight, however, is that Gnosticism permitted differing, even opposing, interpretations and teachings based on a principle of giving an individual what was appropriate to his or her level of spiritual discernment. Therefore, we cannot entirely shut the door on a literal sacramental sexuality—if not in this particular instance, then elsewhere during Gnosticism's varied history.

Further support for a metaphorical reading of the *Gospel of Philip*'s bridal chamber passages comes when the writer suggests that only through this ritual can one escape the power of evil spirits: "And none shall be able to escape them, since they detain him if he does not receive a male power or a female power, the bridegroom and the bride—one receives them from the mirrored bridal chamber." And this bridal chamber, the author adds, "is not for the animals, nor is it for the slaves, nor for defiled women [those who have experienced intercourse, apparently]; but it is for free men and virgins."

Finally, the bridal chamber is mentioned in connection with Christ's incarnation, which in most Gnostic literature is seen as a daring foray into the kingdom of the Demiurge in order to bring the true knowledge to that minority capable of comprehending it. "Indeed, one must utter a mystery," he writes. "The father of everything united with the virgin who came down [Sophia/Barbelos rather than Mary in this instance], and a fire shown for him on that day. He appeared in the great bridal chamber. Therefore, his body came into being on that day. It left the bridal chamber as one who came into being from the bridegroom and the bride. So Jesus established everything in it through these."

In metaphorical terms, then, the bridal chamber ritual united the initiate with his or her "image" or angelic counterpart, an image described in sexual terms but not literally so. Or in other terms, this union may have been viewed as a marriage between the psyche or mental-emotional self and the pneuma or undying spirit. Through this initiation, the text proclaims, the Gnostic became "no longer a Christian, but a Christ."

Such sexual metaphors were not entirely absent from catholic Christianity. Paul, who valued virginity over marriage, goes on to say in the well-known "Husbands, love your wives" passage of Ephesians chapter 5 that he interprets the scriptural passage about the two becoming one flesh as referring to Christ and the church.

And, human nature being what it was, some charlatans undoubtedly flourished, using the language of religion in order to satisfy their own desires. Epiphanius believed that he was denouncing such charlatans when he described men "making fools of poor women and saying, 'Have sex with me so that I may present you to the archon.' With each act of sex they [the Gnostics] name the outlandish name of one of those invented by them, and pray: I make an offering to you, so-and-so, that you may offer to so-and-so. . . . When therefore he has reached the number of 365 lapses, that is of shameful acts and of the names invented by them, from then on he dares to say, 'I am Christ, for I have come down from above by means of the names of the 365 archons.'"

For their part, the bishops of the late first and second centuries viewed these "superior" Gnostic Christians with a great deal of suspicion. They respected some Gnostics for their self-discipline and asceticism, but the Gnostics' constant creation of new personal knowledge and new holy books was a greater threat. Ultimately, orthodox Christians used the Gnostic threat to their beliefs to define precisely what those beliefs were, an endeavor central to second-century Christian theology. This struggle over the key beliefs of Christianity was to produce the whole concept of heresy as evil, something entirely foreign to the Pagan world.

The Origins of Gnosticism
The origins of Gnosticism may be sought in two ways: as a movement and as a worldview. In the latter approach, it is seen as a type of world-weariness that particularly affected dissident intellectuals and people whose worldly status had shifted against their will from higher to lower. Feeling unappreciated and dishonored, these people were receptive to philosophies that rejected the world and the grinding processes of history, replacing them with elaborate spiritual hierarchies though which people of true knowledge could arise. According to the historian of religion Carl Raschke, similar social upheavals produced similar responses during the Romantic movement of the late eighteenth and early

nineteenth centuries, and again during the New Thought and New Age movements of the twentieth century.

As a movement with texts and teachers, however, Gnosticism seems multiheaded. A connection between Gnostic Christianity and esoteric Judaism was hypothesized by the German scholar Kurt Rudolph and others. Prior to the destruction of the Jewish Temple in Jerusalem by a Roman army in the year 70, various strains of Judaism flourished, including the Temple-centered and royally sanctioned priestly sacrificial cult, the politically rebellious and messianic Zealots, the legal and text-minded scribes and Pharisees (ancestors of rabbinical Judaism), and the withdrawn Essene ascetics who lived near the Dead Sea. The Zealots, who hoped to throw off Roman power, treasured apocalyptic writings that predicted the overthrow of evil in a final war, as did some of the more pacifistic Essenes. Rudolph saw Gnostic roots in both apocalyptic writing with its prophetic visions of heavenly hierarchies and the "wisdom tradition," exemplified by the book of Ecclesiastes (written about 200 B.C.), with its pessimistic view of the futility of human endeavors. Although such writings personify Wisdom as an emanation of God, they also depict God as more remote from human affairs, similar to the removed true God of the Gnostics. Parallel to the disillusionment scenario postulated above, some scholars believe Gnosticism was created by dissident, heterodox Jewish intellectuals. Particularly before the discovery of the Nag Hammadi books, however, other researchers found Gnosticism to be more heavily influenced by Greek philosophy or Asian religions.

Jung and Gnosticism

Much of Gnosticism's present-day cachet is due to the value that the famed Swiss psychologist Carl Jung (1875–1961) placed on it as a forerunner of psychoanalysis. In Valentinus's description of the true God's existence before the Demiurge created the world, Jung saw a parallel with—or indeed a metaphorical description of—the personal unconscious, described as a "God without consciousness." Jung then equated the Demiurge with the ego, the organizing principle of consciousness, and Christ as the "complete man," the unified self. "From various hints dropped by [the anti-Gnostic writer] Hippolytus, it is clear that the Gnostics were nothing other

than psychologists," Jung wrote. "Gnosis is undoubtedly a psychological knowledge whose contents derive from the unconscious." He concluded that the entire struggle between the false and true gods took place among the components of the psyche.

Gnostic philosophy, Jung concluded, was continued in late medieval and Renaissance alchemy. In *Aion,* Jung wrote, "Most [of the Gnostics]—Valentinus and *BASILIDES,* for instance, were in reality theologians who, unlike the more orthodox ones, allowed themselves to be influenced in large measure by natural inner experience. They are, therefore, like the alchemists, a veritable mine of information concerning all those natural symbols arising out of the repercussions of the Christian message. At the same time, their ideas compensate the asymmetry of God postulated by the doctrine of the *privatio boni* [privation of good: the doctrine that evil is a diminution of good, the lack of perfection], exactly like those well-known modern tendencies of the unconscious to produce symbols of the totality for bridging the gap between the conscious and the unconscious, which has widened dangerously to the point of universal disorientation."

Although Jung did much to elevate the reputation of Gnosticism—or at least his version of it—in the twentieth century, other novelists, artists, and filmmakers have been drawn to Gnostic themes. A short list would include Philip K. Dick, Jack Kerouac, Zena Henderson, Harold Bloom, and Lawrence Durrell. Even the comic-book and movie story of Superman can be interpreted as a quasi-Gnostic fall from a better world into this one.

Gospel of Mary   See *MARY MAGDALENE.*

Gugliema, Gugliemites   An Italian prophetess in the city of Milan in about 1270, Gugliema was seen by her followers the Gugliemites as incarnating the Holy Spirit, thereby ushering in the Third Age of the world, foreseen by the monk *JOACHIM OF FLORIS* to begin around 1260. Numerous Joachites believed that since the second person of the Trinity had incarnated as a male—Jesus—the third person, the Holy Spirit, would be female for the sake of cosmic symmetry. With her incarnation, new gospels would appear, and women would be spiritual leaders. In Provence, a *BEGUINE* named Prous Beneta was similarly hailed as incarnating the Holy Spirit in the early 1300s.

The idea of a woman incarnating the Holy Spirit has occurred since the Middle Ages. For example, "Mother" Ann Lee (1736–1784), English-born founder of the American sect of celibate utopians called Shakers, taught that she represented God's incarnation in a woman, as Jesus had in a man. Her less well-known contemporary, Jemima Wilkinson (1752–1819), known to her American followers as the Publick Universal Friend, was regarded by many as Christ returned. Wilkinson, who like Lee also founded a community in New York State, was accompanied by two women who were presented as the biblical prophets Daniel and Elijah now "operating in these latter days in the female line."

An unsubstantiated tradition makes Guglielma the prototype of the Female Pope (also called the High Priestess) card in the *TAROT* deck. For more information on similar movements see *APOSTLES* and *FREE SPIRIT*.

Henry of Le Mans　See *PETROBRUSIANS*.

Hippolytus　A puritanical defender of early Christian orthodoxy, Bishop Hippolytus of Rome lived from about 170 to 235. A disciple of *IRENAEUS,* he produced his own polemical book called the *Syntagma* (usually translated as Against all heresies), which served as a source for the later *Panarion* of *EPIPHANIUS*. Hippolytus was particularly concerned with refuting the heresies of *MODALISM* and *PATRIPASSIANISM*.

During one of the periodic struggles over control of the papacy, Hippolytus was briefly elected pope by a purist faction within the Catholic church. Losing the contest, he was banished from Rome but later was reconciled with the church and canonized after his death in recognition of his struggle against heresy. His feast day is 13 August.

Homines Intelligentiae
See *MEN OF INTELLIGENCE.*

Homosexuality　Although accepted in most of the Mediterranean regions where Christianity arose, homosexuality was almost universally condemned by Christian leaders, and by the late Middle Ages homosexuals were liable to be tried and executed as heretics.

Christian condemnation of homosexuality had several roots. Both the Old and the New Testaments contain passages condemning homosexual practices. These include Leviticus 18:22, "You shall not lie with a man as with a woman: that is an abomination," and 20:13–14, "If a man has intercourse with a man as with a woman, they both commit an abomination. They shall both be put to death; their blood shall be on their own heads." While Jesus is not recorded as saying anything on the matter, the epistles attributed to Paul contain several disapproving references to homosexual practices. Romans 1:26–27 describes male and female homosexuality as "shameful passions," while 1 Corinthians 6:9 lists homosexuals among fornicators, adulterers, drunkards, and a variety of criminals who "will never come into possession of the kingdom of God." 1 Timothy contains a similar list.

Beyond this, however, the specific equation of homosexuality with heresy—false doctrine—began in the early centuries of the organized Christian church. It is not surprising that *EPIPHANIUS,* the bishop whose own encyclopedia of heresies provides much of what we know about certain vanished Christian sects, linked homosexuality with the form of Christianity called *GNOSTICISM*. Most Gnostics believed the material world was a prison for human souls who needed secret religious knowledge in order to escape it and return at death to the realm of the true God—who was not the creator of this world. With such beliefs, many abstained from all sexual activity, renouncing sexual pleasure as a trap set by the *DEMIURGE,* the false god. Some Gnostics, however, apparently favored any sexual practice that did not produce children and that therefore did not trap any further souls in physical bodies.

During the Middle Ages, Roman Catholic theologians expanded on the idea that homosexuality was a "crime against nature," and accusations of homosexuality were made against many persons identified as heretics. The *KNIGHTS TEMPLAR,* a powerful order of soldier-monks, were accused of secret homosexual rituals as part of the French king's attempt to break their power and appropriate their wealth. Similar accusations were made against the *BEGUINES* and *BEGHARDS,* groups of women and men who lived communally and took religious vows somewhat like those of monks and nuns but less severe.

During the twelfth and thirteenth centuries, various European city councils and parliaments passed laws against homosexual acts between both women and men. The famed Italian poet Dante Alighieri (1265–1321) gave "sodomites" their own section in his grand description of Hell and its inhabitants. "Penitentials"—handbooks for priests who heard confessions, gave absolution, and prescribed penance for sins—set out specific penances for different degrees of acts, such as for one man kissing another "with emission or embrace." In some cases, the penalties went beyond prayers or fasting; for instance, Richard von Hohenburg, a fifteenth-century German knight, was executed in Zurich after being tried for the "heresy" of homosexuality.

In medieval art, where animals often stood for specific moral qualities (see *PANTHERA*), the hare, the hyena, and the weasel became symbols of homosexuality because of the various bizarre legends about their genital organs.

The connection between homosexuality and heresy has also led some people to argue that the slang term *faggot* for homosexual came from the practice of burning heretics at the stake in fires made from faggots (or fagots), bundles of sticks tied with rope or flexible twigs. The connection is merely coincidence of sound, however; the slang term *faggot* may possibly derive instead from the British public school slang term *fag,* meaning "a younger boy who does menial tasks for an older one."

Hus, Jan; Hussites   The war fought by the followers of Jan Hus against the Holy Roman Empire became largely a question of Bohemian rebellion against German rulers, but Hus himself was a religious reformer influenced by the English theologian John *WYCLIFFE*. Both men were condemned as heretics by the Roman Catholic church, and Hus was eventually executed. Wycliffe's body was also taken from its grave and burned. Meanwhile, the Hussite rebellion illustrated to what extent the currents leading to the Protestant Reformation of the sixteenth century were also carrying notions of

nascent nationalism and the breakdown of kingdoms and empires that crossed linguistic and ethnic boundaries.

Hus was born about 1369 in Bohemia (part of the modern Czech Republic) and studied for the priesthood. He taught theology at the University of Prague and was also a popular Czech-language preacher. At the university he was influenced by Jerome of Prague, a scholar who had studied at Oxford University with Wycliffe, bringing some of Wycliffe's books back to Prague with him. (Bohemian and *LOLLARD* reformers maintained some degree of contact.)

While he was a student, Hus earned money by copying Wycliffe's works (which would have been written in Latin, then the universal European scholarly language) for other scholars. His teaching was influenced by Wycliffe's ideas on scriptural authority, church governance, the denial of transubstantiation, and so forth, and Hus became one of the most popular lecturers. His popularity, however, fed ethnic antagonism between German faculty (representing the colonial German nobles and merchants dominating fourteenth-century Bohemia) and native Bohemians. (Torn by this and other, deeper disputes, the University of Prague, which had only been founded in 1348, was reorganized in 1409 on linguistic and cultural lines, with the German-speaking faculty forming a new university at Leipzig.)

Besides the influence of Wycliffe, Hus inherited the work of earlier Bohemian reformers, particularly Conrad Waldhouser (died 1369); Jan Milíc, a cathedral priest turned wandering preacher (died circa 1374); and Matthias of Janov, a disciple of Milíc and a writer of treatises on individual devotion and clerical corruption. Clerical corruption was on the minds of all Europeans due to the Great Schism, the era between roughly 1378 and 1414, when rival popes based in Rome and Avignon, France, excommunicated each other and struggled for control of the Roman Catholic church. (Between 1409 and 1414, three men each claimed to be pope.)

In the early 1400s, the university's theological divisions often became ethnic ones as well, with the Germans holding the more conservative views and the Czechs, if not followers of Wycliffe, at least supporting the study of his ideas. In 1403 a German professor sought ecclesiastical condemnation of Wycliffe's ideas at Prague, recycling the propositions heard by

Archbishop Courtenay in England 20 years earlier. In fact, by summarizing Wycliffe's ideas ("It is contrary to Scripture that churchmen should have possessions"; "Any deacon or priest can preach the word of God without the authority of the apostolic see [the papacy] and the Catholic bishop"; and so on), his opponents made them easier for people to remember.

When the archbishop in Prague burned some of Wycliffe's books and excommunicated his supporters in 1410, he provoked an uprising by Bohemian students and citizens; the whole affair had also become entangled with other aspects of civil and religious politics.

Hus, now risen to rector of the reorganized university, became leader of the pro-Wycliffe faction. More radical anticlerical reformers, some probably influenced by *WALDENSIAN* ideas, attacked the church for *SIMONY* and the selling of indulgences. In 1412 Hus was excommunicated and forced out of Prague by ecclesiastical authorities, who threatened the city with an interdict (a decree forbidding clergy to perform the sacraments) unless he left.

Protected by aristocratic patrons, Hus continued thinking and writing on church reform and other topics as well, including the grammar of the Czech language. In his major work, *De ecclesia* (usually translated as The church), he followed Wycliffe's ideas on predestination and his rejection of the papacy as divinely ordained.

Another of his proposed reforms—that Catholic priests return to offering the congregation Holy Communion "in both kinds," that is, both bread and wine instead of bread alone—became a key demand in the religious upheavals that followed Hus's death. (Because of its doctrine of transubstantiation, or the physical presence of Jesus Christ in both wine and bread, the church held that bread alone was sufficient, and offering the cup to everyone increased the possibility of a sacrilegious spill of Christ's blood.) Communion in both kinds was the norm in the early church and remained so in the Eastern Orthodox churches; by returning to it, Hus and his followers were attempting to cross the enormous gulf that had grown between clergy and laity.

Hus's downfall came in 1414 when he was trapped, arrested, and executed in the German city of Constance (Konstanz), where the Holy Roman Emperor Sigismund had convened a church council to decide which of several rivals would become pope and to otherwise heal schisms within the church. Promised a safe-conduct pass by Sigismund, Hus ventured to Constance in hopes of redeeming himself before top church officials and imperial rulers, only to be tried along with Jerome of Prague and—posthumously—Wycliffe. After refusing to recant his views despite imprisonment and threats, Jan Hus was executed by burning at Constance on 6 July 1415; Jerome of Prague escaped only to be recaptured and burned to death the following year.

Hus's execution, facilitated by a German emperor, raised Czech-German tensions even higher. Some 452 members of the upper classes in Bohemia and neighboring Moravia joined a protest to the Council of Constance before Hus's execution. Dead, Jan Hus was a martyr to religious reform and Czech nationalism. Hussite churches were formed, with Bohemians demanding the communion cup and free preaching without approval of the hierarchy. Radical priests baptized children in ponds and streams rather than in church, destroyed holy images, and held to the Donatist (see *DONATISM*) position (frequently espoused by medieval reformers) that only sinless clergy could celebrate the Eucharist. The council, still in session, condemned "the lay chalice," or offering consecrated wine to the congregation, and this issue, with its overtones of anticlericalism on the reformers' part, became hugely symbolic in the subsequent struggle. (The position favoring communion in both kinds is also known as Utraquism.) When the Hussite party failed to gain control of a particular church, it often held services in barns, other buildings, or outdoors. Some radicals began celebrating the Mass in Czech instead of Latin and otherwise altered the liturgy to fit their own demands.

Moderate and radical reformers eventually met in 1418 and attempted to set some standards. In effect, they organized a reformed pre-Protestant church, blending Roman Catholic practices (such as infant communion) with modernizations such as reading the epistle and gospel selections in Czech.

Meanwhile, pushed by the hard-line Pope Martin V (the same pope who saw to it that Wycliffe's body was disinterred and burned), King Wenceslas IV of Bohemia, the emperor's

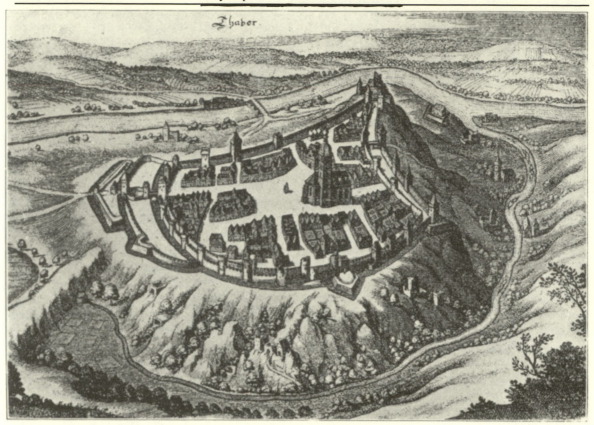

Tabor, a Hussite army fortified camp that was named after the biblical Mount Tabor. (From a copperplate engraving by Hans Merian.)

older brother, prepared a crusade against the Hussites. After the king's death in 1419, Sigismund himself stepped in and began an 11-year campaign against the Hussites, legitimized as a Crusade by Martin V.

The Hussites themselves split into two factions, one moderate, one radical. The moderates, sometimes referred to as Calixtines, favored communion in both kinds; the radicals went further and rejected all sacraments except baptism and the Eucharist, demanding a return to the primitive, apostolic Christian community. The Hussite radicals were often known as Taborites after they renamed a hill used as a gathering place for the biblical Mount Tabor. Later, in 1420, when the radicals took over an abandoned royal castle and refortified it, they also referred to it as Tabor.

Attempts by the authorities to quell Utraquism were interpreted by some of the Taborites as signaling the Last Days and the imminent Second Coming of Christ. When they withdrew from the towns to worship and eat communal meals on hills (much in the spirit of Mark 13:14), they saw themselves as preparing for the Apoca-lypse. In Prague, demonstrations by Utraquist and Catholic factions turned into violent riots. One incident became known as the denefestration of Prague: An armed mob led by Jan Zelivsky, a radical preacher, entered Prague's New Town Hall on 30 July 1419 and captured several town councilors who, although Czechs, represented the Catholic, pro-imperial faction. When the councilors refused to release certain Utraquists from prison, the mob threw 13 councilors from upper-story windows; those who did not die from the fall were killed by rebels in the street below.

The "defenestration of Prague" preceded King Wenceslas's death from natural causes by a few days and launched the rebellion, which, as stated above, was pointed at both the Roman Catholic church and the chiefly German Holy Roman Empire. Jan Zizka (circa 1360–1424), a Taborite and veteran of imperial wars against the Poles, Turks, and French, became leader of the improvised Hussite army.

Because of Zizka's military genius, the Hussite wars produced a footnote to military history. Under his command, the Hussites produced a forerunner of the tank. Heavy wagons were built up and protected with improvised armor, then mounted with small, primitive cannons. These wagons could be deployed in various formations in the field, giving the Hussite fighters what were in effect mobile forts, referred to in German as *wagonburg*. The *wagonburg* could not be used offensively: Zizka's genius lay in enticing his enemies to attack it under conditions favoring the Hussites. (According to military historians, he may have gotten the idea from medieval Russians, who used wagon formations to protect bowmen against onslaughts by Mongol cavalry.)

Despite losing his sight partway through the campaign, Zizka initially defeated Emperor Sigismund's more professional, knightly army. The Hussites, however, also fought among themselves. The moderates, who were open to religious reform but not interested in violent social change, lost to the Taborites under Zizka. So did the even more radical Adamites, who apparently advocated even less central control than did the Taborites. The Hussite factions reached a truce in 1424 and agreed to fight Sigismund's forces together under Zizka's leadership, but in that year the general died of the plague. Zizka was replaced as military commander by Andrew Procop, who led the Hussites to victory against the Crusades of 1426, 1427, and 1431 and occasionally carried the war into Germany.

Internal conflict broke out again between moderate Calixtines and radical Taborites in the 1430s; this time, an alliance between moderates and the nobility carried the day. Although many nobles supported the Hussites' religious reforms, they were threatened by the Taborites' social radicalism—for example, peasants' refusal to pay rent to landowners on the ground that the Last Days were at hand.

In 1434, a settlement between the moderates and the Roman Catholic church left Bohemia with a large degree of religious self-governance, including the right to receive communion in both kinds and to have preaching in the Czech tongue.

Huss, John   See *HUS, JAN*.

Hypatia   Killed by a Christian mob in 415, the philosopher Hypatia has been held up ever

since as an example of the intellectual woman hated—or at least mistrusted—by the institutional church.

Daughter of Theon, a Greek mathematician living in the cosmopolitan Egyptian city of Alexandria, Hypatia was probably born around 370. Little is known of her early life, but she apparently was tutored by her father and assisted him with his writings and lectures on philosophy and mathematics, which in the Greek tradition were closely intertwined. She became a leading philosophy teacher in her own right and was considered the chief Neoplatonist (see *NEOPLATONISM*) thinker in Alexandria. She was widely known and respected, and magistrates and political leaders consulted her for her wisdom. Although she is described as a beautiful woman, various anecdotes about Hypatia depict her as valuing intellectual concerns over physical beauty and bluntly rebuffing those male students who had crushes on her.

Several years before Hypatia's death, hatred and violence began to increase between members of Alexandria's large, established Jewish community and increasingly power-hungry Christians led by their bishop, Cyril. (Cyril was the nephew of another bishop who had actively destroyed Pagan temples, including the famous library housed in the temple of Serapis, in 391.) As the violence mounted, volatile members of the Christian and Jewish communities fought in the streets and attacked each other's churches and synagogues. The Roman prefect in charge of the city, Orestes, tried to keep order, but he gained Cyril's hatred for hampering the bishop's efforts to turn Alexandria into a purely Christian city. Although Orestes was probably at least a nominal Christian, Cyril's followers, headed by a group of 500 fanatical monks brought in from desert monasteries, mobbed the prefect's carriage in the streets, accusing him of Paganism. The fact that Orestes was a friend of Hypatia and had attended her lectures was one of the things held against him by the Christian fanatics.

When one of the monks was killed by Orestes' guards after attacking the prefect physically, Cyril proclaimed the dead man to be a saint and used his death to whip up more feeling against Orestes. But because Orestes was too powerful to attack directly, the fanatics turned on, among others, Hypatia. During Lent she was seized in the street, dragged into Cyril's own patriarchal church, stripped, beaten, and stabbed to death with pieces of broken pottery. Her body was hacked into pieces, carried triumphantly into the streets, and later burned. For whatever reason—perhaps Orestes' desire not to create more martyrs—no one was punished for her murder.

Several causes can be offered for Hypatia's death. Both her sex and her position as a spokeswoman for the type of Pagan intellectualism that was in increasingly popular disfavor made her vulnerable when she was drawn into the Christian-Jewish factional conflict by the sequence of events. Imperial Roman persecution of Christians had ceased in the early 300s, with the brief exception of the rule of *JULIAN THE APOSTATE* (361–363). By the 370s the puritanical bishop *EPIPHANIUS* was attacking heresy and Greek philosophy alike in his *Panarion;* sometime in mid-century the heterodox book collection known as the *NAG HAMMADI* library was hidden in the Egyptian desert. By the early 400s, admitted Pagans were gradually being excluded from high administrative and military posts by a series of imperial edicts; Pagan intellectuals were increasingly likely to quietly withdraw from society or to exile themselves to nations outside Christendom, such as Persia.

Iamblichus Born at Chalcis in Syria about 260, Iamblichus has been regarded both as a successful synthesizer of intellectual *NEO-PLATONISM* with late classical Pagan religion and as an idolatrous mystagogue spoiling the purity of Platonic thought with Eastern mysticism. "During the predominance of [his] school Platonism becomes a mere adjunct, a mere excuse for theosophy," wrote one disapproving Victorian commentator.

To his Hellenistic contemporaries, however, Iamblichus was divine. *JULIAN THE APOSTATE,* Rome's last Pagan emperor, wrote of him after his death that "he was posterior indeed in time but not in genius to Plato." Iamblichus died about 330, some 25 years before Julian's birth, but several of the mystic philosopher's students were instrumental in persuading Julian to abandon Christianity himself and to remove it from the privileged imperial position it had gained under his predecessor *CONSTANTINE* the Great.

In brief, unlike some of his purely intellectual predecessors, Iamblichus held that one could approach the One, the highest level of Deity, through theurgy—sacramental magical rites—as well as through pure contemplation. Iamblichus granted that the latter method was valid for the philosophically inclined, writing in his *Exhortation to Philosophy,* "We shall worship the Deity rightly if we render our intellect pure from all vice as from some kind of stain or disgrace." But he also advocated ritual methods by which the philosopher, by conjuration of spirits or divine manifestations, could confirm the results of intellectual contemplation. In so doing he gave rise to legends about his own miracle-working abilities that resemble those surrounding some Christian saints. For instance, his disciples said that when praying he was at times elevated ten cubits (roughly 16 feet) above the ground.

Iamblichus's surviving works include *De Mysteriis Ægyptiorum* (On the mysteries), a defense of the practice of theurgy that he (or one of his followers) wrote in response to a skeptical letter by his predecessor, the important Neoplatonic philosopher *PORPHYRY*. It countered Porphyry's skepticism with a defense of ceremonial religion as being appropriate and beneficial for the majority of the population, who are not capable of living the purely philosophical life. His *Exhortation to Philosophy*, quoted above, apparently represents lecture material and presents Platonic and Pythagorean philosophies' attraction in a rather didactic way that may have been influenced by a perceived need to counter the attraction of Christianity among the educated classes. Many of his other works were lost or are preserved only in fragments.

Another work falsely attributed to Iamblichus by the nineteenth-century French translator Christian (pen name of Jean-Baptiste Pitois) is entitled *Egyptian Mysteries: An Account of an Initiation*. Probably written by a German occultist of the late eighteenth century, it describes the long preparation and training of an ancient Egyptian boy who is eventually admitted into the fraternity of magicians during a ceremony in hitherto undiscovered chambers beneath the Great Pyramid. Because the work describes a long room painted with the images of the *TAROT* greater trumps, it has been mistakenly cited to support the claim that that portion of the Tarot deck was designed in ancient times rather than, as is more likely, during the early Renaissance. See also *HYPATIA; PLOTINUS.*

Iconoclasm A controversy over the use of holy pictures and images among Eastern Christians, Iconoclasm deeply affected the Eastern (Byzantine) church in the eighth and ninth centuries. (The name comes from Greek words meaning "image-breaking.") The use of icons was at least partly a carryover from Pagan times, but several tendencies within and without Christianity led to a reaction against their use. The rise of Islam also had this effect. Muslims, who also honored Moses as a prophet, carried forward the second of the Ten Commandments: "You shall not make a carved image for yourself nor the likeness of anything in the heavens above, or on the earth below, or in the waters under the earth. You shall not bow down to them or worship them; for I, the Lord your God, am a jealous god." The Muslims at first forbade even secular sculpture and painting; their fierce attitude toward such images corresponded with the feelings of some Christians, particularly those of Semitic background. Icon worship was strongest among Greek Christians, adding an ethnic cast to the conflict. *MONOPHYSITE* Christianity was particularly strong in the empire's eastern provinces before those areas (such as Egypt, Palestine, Mesopotamia, Syria, and parts of present-day Turkey) were conquered by the Muslims, and Monophysites were less prone to icon worship.

In 726 Leo III, ruler of the Byzantine Empire from 717 to 741, issued the first of several edicts forbidding the worship of icons of Jesus and the saints, a traditional practice that was permitted by most of the Eastern Orthodox hierarchy. His action pitted him against Germanus I, patriarch of Constantinople, and against many Greek monks and civil servants. From Rome, Pope Gregory II joined the patriarch in denouncing Leo, who responded by forcing Germanus to resign. Germanus was replaced by a patriarch who agreed with the emperor's position, but Leo's edicts did not carry equal weight in all parts of the empire. During the 730s, enforcement of Leo's iconoclastic edicts led to the destruction of monasteries and the killing or forced secularization of their inhabitants, actions that continued to widen the divide between the Western and Eastern churches.

The iconoclasts not only cited the Second Commandment to justify their actions, but, echoing the earlier *ARIAN* and Monophysite controversies over the nature of Christ, claimed that his human and divine natures could not be contained in a statue or picture. To make a picture or statue representing Christ, they said, was a vain attempt to place limits on the divine. According to the iconoclasts, his only correct representation was in the Eucharistic host. Likewise, a graphic representation of a saint was wrong because the saints were free from their material bodies.

In the 780s, Irene, widow of the emperor Leo IV, assumed the throne as regent for her son. An *iconodule* (servant of the icons), she convened a church council that reaffirmed the "relative" worship of icons. In other words, by venerating an icon a believer was honoring the divine person or saint it depicted.

In succeeding decades, however, iconoclasts and iconodules continued to clash as emperors and ecclesiastics favored one side or the other. The empress Theodora restored icon worship in 843, the position held by the Eastern Orthodox churches to the present day. Nevertheless, during the Protestant Reformation in Western Europe, the religious use of images again became an important issue, leading at times to the destruction of much religious artwork, for example, during the English Civil War (1642–1652). See also *NICAEA, COUNCILS OF.*

Inquisition As an institution, particularly in its later, Spanish phase, many of the Inquisition's activities are outside the scope of this encyclopedia, dealing as it does with heresy before the Protestant Reformation. Indeed, many of the WITCHCRAFT persecutions were actually performed by Protestants and occurred not during the Middle Ages but during the religiously troubled sixteenth and seventeenth centuries. During that period, the people of Western Europe, having seen the monolithic Roman Catholic church shaken to its roots by the great reformers, lost some of their old certainties and perceived Satanic evil lurking closer than ever before. In contrast, from the days of the early church until the rise of *ALBIGENSIAN* and *WALDENSIAN* heresies around 1200, heresy hunting was primarily the concern of individual bishops.

The execution of a woman declared by the Inquisition to be possessed by demons. (From Rappresentatione della Passione, *Florence, 1520.)*

The Albigensians, however, posed such a threat that although they were suppressed militarily by the Middle Age's one permanently successful crusade, the Inquisition (as well as a new monastic order, the Dominicans) was created for the purpose of further rooting them out and for uncovering any future heretics. This new unified bureaucracy could locate, imprison, and try heretics and then, if they were found guilty, turn them over to the secular authorities for punishment. Earlier heretics had usually been punished by excommunication if they were laypeople and confinement in a monastery if they were clerics. (Exceptions include the *ORLÉANS* heretics and some of the *BOGOMILS*.) From this point on, the Western church returned in essence to the old Roman practice of treating heresy as a crime against the secular government as well as against ecclesiastical authority. The church no longer relied on persuasion or moral authority to enforce its doctrines, but turned instead to naked force, cloaked with the pious deception that it was not actually the church imprisoning or executing but rather the secular authorities. The church saw heresy as endangering not just society's body—like common criminality—but its very soul. Dissenters came to characterize the church as the "woman drunken with the blood of the saints"

described in Revelation 17:6. But in setting up the Inquisition, the church was only continuing the tendency found throughout the Old and New Testaments to read spiritual messages in political events; to see heresy as a threat to the state was a logical outgrowth of that tendency.

The medieval Inquisition, which reached its pinnacle of power in the late thirteenth century, was largely staffed by Dominican monks, members of a preaching order begun by St. Dominic in 1216. These monks frequently made a pun on their name in Latin: *domine cani* or, loosely, "God's dogs"—a pack of black-and-white hounds pursuing heretics. By the 1220s, some *FRANCISCAN* monks were also employed by the Inquisition for their skill in preaching and turning the people away from heretical doctrines; they were officially called to inquisitorial work by Pope Innocent IV in 1246.

Although earlier church councils had required rulers to prosecute heretics, the Inquisition's formal beginning is often dated to a decree of Pope Gregory IX, who in 1231 ordered that repentant heretics be imprisoned for life and those who refused to recant their heresy be turned over to secular authorities for execution. (By doing so, Gregory apparently was trying to keep the Inquisition under central church control rather than having various bodies controlled in whole or in part by the German emperor, other rulers, or independent-minded bishops.) Unlike heretics condemned by bishops, those condemned by the Inquisition were not supposed to be able to appeal their sentences to the pope although some were occasionally

Excommunicamus (We excommunicate), contained various provisions in addition to those mentioned above. These included instructions to dig up and destroy the bones of dead proven heretics and to demolish the homes of convicted living heretics. Albigensians and Waldensians were excommunicated, and so were their friends,

An example of how the Inquisition obtained confessions from people accused of witchcraft. (From Bambergische Halsgerichtsordnung, *1508.)*

able to do so in later decades. At first inquisitors made circuits through areas where heresy had spread; but as the bureaucracy—and the archives—grew, it was easier to set up regional tribunals and summon heretics to them. For instance, Toulouse, a city in the south of France, was selected as one such headquarters because it lay squarely in Albigensian territory.

Pope Gregory's constitution for the Inquisition, known by the first words of its Latin text,

defenders, and anyone who failed to denounce them. Gregory's first inquisitors were mostly Dominicans, but the man he sent to Germany to exterminate *WALDENSIANISM* was a secular priest, *CONRAD OF MARBURG.*

A subsequent pope, Innocent IV, further strengthened the Inquisition. His bull *Ad Extirpanda* (To extirpate) permitted the use of torture to gain confessions, reinforced the use of burning at the stake as the chief method of execution, and heightened the persecution of heretics in Italy in particular. It provided for the confiscation of not only heretics' property but that of their heirs as well, thus further increasing the possibility of corrupt inquisitors looking for rich so-called heretics.

In a subsequent bull, Innocent IV divided Europe between the Dominicans and the Franciscans for the purpose of heresy hunting. The Franciscans were given central and northeastern Italy, plus southeastern France, Poland, Dalmatia, Bohemia, Croatia, Serbia, Hungary, and Christian-controlled parts of Palestine and Syria. The Dominicans were given other parts of Italy, northern and southwestern France, Germany, and Austria. Both orders operated in Burgundy and Christian-controlled portions of the Iberian peninsula.

As inquisitors searched for heretics, they needed uniform processes and procedures to follow. Although the most notorious of these, the *MALLEUS MALEFICARUM* (Hammer of witches), was not written until the 1400s, earlier inquisitors' manuals were prepared in the years following Gregory IX's constitution. A few years' experience showed ecclesiastical authorities that freewheeling inquisitors such as Conrad of Marburg and *ROBERT LE BOUGRE* got into trouble because they did not follow consistent procedures. Two important early manuals were the *Directory of Raymond of Peñafort,* prepared for the Inquisition in Barcelona in 1242, and the *Processus inquisitionis,* used in southern France. The famed inquisitor Bernardo Gui, who headed the Inquisition at Toulouse from 1307 to 1324, produced a longer, more complete manual setting out all the boilerplate texts that inquisitors would need.

Raymond of Peñafort's directory, designed for use against the Albigensian Cathars, began by defining a heretic—anyone who professed Cathar beliefs, listened to the Cathars' sermons, or believed them to be good people. But it also included as worthy of prosecution anyone who knew of heretics' presence but did not report them and anyone who, having once repented of heresy, returned to it. The language of this and other manuals effectively prevented an accused heretic from being represented at his or her trial by either a cleric or a secular lawyer, since anyone helping a heretic in any way was automatically a suspected heretic

too. The manual also set out a schedule of punishments, from simple penances through imprisonment, excommunication, and finally transfer to secular authorities for execution. In addition, the manual advocated the same treatment that was given to the bones of the scholarly heretic *AMALRIC OF BENE*: "If during the inquisition it is revealed that heretics or Cathars or believers [those Cathars who did not rank as "perfects"] are buried in the cemetery, their bones are to be exhumed and burned if they are recognizable."

The *Processus inquisitionis* contained additional material, including numerous fill-in-the-blank legal formulas. It required that each local inquisition begin by calling together the residents of each parish, defined as all males over 14 and females over 12, to hear a general sermon, after which those heretics who submitted themselves voluntarily would escape imprisonment (the period of grace). It provided set questions for the inquisitors to ask suspected heretics and laid out their punishments. Again, the legal maneuvering that permitted authorities to claim that the Inquisition never executed anyone was displayed: Confessed heretics were to take themselves to prison, and if they failed to do so, secular rather than ecclesiastical authorities were to take them there.

Subsequent papal bulls expanded and further defined the inquisitors' authority and powers. Although local bishops were supposed to approve inquisitors' verdicts, at times they were outmaneuvered. Some inquisitors were scrupulous, but others were able to use the system's secrecy and power to destroy people of any social rank and confiscate their possessions. Stubborn defendants could be imprisoned or tortured to whatever degree was necessary to extract a confession.

In southern France, the Cathar stronghold, the Inquisition continued its work into the 1400s; in other areas it declined, partly because increasingly independent secular rulers and parliaments resented dealing with an arrogant outside authority. In Spain, however, the Inquisition was revitalized under the notorious Tomás de *TORQUEMADA,* who helped create an organization (under royal rather than papal control) that lasted until the early 1800s and that undertook *autos da fé* (acts of faith—mass penances and burnings of heretics) in the Spanish colonies of Mexico, Peru, and Colombia.

The papal Inquisition was never such a force in England, the Low Countries, or Scandinavia, although the English parliamentary act of 1401, *DE HERETICO COMBURENDO,* passed to combat the *LOLLARDS,* replicated many of its features. (The Spanish Inquisition, however, would carry out a bloody persecution of Dutch Protestants.)

The modern equivalent of the Inquisition is a section of Vatican bureaucracy known as the Congregation for the Doctrine of the Faith, which periodically condemns certain Catholic theologians and professors for heretical tendencies. One example is the one-year "silencing" of the Dominican priest Matthew Fox of Holy Names College in Oakland, California, in 1988.

Irenaeus Much of what is known about the *GNOSTICS* and other early heretics comes from the work of Irenaeus. Although born in Asia Minor about 130, he became a presbyter (priest) and ended his life as bishop of Lyons in the Roman province of Gaul (France). He died in the early third century. He is best known for the book usually called *Adversus Haereses* (Against heresies), whose full title translates as "the refutation of gnosis, falsely so-called." It also includes his view on the apocalypse and ensuing millennium, the prophesied thousand-year rule of Jesus Christ on earth. The book's main task, however, was to strengthen the early church's apostolic tradition against the Gnostics' and other groups' claims of secret teachings and subsequent prophecies and revelations. Although Irenaeus lived before the final adoption of the canonical New Testament books, he defended the gospels attributed to Matthew, Mark, Luke, and John as being the only valid gospels, as opposed to other gospels—some of them Gnostic in viewpoint—then circulating. (See *NAG HAMMADI.*) A great deal of what is known about Gnostic teachers and their congregations comes from Irenaeus's decidedly negative outlook on them.

The goddess Isis, as depicted in a book from the seventeenth-century occult revival. (From Anthanasius Kircher, Oedipus Aegyptiacus, 1652.)

Isis The Queen of the Egyptian gods, Isis (in Egyptian, *Ashet*) was worshiped throughout the late Roman Empire. As a preeminent image of female divinity, Isis became blended in devotion with the Virgin Mary and, as the embodiment of divine wisdom, may have influenced the *GNOSTIC* cult of *SOPHIA* or Wisdom. A passage from *Thunder, Perfect Mind,* one of the best-preserved but most enigmatic of the *NAG HAMMADI* texts, suggests a possible identification of Isis with Sophia, the personified wisdom of God. The work is given as the revelation of a transcendent deity who speaks chiefly in a series of antithetical statements, for example:

> I am the first and the last.
> I am the honored one and the scorned one.
> I am the whore and the holy one.

At several points the verses suggest the stories of Isis told by the ancient Egyptians and other worshipers of the goddess after her cult spread through the Roman Empire. In these stories, she and her brother/husband Osiris lived for a time on earth. After Osiris's evil brother, Set (or Seth), killed him and scattered the pieces of his body throughout Egypt, Isis reassembled them and reanimated them through her divine power, enabling the couple to create their divine child, Horus. During the Roman period Isis became a universal mother goddess. Legal worship of Isis was retained in Egypt into the sixth century, by which time many of her attributes and titles, such as Queen of Heaven, had been transferred to the Virgin Mary.

The following lines might be suggestive of the cult of Isis, which included a mystical, initiatory side:

> I am the mother of my father
> and the sister of my husband
> and he is my offspring. . . .
>
> For I am the wisdom of [the] Greeks
> and the knowledge of [the] barbarians.
>
> I am the judgment of [the] Greeks
> and of the barbarians.
>
> [I] am the one whose image is great in Egypt
> and the one who has no image
> among the barbarians. . . .

(As in all the English translations of the Nag Hammadi texts, square brackets are used to show a word or words missing in the original books, which lay buried in Egypt for nearly 1,600 years.)

Jeanne d'Arc   See *JOAN OF ARC*.

Joachim of Floris   Benedictine abbot and medieval prophet Joachim of Floris (Gioacchino da Fiore) offered a three-part view of history that became highly influential among unorthodox religious groups in the thirteenth century and afterwards.

Born in Calabria in southern Italy, Joachim lived circa 1135–1202. Based on his study of the Bible and on particular moments of illumination, Joachim declared that human history could be divided into three stages that corresponded to the persons of the Trinity: the age of the Father, the age of the Son, and the age of the Holy Spirit. (In Latin he referred to each age as a *status*.) In particular, he was moved by the passage in Revelation 14 that speaks of "an angel flying in mid-heaven, with an eternal gospel to proclaim to those on earth, to every nation and tribe, language and people."

According to Joachim's presentation of the eternal gospel, the age of the Father corresponded with Old Testament times; it was characterized by its emphasis on law and God's role as a lawgiver and the absolute authority over his people. Joachim also referred to this as the age of St. Peter, and it was the age of the servants of God.

The age of the Son—also called the age of St. Paul—was the age of the New Testament and of the church; its keynote was divine grace. Following Matthew 1:1–17, which listed 42 generations between Abraham and Jesus Christ, Joachim calculated that the age of the Son would also last for 42 generations, meaning that it would end around 1260, to be succeeded by the age of the Holy Spirit—but not without enormous upheaval and the brief rule of the Antichrist. The second age was the age of the sons of God.

In the age of the Holy Spirit, love and liberty would reign, and faithful humanity would become the friends of God. Joachim aligned the third age with St. John, alleged author of Revelation.

Likewise, Joachim saw the forms of human life altered by the three ages. The first age was the age of the householder-priest, symbolized by the Hebrew patriarchs, and the second took its spiritual direction from the monks and clergy. In the third, paradisiacal age, all people would live like monks and nuns in religious contemplation and ecstasy.

The idea that paradise would arrive on earth through a historical process ran counter to Catholic teaching, although we see it repeated in socialism, Marxism, and other later political and utopian movements. The workers' paradise, the Age of Reason, and the New Age all follow similar schemes of historical progression, assigning definite values to past, present, and future.

Although many people of different social classes embraced Joachim's teachings (the Italian poet Dante placed him in his literary Paradise), the abbot's ideas alarmed the church. His prophecy left the church in a marginal role, and his three-part history could be read as a criticism of the church as it existed. Joachim's followers took the concept of the three ages further, some saying (along with numerous other medieval reformers) that the Catholic church had become corrupt, that baptism and priestly absolution were no longer efficacious, and that personal holiness counted for more than ordination as a priest.

As the years progressed, Joachim's ideas were taken up by members of the Franciscan order and by popular preachers inside the church, such as *AMALRIC OF BENE,* and outside it—including *BEGHARDS* and members of the brotherhood of the *FREE SPIRIT.* Meanwhile, his doctrines were officially condemned by theologians at the University of Paris, the leading university of the age, and by Pope Alexander IV in 1263, after a Franciscan had rewritten Joachim's ideas in a book called *Introduction to the Eternal Gospel.*

Joan of Arc   "I never had to do with wicked spirits: But you, that are polluted with your lusts, / Stain'd with the guiltless blood of innocents, / corrupt and tainted with a thousand vices, / Because you want the grace that others have, / You judge it straight a thing impossible / To compass wonders but by help of devils." William Shakespeare puts these words in the mouth of Joan of Arc shortly before her execution in his play *The First Part of Henry VI.* Although the English lords denounce her as being in league with the devil, Joan, "La Pucelle," insists that she is a pure virgin whose death heaven will avenge. Yet earlier in the same play, Shakespeare shows her speaking with spirits that she feeds with her blood. Perhaps the playwright was trying to please everyone: any admirers of Joan who might have walked in England a century and a half after her death as well as those in the audience who saw her as a sorceress justly burned—a sorceress who served England's old enemy, France, at that.

Born in 1412 to a peasant family of Domremy in Lorraine, Joan played a short but significant part in the Hundred Years' War, the long struggle by the English kings to retain their holdings in France. (Her birth came three years before the battle of Agincourt, a notable English victory.) At about age 13, Joan claimed to hear voices and see visions; she became convinced that various saints such as St. Michael, St. Margaret, and St. Catherine were speaking to her. (Saints Catherine and Margaret were the objects of popular devotional cults at the time, and St. Michael was symbolic of France in the way that St. George was associated with England.)

In 1429, as the English army was threatening the city of Orléans, Joan appeared before the dauphin (crown prince) Charles, claiming that she had been divinely appointed to save France from the English, who controlled about half of it on the basis of feudal holdings, alliances with local rulers, and military conquests. She also convinced church authorities of her mission, and with their approval Charles gave her armor, weapons, and soldiers to command, together with a distinctive white banner.

Inspired by Joan, the French turned back the English besiegers; Charles, able to assert his claim to the throne against the counterclaim of Henry VI of England, was crowned king of France with Joan standing nearby.

The war, however, continued, and in 1430, after a military career that lasted only nine months, Joan was captured by soldiers from Burgundy, an area that is now part of France but whose duke at that time was an English ally. Joan was handed over to the English and then to a church court to be tried for heresy and sorcery. The charges against her included claiming to believe that she was directly responsible to God rather than to the church and wearing men's clothing. She was condemned to death, but when she repented, the sentence was changed to life imprisonment. When she again put on men's clothing in prison, the ecclesiastical authorities decided that she had relapsed into heresy. She was also convicted of idolatry on the grounds that she claimed to have seen the saints physically and to have embraced their feet. On 30 May 1431, she was burned at the stake in Rouen, a French city then in English-held territory.

Joan, however, had become a national heroine to the French. Some 25 years after her execution, Charles VII, the dauphin whom she had helped rise to the throne, arranged a retrial, and she was pronounced innocent. She was canonized in 1920, largely due to the lobbying of the right-wing group Action Française, which saw in her a symbol of Catholic, monarchist France. Roman Catholic churches as far away as the United States have been dedicated to her, and her memory still serves as the main attraction of excursion tours of northern France. In addition, her story has inspired numerous artists, poets, playwrights, and other writers.

The English playwright George Bernard Shaw, for example, made her the heroine of his play *Saint Joan* (1921). In the preface he wrote that he considered her a Protestant martyr, despite the fact that she lived before the Protestant

Reformation, because she followed her own conscience ahead of the Roman Catholic church's teachings. Shaw also used Joan as a convenient symbol for a change from the medieval pattern of feudal landholdings—in which a powerful aristocrat might control lands, castles, and towns in different places—to the modern concept of nations with unchanging boundaries regardless of who governs them. In that context, Joan remains a permanent symbol of French nationhood; for example, a modern French aircraft carrier was named for her.

Historians are inclined to view Joan's brief public career and her subsequent trial and execution as more politically than religiously motivated. The ecclesiastical panel that first approved her mission was a French panel; the tribunal that condemned her bent before an English breeze. Medieval people were open to the sudden appearance of the miraculous in their midst, and Joan's military success was not totally unique—other armies had been led by figures just as unlikely. But as a prisoner of war she fit no accepted category. Had she been a male common soldier, she would not have been worth taking prisoner. Had she been a nobleman, she would have been worth holding for ransom, since that was how aristocrats played the game of war. As a woman who dressed as a fighting man she was neither, but she was probably a witch. An illiterate country girl constantly hammered by teams of church experts, Joan might have been tricked into admitting the charges against her. Or she may have welcomed execution compared to the alternative: indefinite confinement on bread and water, probably compounded by rape and other abuse. Considering that her resumption of male attire figured into the matter, some historians have suggested that her female clothing was removed and male clothing left nearby, giving her a choice between chilly nudity or heresy. Whatever the facts, Joan paid the price for upsetting the social and ecclesiastical hierarchy of her day.

Jovinian A monk active in the late fourth century, Jovinian was persecuted for advocating a moderate position on the spiritual value of virginity and perpetual *CHASTITY*. Although he had lived the austere life typical of early monks himself—refusing to wash or wear clean clothes, eating only simple food, and avoiding contact with women—Jovinian, unlike many of his colleagues, came to believe that all baptized persons could be equally holy, that God had commanded marriage and procreation in Matthew 19:6 and Genesis 1:28, and that vegetarianism and abstaining from alcohol produced no special virtue in and of themselves.

Jovinian's views ran counter to the more radical asceticism preached by church fathers such as the great Bible translator Jerome or the ex-Manichaean Augustine. He was condemned by Pope Siricius and excommunicated, but his views found favor among many Christians, and he refused to be silenced. Jerome, holding that all sexual intercourse was unclean, denounced Jovinian at length and accused him of following the ancient hedonistic philosopher Epicurus. Although Jovinian himself is not well known as a heretic, Jerome's book *Against Jovinian* circulated widely due to its author's fame and helped fix the church's position on sexual matters.

Julian the Apostate Born in 331 and ruler of the Roman Empire from 361 until his death in 363, the emperor Flavius Claudius Julianus is known to history as the apostate because he formally renounced the Christian religion in which he had been raised and tried with only partial and ephemeral success to revive old Roman Paganism, placing himself at its head as high priest and philosopher-king.

Julian was born in Constantinople, the new imperial capital established by *CONSTANTINE* the Great. His father, Julius Constantius, was Constantine's half-brother and spent most of his life excluded from power by Constantine (who feared him as a possible rival to the throne); he was eventually murdered by Constantine's son and successor Constantius when Julian was five. Julian's mother had died shortly after his birth. The young Julian spent most of his boyhood under what amounted to house arrest in luxurious imperial villas, surrounded by nurses, slaves, and tutors. The whole establishment was supervised by Eusebius, a Christian bishop. For a time, Julian was also allowed to make extended visits to his grandmother's country estate; otherwise, aside from rare visits from his half-brother Gallus, he was without family contacts. He was raised a Christian but educated in the Pagan classics—the only books of literature, philosophy, and science available—such as the works of Homer and

Plato. In his teens he was baptized and ordained a "reader," the lowest step on the clerical ladder, charged with giving the lessons from the Old and New Testament during worship services. Later in life, he wrote of those years of gilded exile: "No stranger came near us [i.e., Julian]. None of our old friends was allowed to visit us. We were cut off from any serious study and any contact with free men; surrounded by a splendid entourage, we had no companions but our own slaves."

Despite his carefully guided Christian upbringing, Julian was drawn to the competing philosophy of *NEOPLATONISM,* Christianity's chief intellectual rival and an irresistible influence on it. He had also experienced moments of mystic insight that did not seem to fit into a Christian worldview. By his twentieth birthday, he had decided privately that he was philosophically a Pagan, although he had never encountered Pagan religion in practice. At about the same time, the political climate changed, and Julian was allowed to travel where he liked as long as he stayed out of political affairs. His studious nature led him to Aeidesios, a student of the late Neoplatonist teacher *IAMBLICHUS.* Through other of Aeidesios's students, Julian heard of *MAXIMUS,* a charismatic man who was a combination philosopher, ritual magician, and free-lance Pagan priest. Using the works of Iamblichus, which countenanced ritual magic as a step in the soul's journey toward the One—the source of all existence—and other magical -texts such as the second-century *Chaldean Oracles,* Maximus offered initiation into what amounted to a secret, esoteric Neoplatonic religion. Julian became his initiate. Later he was also initiated into the all-male cult of *MITHRAS,* the Persian sun god widely worshiped in the Roman army. Mithraism, with its ranks and lodges, filled a place somewhat similar to modern Freemasonry for soldiers stationed far from home.

Julian's brother Gallus was appointed caesar (regional military commander) of part of the eastern empire under the emperor Constantius, but he was eventually accused of treason and executed like so many others. Meanwhile, Julian continued his philosophical and magical studies while keeping the outward appearance of pious Christianity. But eventually the emperor's net caught him too. Accused of plotting treason, he was summoned to Constantius's headquarters in Milan. On the way he visited the city of Troy (much reduced from its Homeric glory) and was escorted by a bishop to the shrines of the goddess Athena and the hero Hector. Both shrines were still in use, which did not seem to offend the bishop, and both the continuance of Pagan practice and the bishop's tolerance—perhaps even approval—affected Julian deeply.

Unlike his half-brother, Julian escaped execution but was held for a time under house arrest and then exiled to Athens, a political backwater but still an important center of learning. There he continued his studies and was initiated into the ancient cult of the goddess Demeter at Eleusis. But in 355, after less than a year, he was recalled to Milan; facing another coup attempt, Constantius decided to summon his sole adult male relative and invest him as his deputy, even though he had destroyed Julian's father and brother.

The quiet, scholarly 24-year-old gave up his philosopher's beard and gown. Suddenly he was a high officer: caesar of Gaul, Britain, and Spain. He also undertook a political marriage with Helena, Constantius's sister, who was about 30. In reality, he was only a figurehead; military and civil decisions were made by other men Constantius had appointed.

Swept into a campaign already under way against the German and Frankish tribes, Julian studied the craft of war from veteran officers and garnered some small initial successes, which enhanced his popularity among the legionnaires and people. After his outnumbered troops—with Julian in the thick of combat—defeated a larger coalition of German tribesmen on the Rhine at Strasbourg, his popularity rose even faster in the army. Too much popularity, however, could be unhealthy. Once a figurehead, Julian was now Constantius's potential rival.

The flash point came in 360 when Julian, headquartered in Paris, was requested by the emperor to send six legions—many of them romanized Germans—far to the east for a campaign against the rising Persian Empire. Although he tried to comply, the soldiers refused to go, proclaiming him to be their emperor. They surrounded his palace all night, chanting

"Iulianus Augustus!" (Julian for emperor). In the morning, he came out and was lifted high, standing on a shield held by a group of soldiers—a German ritual of tribal chieftainship transplanted to the Roman legions.

Thrust toward civil war, Julian tried negotiating with Constantius. The negotiations dragged on: Constantius was commencing a campaign against the Persians while Julian continued punitive expeditions against the German tribes. In the summer of 361, however, the Persians backed down, and Constantius began to prepare for war with his former subordinate, who in turn moved down the Danube to meet the emperor in the eastern empire. But Constantius died between Antioch and Constantinople in November 361; Julian was able to reach Constantinople in time to meet the late emperor's corpse as it was brought to the capital.

Now emperor at age 29, Julian tried to become Plato's philosopher-king. He trimmed the extravagant imperial court and issued edicts of religious toleration. Not only did he permit Pagans and Christians their religious practices equally, but he stopped the Christian clergy's government salaries and refused to intervene in disputes over heresy. In fact, he ordered that Christian clerics exiled for heresy by his predecessor be allowed to return home. He issued a decree ordering that Pagan temple property confiscated under Constantine and his successors be returned to its original owners; in some areas, this provided an excuse for anti-Christian looting and the martyrdom of some believers. But beyond that, he tried to turn educated people and the upper classes away from Christianity. He encouraged Pagan theologians, who were a novelty, since classical Paganism had done without theologians, having only poets and priests.

Julian's potentially most far-reaching edict forbade Christians from teaching grammar or rhetoric—what teachers today would call literature and language arts—in private or municipal schools. It did not, however, forbid young Christians from attending such schools, for that was part of Julian's plan to make Christianity less appealing to the educated portion of the populace. (Some Christian historians of the following century did falsely accuse Julian of banning Christian students, however.) He was not asking Christian teachers to abandon their faith, he explained; he merely wished them to stop teaching the literary classics—for example, Homer's *Iliad* and *Odyssey*—as literature while condemning the religious views expressed in those and other pre-Christian works. "If they [teachers] are real interpreters of the ancient classics, let them first imitate the ancients' piety towards the gods. If they think the classics wrong in this respect, then let them go and teach Matthew and Luke in the church," the young emperor wrote.

Julian's edict presented both Christian teachers and parents with difficult choices. The former group faced an obvious threat to their livelihoods. With no tradition or law of academic freedom to protect them, they had to either live and teach a lie or face firing. Parents, meanwhile, had to either pull their children out of the very schools that would put them on the path to careers in law or government or risk exposing them to openly anti-Christian faculties. Had Julian not died only months later, he could have seriously hurt Christianity's rising prestige.

While trying to block Christians from teaching, Julian also wrote and encouraged others to write anti-Christian books that paradoxically reflected how powerful Christianity had become. He sought to unify Pagan theology and to elevate Pagan priests into full-time religious workers like their Christian counterparts, complete with ecclesiastical hierarchies, culminating in the person of Julian himself as *pontifex maximus,* or high priest of the entire empire. In a letter to a Pagan religious dignitary, Julian wrote, "Do we not see that what has most contributed to the success of atheism [what educated Pagans considered Christianity to be] is its charity towards strangers, the care it takes of the tombs of the dead, and its feigned gravity of life?"

He also underwrote reconstruction of the Jewish temple in Jerusalem, destroyed by Roman armies 300 years earlier. The combination of an earthquake in Jerusalem, Julian's death, and opposition from the rabbis (who were now the Jews' spiritual leaders in place of the former temple priesthood) put an end to the project shortly after work on it had begun.

But Julian's efforts to damage Christianity and restore the old cults in a Neoplatonic synthesis with himself as leader were cut short by events. In 363 he led an army east toward the Persian frontier in an attempt to contain the Persian Empire and stabilize Roman boundaries. In one of several clashes along the banks of the Euphrates River, Julian was fatally wounded by a Persian cavalryman's lance. According to the most reliable accounts, he rushed into a melée without his armored breastplate and was wounded. He was carried to his tent, where he died later in the day. Pagan chroniclers depicted him as discussing philosophical issues with Maximus and others until losing consciousness. However, the fourth-century church historian Theodoret (one of those who misdescribed Julian's school edict) portrayed the emperor as admitting spiritual defeat with the words *Vicisti, Galilæe*—Thou hast conquered, O Galilean (Jesus).

The imperial preference for Christianity was reasserted by Julian's successor, Jovian. Under subsequent emperors the decline and fall of the empire continued, with its western portions being abandoned to various Germanic and other non-Roman kings a century later.

Justin the Gnostic   Little is known about this Gnostic teacher except that he considered the Pagan deity Priapus to be the creator of the world, "the one who made creation even though nothing existed before."

Knights Templar   In simple historical terms, the Knights Templar (or simply the Templars) were a group of European knights organized like a monastic order and responsible for protecting pilgrims and defending the Christian kingdom in Palestine, which dated from the capture of Jerusalem by the men of the First Crusade in 1099 and included most of the modern nations of Israel and Lebanon. Founded in 1118 and officially recognized by the papal Council of Troyes in 1128, the order lasted until 1314, when it was destroyed by King Philip I (the Fair) of France, who had its leaders burned at the stake on charges of heresy.

The order's organizers, two French knights named Hughes de Payn and Godefroi de St. Omer, were part of a second wave of crusaders that came to the Holy Land after the First Crusade had conquered it and established a Christian kingdom that included most of present-day Israel and Lebanon. They were given permission by King Baldwin to start an order of fighting monks—a cavalry corps that lived communally; took vows of poverty, chastity, and obedience; and when not at war followed the monastic round of religious services. The order was financed by donations and later by loot as well. Returning to Europe in 1127 to raise money, Hughes de Payn persuaded the great monastic organizer St. Bernard, abbot of Clairvaux, to line up church backing for the order, basing its organization on his own Cistercian monastic way of life. Bernard, who had no delusions about the fact that most medieval nobles lived for war, conquest, and pillage, saw the Knights Templar as a means of turning those destructive energies to religious purposes through the consecrated slaying of Muslim infidels. He also knew that many of the men who went on crusades did so because they were in trouble at home for breaking either secular or religious laws. It was no coincidence that the Templars frequently recruited knights who had been excommunicated, but once in the order they were able to receive the sacraments from the order's own priests. "The soldier of Christ kills safely," the great abbot argued.

The Templars were headed by a Grand Master, with his lieutenants the Marshall and the Seneschal. Preceptors were in charge of regional Templar organizations in Europe (for instance, Normandy).

Despite their large holdings in Palestine and Western Europe—estates, castles, and churches—the Templars were not numerically a large order. Modern historians estimate that at their height there were no more than 300 knights in Palestine, supplemented of course by non-noble fighting brothers, servants, and mercenary soldiers hired in Turkey and elsewhere. In Palestine the order also accepted European knights who signed on for a period of years but did not take Templar vows. Other brothers included sergeants, who rode horseback and carried knights' weapons but wore brown or black mantles instead of the Templars' distinctive white mantles. Below them came a rank of esquire, and below them ranks of rural brothers and servant brothers who ran the houses, stables, and rural estates.

During the 1100s the Templars grew rich and powerful. They had a network of castles and estates from Jerusalem to northern Spain, and they answered to no king—only to their Grand Master and the pope. Because they transferred large amounts of money between their various domains, they also acted as financial couriers and later bankers to rulers and the nobility. But in the late 1100s, the Saracens, or Muslims, took the military offensive against the

Christian kingdom. In 1187, a Christian army including many Templars was smashed near the Sea of Galilee at the battle of the Horns of Hattin, named after a rock formation. Jerusalem fell to the sultan Saladin that same year; after months of fighting, King Richard (the Lion-Hearted) only succeeded in getting a Muslim guarantee of safe passage for Christian pilgrims into the holy city. Retaken by the Christians under the German (Holy Roman) emperor Frederick II in 1228, Jerusalem fell again to the Muslims in 1244. The Christian enclave shrank slowly until it included just a few castles on the coast; the last one, Acre, fell in 1291. Its Templar defenders, including the current Grand Master, were killed in battle; only a few knights escaped by boat.

Medieval people saw the judgment of God played out in history, and although the order of the Knights Templar was still powerful, it had lost its reason for being when it was pushed out of the Holy Land. People now found it easier to criticize the knights for their wealth, arrogance, and perceived greed. The last Grand Master, Jacques de Molay, resisted suggestions from European monarchs that the order merge with a somewhat parallel group, the Knights of St. John of Jerusalem, or Knights Hospitaler, in a grand new crusade against either the Muslims or the Orthodox Christian Byzantine Empire, the merger being a favored plan of King Philip I of France, the most powerful Western European monarch of the day.

Frustrated by Templar stubbornness and jealous of the order's immense wealth, Philip set out to destroy the knights. On 13 October 1307, his agents arrested Jacques de Molay, other Templar leaders, somewhere between 50 and 100 knights, plus sergeants, esquires, and servants—for a total of around 500. They were charged with heresy and idolatry, particularly that they worshiped a mysterious "head." Such religious charges might have been more proper coming from the church than from a king, but Philip's ministers argued that the king's duty to protect his people required him to act. Besides, Philip's ancestors had enforced orthodoxy decades earlier when they rode south to destroy the *ALBIGENSIAN* heretics in Provence.

Under torture, the Templars confessed to a variety of offenses: denying the divinity of Christ, trampling the cross, committing sodomy

(see *HOMOSEXUALITY*), and worshiping an idol of Baphomet (a garbled medieval name for Muhammad, the prophet of Islam). No idols were ever found, however, and the descriptions of heretical rituals dragged from the Templars by torture did not necessarily agree with one another. King Philip defied theologians who questioned his right to try the Templars, and eventually Pope Clement V gave orders that Templars in all nations were to be examined and tortured, if necessary, to determine whether they were heretics. A separate papal commission was created to oversee the task. Proceedings dragged over months and years; an ineffectual Templar legal challenge died, and in 1310 some 54 members of the order were burned at the stake in France. Finally, in 1314, Jacques de Molay and three other top officers were similarly burned alive in Paris. Some members of the order, notably in Cyprus, Scotland, Portugal, and the Spanish kingdoms, survived its suppression. In some cases, they were permitted to join the Hospitalers. Other Templars probably shaved their distinctive beards and faded into feudal society as best they could. The order's wealth was in theory given to the Hospitalers as well, but King Philip of France and King Edward II of England diverted much of it to their royal treasuries.

The Templars' failure to adequately defend themselves, either in court or by military action, has led to a variety of theories. Most likely their own loss of morale and organizational purpose after losing their foothold in the Holy Land, combined with difficulties of communication, caused their inaction.

Had the Templar order truly ended in 1314 with the execution of Jacques de Molay, the knights' place in the history of heresy would be slight. What makes their story remarkable is that they would be seen in the future not just as heretics, but as hidden masters of Oriental wisdom and conduits of esoteric thought from the Middle East to Europe. At the time of the trials, alleged Templar heresy was linked vaguely to that of the *ALBIGENSIANS*, who were still alive in southern France, but Templar imitators from the eighteenth century to the present have made much more of their story.

Because the Templars were suppressed by a royal government supported by the church, their story appealed in those in the eighteenth century who were looking for a hidden current in the Middle Ages, something opposed to church orthodoxy and secular power. The idea that the Templars might have guarded a flame of secret teaching struck the imaginations of the same men who founded new Masonic and Rosicrucian secret societies in Western Europe. Even earlier, one of the best-known Renaissance writers on occultism, Henry Cornelius Agrippa, a sixteenth-century German scholar who sought to define a pure, Neoplatonic (see *NEOPLATONISM*) form of magic, discussed the Templars in his book *De Occulta Philosophia* (published in English as *The Philosophy of Natural Magic*), printed in 1531. It included hints that the Templars were indeed heretics who practiced black magic.

However, it took the particular combination of literary nostalgia, a search for secret teaching, and the whole Romantic movement to revive the Templars as a positive model of magic. The founders of Freemasonry included the Templars in the lineage of those who guarded Masonry's purported ancient wisdom from earlier centuries.

New Templar orders were founded, particularly in Germany, around 1760. A prosperous landowner from Saxony, Karl Gotthelf von Hund, was the most successful organizer; after his death in 1776 he was buried in the regalia he invented for himself as Provincial Grand Master.

German neo-Templar orders spread to Britain and the United States, appealing to men who wanted esoteric religious teaching in an aristocratic atmosphere. In France, however, the would-be Templars had to face political suspicion based on the notion that the historical Templars were enemies of the royal house. According to one legend, when King Louis XVI was executed in 1793, a voice from the crowd had shouted, "Jacques de Molay, you are avenged!" When royal government was reinstated after the Napoleonic Wars in the early nineteenth century, the new Templarism remained tainted by suspicions of anticlericalism and antimonarchism. Some writers alleged that the Cathars were linked to the Templars, who in turn were linked to the Jacobins, the revolutionaries who led the overthrow of Louis XVI.

During the nineteenth century, other Masonic Templar orders were invented, one in 1808 on the anniversary of Jacques de Molay's execution and others later in the century. Their name was evoked again in the early 1900s when a German named Theodor Ruess began a magical order—Order of the Eastern Temple—whose Latin initials were O.T.O. It too has various offspring.

Indeed, in the years since 1314, the Templars have been described as simple soldiers who confessed anything imaginable under torture; as guardians of secret wisdom learned in the Near East; as political radicals bent on destroying kings and creating world government; and as participants in conspiracies that stretched over centuries with the purpose of protecting some secret tradition of Christianity, such as the purported flesh-and-blood offspring of Jesus or the so-called Holy Shroud of Turin, which some suggested was the idol they were accused of worshiping. When European (and some American) writers seek to suggest that a secret society controls world history, the Templars are often given a part in the conspiracy.

Kyteler, Alice Ireland was generally free of persecutions of heretics and so-called witches during the Middle Ages, with the case of Lady Alice Kyteler being a notable exception. For one thing, outside of the Anglicized *pales* or locales surrounding Dublin, Cork, Wexford, and Limerick, the rest of Ireland was somewhat turned in upon itself, with the descendants of Normans and Vikings joining the Gaelic Irish in the old Celtic pastimes of cattle raiding, feuding, and other manifestations of tribal politics. During the sixteenth and seventeenth centuries, when the *WITCHCRAFT* persecutions raged on the European continent, Ireland was being contested between the English crown (or the dictator Oliver Cromwell) and various Irish leaders in a long, bloody cycle of rebellion and pacification. Since the conflict was cast in religious terms—Catholic versus Protestant—from the time of Elizabeth I onward, heresy and dissent were nonissues, drowned out by and subsumed in the larger religious war.

In 1324, however, Ireland was probably no more or no less warlike than other European countries. Along with the castles and tower houses of the Hiberno-Norman aristocrats, stone churches and large monasteries were built. The *FRANCISCANS* had several large houses in Ireland, and it was a French-trained Franciscan priest made Bishop of Ossory, Richard de Ledrede, who accused Alice Kyteler, the wealthiest noblewoman of Kilkenny, of sorcery and heresy.

The bishop accused Lady Alice, her son by her first marriage (she was on her fourth husband at this point), and several other persons of half a dozen charges. To begin with, they were accused of denying God and the Catholic church; parodying religious ceremonies; seeking knowledge of the future from evil spirits; sacrificing cocks and other animals to a demon named Robin Artisson; and preparing magical potions, powders, and ointments. Lady Alice, in particular, was accused of having sexual relations with Robin Artisson, who would appear as a cat, a black dog, or a shaggy man carrying an iron rod.

Lady Alice, a fiery specimen of the Norman nobility that became "more Irish than the Irish," retaliated by summoning her retainers and imprisoning the bishop, who had excommunicated her. He in turn announced that his diocese was under interdict, meaning that no one could receive the sacraments—baptism, communion, marriage, and so on. Now the conflict moved into the secular courts, with the Lord Justice ordering the bishop to lift the interdict and having him thrown out of court when he protested.

Bishop de Ledrede in turn demanded that Lady Alice and the rest be charged with sorcery under civil law. She prudently decided that she needed to visit England for a time and seek the protection of King Edward II. The bishop managed to imprison her son William and also her maid, Petronilla de Meath. Petronilla was tortured by flogging until she confessed to a typical menu of diabolism: She and Lady Alice had indeed consorted with demons, attended Satanic orgies, and all the rest. With Lady Alice beyond his reach, the bishop had to be satisfied with seeing Petronilla burned at the stake in Kilkenny on 3 November 1324.

Alice Kyteler's accusation and Petronilla's death mark the slow birth of witchcraft trials and a move away from the position established by the *CANON EPISCOPI*—that belief in witchcraft's reality was itself a heresy. By comparison, the first recorded trial for witchcraft in France took place in a secular court in 1390.

Lady Alice's case also contributed a piece of evidence that is frequently cited in the argument that medieval witches used psychedelic drugs. In searching her bedroom, her accusers found a "pipe of ointment" with which they said she would "grease a staff, upon the which she ambled and galloped through thick and thin, when and in what manner she listed." To some historians, this suggests the use of a rounded stick to apply a drug-containing ointment to the sensitive membranes of the female genitals, permitting it to rapidly enter the bloodstream.

La Pucelle d'Orléans   French for "the maid of Orléans," this term is occasionally used to refer to *JOAN OF ARC*.

Lollards   Itinerant preachers commissioned by the heretical reformer John *WYCLIFFE* (or Wyclif) in fourteenth-century England, the Lollards were probably so nicknamed from a slang term meaning "mumbler"—in other words, someone who prays frequently. Wycliffe, a prominent English critic of the papacy and of clerical corruption, believed (like the *WALDENSIANS*) that the people needed to be able to read the Bible in their own language, not Latin.

Although he was himself in holy orders, Wycliffe sided with King Edward III in a dispute over money demanded by Pope Urban V in the 1360s. When Wycliffe was reprimanded in 1377 by William Courtenay, the bishop of London, the whole controversy took on a nationalist cast with Wycliffe receiving the support of royal officials. From this dispute, Wycliffe de-

A demonized portrait of the pope with the Latin inscription Ego sum Papa, *meaning "I am the pope." Such propaganda led to Roman Catholic persecution of the Lollards. (Woodcut by Eduard Fuchs, from* Die Karikatur der Europaischen Volker, *sixteenth century.)*

veloped a position that the entire Catholic hierarchy constituted an affront to true Christianity and that the pope—any pope, not just Urban V—had become the Antichrist. Furthermore, he attacked Catholic doctrine on the sacraments, particularly the doctrine that Christ was physically present in the sacraments of bread and wine (transubstantiation). Even the Franciscan monks, *FRANCIS OF ASSISI*'s barefoot friars, had become corrupted from their founder's ideals, he declared. When four Franciscans visited him during a severe illness and advised him to withdraw his views and die in sanctity, Wycliffe is said to have sat up in bed and shouted, "I will not die; I am going to live and denounce the evil deeds of the mendicant monks!"

To renew his vision of Christianity, Wycliffe organized his own teams of evangelical men, the Lollards, around 1380. It is not known whether he was aware of the similar Waldensian preachers in earlier centuries, but he chose a similar tactic. His preachers wore plain garments, went forth in pairs, and had no permanent homes but taught wherever they could find hearers—in marketplaces, church-yards, private homes, or country fields.

To help them, he prepared the first English translation of the entire Bible, thus challenging the Catholic doctrine that only the trained clergy were qualified to preach from the Scriptures. Wycliffe himself is credited with most of the translation from the Latin Bible then in use; some colleagues from Oxford University completed it. His translation, his other writings, and his personal example inspired other reformers in Europe, particularly Jan *HUS*.

Almost immediately, some of Wycliffe's followers, although not Wycliffe himself, became embroiled in the Peasants' Revolt of 1381, in which angry countrymen stormed London in protest of a per capita tax they had been forced to pay annually since 1377. (The revolt is also known as Wat Tyler's Rebellion after one of its principal leaders.) The rebels succeeded in forcing King Richard II to temporarily remove the tax, but some alarmed aristocrats blamed Wycliffe's religious ideas for inspiring the peasants to such seditious behavior. The ruling class's alarm undoubtedly lay behind a decision the following year by the archbishop of Canterbury to try Wycliffe for heresy and have him expelled from Oxford University.

Lollardism, meanwhile, continued without Wycliffe's active leadership, becoming more and more identified with social issues and consequently more suppressed by the local authorities. Unlike the comparable Hussites, the Lollards—at least the more moderate among them—never succeeded in winning the support of an influential portion of the nobility, clergy, and merchants. It was not an organized movement, but more a movement of opinions led by laymen and rebellious clerics. Throughout the late fourteenth century, small groups of Lollards were periodically tried for heresy. After one group publicly called for ending taxes that supported the church, a

A Renaissance depiction of Lucifer. (From Ricchierus, Lectionum Antiquarum, 1517.)

church convocation in the archepiscopal city of Canterbury petitioned the king to execute convicted Lollards, a "cunning and bold sect of anti-Christians."

After his ascension to the throne in 1399, Henry IV did indeed approve legislation providing the death penalty for anyone found guilty of Lollardism, thus making Lollards criminals as well as heretics. (See *DE HERETICO COMBURENDO*.) Initially only two men were burned after heresy trials during Henry's reign, but Lollardism helped fuel the futile rebellion of Sir John Oldcastle in 1414. Oldcastle, a nobleman with Lollard sympathies, was charged with harboring and supporting these heretics in 1413. Imprisoned in the Tower of London, he escaped and tried to organize a rebellion, but his expected 20,000 followers turned out to be only a few hundred, a number of whom were executed even though their leader escaped and remained on the run until he was captured and burned in 1417.

For the next two decades, Lollards were periodically tried and executed, and after Oldcastle's rebellion they were often accused of acting in collusion with foreign powers to overthrow the government. Another Lollard rebellion, that of William Perkins (Jack Sharpe of Wigmorland), set out to overthrow religious and royal rule in 1431; it too fizzled, and its leaders were executed. (See map on page 83.)

Luciferans   Following the pantheistic doctrine that God is present in all of creation, some medieval sectarians held that God and the devil were one. (This view is similar to the doctrine of the small but highly publicized Process Church, which operated in England and North America in the late 1960s and 1970s.) Since the Catholic church (and later Protestants) frequently referred to Satan as "the ruler of this world," breakaway groups of antinomian heretics would therefore declare that Satan (Lucifer) should indeed be worshiped, for he was one of God's creations and would one day be restored to his rightful place in heaven.

Since many medieval heretics came to be accused of making pacts with Satan and wor-shiping him, it is difficult to tell who the real Luciferans were, but groups with this theology are mentioned as existing in thirteenth-century Germany. See *ANTINOMIANISM*.

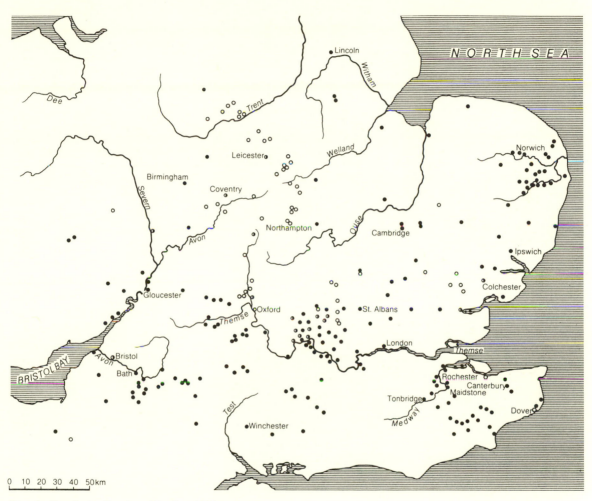

The Lollards in England in the 15th century

Towns and places

o Participation in the uprising of 1414

● Lollards in the 2nd half of the 15th century

ø Participation in the uprising and
Lollard activities in the 2nd half
of the 15th century

Sites associated with Lollard activity in England during the fifteenth century. (Map by Matthias Weis, reprinted, by permission of the publisher, from Erbstösser, Heretics in the Middle Ages, *Edition Leipzig, 1984.)*

Magus, Simon   See *SIMON MAGUS*.

Malabar Christians
See *NESTORIAN CHRISTIANS*.

Malleus Maleficarum   Written in Germany in the 1480s, the *Malleus Maleficarum* (Hammer of witches—technically, female evildoers) became perhaps the most notorious and far-reaching document of the papal *INQUISITION*. Overriding an earlier document, the *CANON EPISCOPI*, which had made it a heresy to believe in the reality of *WITCHCRAFT*, the *Malleus Maleficarum* stated that because the Bible mentioned witchcraft negatively, as did later theologians, witchcraft itself could be counted as an organized heresy worthy of persecution. Reversing earlier church doctrine, its authors wrote: "A belief that there are such things as witches is so essential a part of the Catholic faith that obstinately to maintain the opposite opinion is heresy."

During the height of both Catholic and Protestant witchcraft persecution, which began in the mid-fifteenth century and lasted until the late seventeenth century, the *Malleus Maleficarum* was reprinted at least 28 times. Because of its widespread influence, it undoubtedly helped cause the death of thousands of innocent Europeans and, indirectly, those Massachusetts colonists executed in the 1690s.

The *Malleus Maleficarum* was written by two Dominican inquisitors, Heinrich Krämer (his name sometimes Latinized as Institoris) and Jakob Sprenger. It followed Pope Innocent VIII's issuance of the bull *Summus desiderantes affectibus* in 1484, which not surprisingly gave the Inquisition rather than the secular courts jurisdiction over witchcraft as heresy and directed the Bishop of Strasburg in particular to give the two inquisitors his assistance. Both men had previous reputations; Sprenger was dean of Cologne University, and Krämer had already served as an inquisitor in parts of Germany. (Because of his extreme tactics, he fell afoul of one bishop, who forced him from that particular diocese.)

Divided into three parts, the treatise begins with the declaration that it deals with "the three necessary concomitants of witchcraft, which are the devil, a witch, and the permission of Almighty God." It established the biblical basis for a belief in witchcraft, thus overcoming the earlier position against such a belief. Based on verses such as Exodus 22:18, "You shall not allow a witch to live" (a mistranslation of a Hebrew word meaning "poisoner"), and Leviticus 20:27, "Any man or woman among you who calls up ghosts or spirits shall be put to death," the two Dominicans argued that "any man who gravely errs in an exposition of Holy Scripture is rightly considered a heretic." Thus anchored, they proceeded to define the witchcraft heresy as a renunciation of the Catholic faith combined with a new allegiance to Satan, formalized by parodies of Christian ritual and sometimes a written document. This alleged pact with the devil carried more weight in prosecuting someone for witchcraft than did any charge of poisoning, damaging crops and livestock, influencing the weather, and so on.

Even when skeptics doubted witches' ability to do such things, they still advocated prosecution of accused devil worshipers. Even so-called white witches or blessing witches could be accused of making pacts with the devil, although they tried to help rather than harm their neighbors. Here, too, biblical sanction was sought, the inquisitors basing their belief in such pacts on Isaiah 28:15, "We have made a treaty with Death and signed a pact with Sheol." Most of all, the first section of the *Malleus Maleficarum* lays the blame for witchcraft on women, who are "naturally" weaker, more lustful, and more prone to magical evildoing than are men.

In its second part, the treatise covered the traditional works of *maleficia* or "evildoing"—causing disease and death, having sex with demons, flying through the air, damaging crops, and so on—and discussed ways of dealing with them. It included chapter headings such as these:

An illustration from the 1497 Paris edition of the Malleus Maleficarum.

Of the several methods by which devils through witches entice and allure the innocent to the increase of that horrid craft and company

Of the way whereby a formal pact with evil is made

Here follows the way whereby witches copulate with those devils known as Incubi

How witches impede and prevent the power of procreation

How, as it were, they deprive man of his virile member

How they raise and stir up hailstorms and tempests, and cause lightning to blast both men and beasts

The third part, however, was most sinister. There the inquisitors laid out a handbook for accusing, questioning, torturing, trying, and sentencing people for witchcraft. All possible gambits of victims and witnesses were antici-pated; armed with the *Malleus Maleficarum,* an inquisitor could handle almost any circumstance. And when the inevitable guilty verdict came, the book furnished the judge with the proper words to use: "We have exerted our utmost endeavor by various fitting methods to convert you to salvation, but you have been given up to your sin and led away and seduced by an evil spirit and have chosen to be tortured with fearful and eternal torment in hell, and that your body should here be consumed in flames."

The book's anti-feminine character is frequently cited. Not only did the book's authors change the gender of its title to the feminine (compare an earlier work, *Flagellum Maleficorum*), but they indulged in such Latin wordplay as breaking *femina* (woman) into *fe minus* (less faith). Women, who are more fleshly and less spiritual than men, have seven reasons for falling into witchcraft, they said: They are more credulous and less experienced than men, more curious, more impressionable, more ill-natured, more likely to seek revenge, more susceptible to despair, and more prone to gossip. "When a woman thinks alone, she thinks evil," Krämer and Sprenger wrote. "All witchcraft comes from carnal lust, which in women is insatiable."

The book's influence continued into the twentieth century among those convinced of the reality of medieval and Renaissance devil worship. It was translated into English by Montague Summers (1880–1948), an eccentric Catholic priest (although there is some question about whether he was actually ordained) who, unlike most of his contemporaries, believed that the witchcraft persecuted during the fifteenth, sixteenth, and seventeenth centuries was indeed "hideous and horrible fact" and that there was a "powerful secret organization [of witches] inimical to Church and State" in those centuries.

Mani, Manichaeism Although its founder, Mani (circa 216–277), grew up within a Middle Eastern Christian sect, the religion of Manichaeism ultimately had followers from North Africa to China. It offered them salvation from the world's snares and the long struggle between good and evil. Despite Mani's own martyrdom at the order of the Persian monarch Bahram I and persecution of his followers in the Roman and Chinese empires as well, pockets of Manichaeism lasted into at least the eighth century in North Africa and even later in China. Mani himself was variously described as another Buddha, a reincarnation of the legendary Chinese philosopher Lao-Tsu, or a great prophet who renewed the teachings of Jesus or the Persian teacher Zarathushtra, depending on the region.

Through the Middle Ages, Christian writers used the term *Manichaean* loosely to describe any dualistic heresy, whether derived from Mani's teachings or not. Modern scholars, however, do not consider Manichaeism to be a heresy in the strict sense of the word but rather a separate religion from Christianity.

Mani's family, Persian in origin, lived near Babylon in present-day Iraq, a crossroads where he would have been exposed to diverse religious and philosophical traditions: Judaism, different Christian groups, Persian Zoroastrianism, Greek philosophy, Chaldean astrology, plus Buddhism and other Asian doctrines. Well-born, artistic, and multilingual (but according to legend, sickly or lame), Mani is said to have experienced his first religious vision at age 12—the appearance of an angelic being who seemed to mirror himself. This was followed at age 24 by another visit by the same angel, called *al-Tawm,* "the twin." Until that time, he and his parents had been members of an ascetic Judeo-Christian community of "baptists" founded by a man known variously as Elkesai to Christians or al-Khasayh to the Arabs. Both visions were related to Mani's future prophetic role—the first telling him he must leave the Elkesaite community at a later date, and the second telling him that that time had come: "The time is now come for thee to manifest thyself publicly and to proclaim thy doctrine aloud."

As the new "apostle of light," Mani came into immediate conflict with the legalistic Elkesaites. In opposition to their ritual ablutions, baptisms, and dietary and other rules, Mani set forth an essentially *GNOSTIC* teaching. Good and evil were locked in conflict, and the earth was ruled by evil powers. People must learn to separate themselves from their bodies and the world, respectively described as "the great calamity" and "the burning abode," and return to their true spiritual natures. Mani's pessimistic appraisal of the world resembled both Buddhism and other Gnostic teachings, and both have been claimed as influences on him, but the greatest single influence other than Christianity was probably the Persian religion of Zoroastrianism.

Leaving Mesopotamia, Mani traveled northeast toward India, then turned back into Persia at the summons of Emperor Shapur I (of the Sasanian dynasty), to whom he dedicated a theological work in the 250s. Shapur accepted the new doctrines and became a strong supporter of Mani's universal religion, much to the disgust of the Magi, the official Zoroastrian clergy, who rejected the new foreign cult. The date on which Shapur gave Mani permission to preach throughout his kingdom has been calculated as either 21 March 242 or 9 April 243; this date was as important to Manichaeism as the Roman emperor Constantine's battlefield dream in 312 and his subsequent turn toward Christianity. From an initial nucleus of his father and two other disciples, Mani's following grew. Missionaries were sent throughout the Middle East, to the Roman colonies of North Africa, and to Central Asia and China.

Although Shapur's son favored Mani, the next Persian ruler, Bahram (or Vahram) I, prodded by the Magi, ordered Mani arrested, interrogated, and imprisoned. According to Manichaean tradition, the questioning lasted four days, followed by 26 days of imprisonment in heavy chains before the prophet's death. Bahram ordered Mani's head stuck up on the city's gates and his body thrown to the dogs; persecution of his followers within the Persian Empire then commenced.

To commemorate these events, Manichaeans fasted for 30 days each year, leading up to the festival of the Bema (from the Middle

Persian for "throne" or "tribunal"), which occurred at the spring equinox. Other rules and observances included fasting on Sundays, avoiding violence, monogamous marriage, four daily prayers, and tithing to support the clergy, who took even stricter vows.

Manichaean temples contained a physical *bema,* a throne with five steps, in which no one sat. It symbolized Mani himself as discarnate guide for the faithful and/or the Last Judgment. The five steps may have symbolized the laity and the four classes of clergy: 12 teachers or apostles, 72 deacons, 360 stewards, and the larger group of the chosen or elect from which the three higher grades were drawn. The greatest holy day was the spring equinox, when Manichaeans celebrated Mani's last days, sang hymns, read sacred texts, and offered a banquet to the elect.

Although he recognized the validity of other religions, Mani claimed to have extracted their essence; his scriptures were offered as more accurate, more comprehensive, and less corrupted by human error than, say, the Christian scriptures.

The Manichaean Cosmos

Because Mani was in a way competing with other religions, the mythology and metaphors he developed to carry his teachings were perhaps less sharply drawn and less tied to any one people or place than those of Judaism, Christianity, or Buddhism. He divided the history of the universe into three periods. In the beginning, the powers of good and evil, light and dark, were separated. The principle of light was divine and spiritual; the principle of dark was evil and material. They were personified respectively as the Father of Greatness and the Prince of Darkness. These beings and others created during their cosmic battles could be identified or syncretized with the deities of other religions, as will be shown below.

Over time, the chaotic world of matter began to penetrate the ordered world of light. Then the Father of Greatness (God the Father or the Iranian Zurvan) produced the Mother of the Living (or Mother of Life), who in turn gave birth to Primordial Man to battle cosmic evil. The Father created a second divine person, the Living Spirit, who with Primordial Man battled the forces of darkness. In the ensuing battle, the physical earth was created. Although the Prince of Darkness (the Iranian Ahriman or the Christian Satan) defeated Primordial Man and ate his five children, some of their light escaped him and produced the heavenly bodies. The Living Spirit rescued Primordial Man and, from the demons' bodies, the Spirit created the visible earth.

A third of the Father's emanations, the Third Messenger, set out to capture the remaining light. The waxing of the moon each month represented the addition of particles of light to it; as it waned, these particles were passed on to the sun and finally to the highest heaven.

Humans, however, were produced by the mating of demons who had swallowed particles of light. Adam, the first man, was awakened by the Son of God and realized that he contained a spark of the divine light within him. At the return of Jesus, the world would collapse into fire, and after 1,468 years of flaming would be destroyed, with the demons and the damned imprisoned forever.

At their deaths, souls of the Manichaean elect were carried directly to the kingdom of light; those of the hearers who had not taken final vows reincarnated. In this we see Christian and Hindu ideas, blended with the traditional Iranian duality of light and darkness. Like the Jewish and Christian Gnostics, Mani taught that salvation from the evil forces was achieved through a deeply experienced knowledge (*gnosis*) of reality's true nature and the true makeup, history, and future of the universe. The visible world and human life itself were products of evil's partial victory over good and were negated. (Deliberate suicide, however, was forbidden.) Through the Third Messenger and Jesus, the Son of God, the Father was trying to regain lost parts of himself—separated human souls.

Mani and his many missionaries emphasized empiricism, personal experience, and reason; a Manichaean text, the *Kephalaion,* said, "Man should not believe what he has not seen with his own eyes."

Thus, the core of Manichaean belief was condensed into the two principles and the three stages. The two principles were coeval light and darkness; the three stages were the past, present, and future. As one Chinese Manichaean text put it, in the prior stage heaven and earth did not exist, only light and darkness separated. The second, as described above, was the battle between the two cosmic principles, and the third represents a time when "light has returned to the great light" and the original separation is restored.

According to *AUGUSTINE OF HIPPO*'s later telling (see below), Manichaeans taught that both God and evil had substance, evil being "a shapeless, hideous mass, which might be solid, in which case [they] called it earth, or fine and rarefied like air. This they imagine as a kind of evil mind filtering through the substance they call earth. . . . that there were two antagonistic masses, both of which were infinite, yet the evil in a lesser and the good in a greater degree."

Mani and his followers produced beautifully illustrated religious books as well as psalms and hymns. Compared to early Christian productions, Manichaean works were indeed artistically developed: One well-known codex (bound book) from central Asia was written on thin white leather pages with artistic script and illustrations.

Manichaeism's Later History

Geographically, Manichaeism was situated among a rising Christianity, Roman state Paganism, Persian state Zoroastrianism, expanding Buddhism, and—after the seventh century—aggressively expanding Islam, which swept over Iraq and Persia in the mid-600s and soon conquered North Africa as well. All regarded Mani's teachings as a threat, as did the later Christian Eastern Roman Empire centered in Constantinople. (In the sixth century, the Christian emperors Justin and Justinian ordered convicted Manichaeans executed.) Greek philosophers of late antiquity were also hostile to Manichaeism; the noted Neoplatonist *PLOTINUS* wrote and lectured against it. Nevertheless, Manichaeism persisted in the former Western Roman Empire until at least the sixth century, particularly in Sicily, Spain, and southern France. Despite the geographical connection, there is no proof of an uninterrupted Manichaean presence from the 500s until the rise of the Albigensian heresy in the 1100s. The term *Manichaean* was employed, however, by a number of earlier medieval writers as a synonym for heretic, probably due to the influence of Augustine.

Pushed east by persecution in Islamic lands, Manichaeism enjoyed some success in central Asia, where Samarkand became its new religious capital. Chinese emperors were more tolerant than their Byzantine counterparts; in 732 the Religion of Light was officially recognized as acceptable to the rulers of the Middle Kingdom. Imperial Chinese toleration was withdrawn a century later, but Manichaeism persisted in a minor way until the fourteenth century through a network of secret societies.

Augustine and the Manichaeans

Manichaeism is best known in the West through the writings of Augustine of Hippo (354–430), author of *The City of God* and *Confessions* and the leading early Christian theologian. Although raised by a Christian mother, Augustine became a hearer of Mani's teachings as a young man and followed Manichaeism for nine years until his conversion to Christianity. In his autobiographical *Confessions,* written from a Christian perspective, he derided his Manichaean teachers as "men with glib tongues. . . . These names [God the Father, God the Son, and God the Holy Ghost] were always on the tips of their tongues, but only as sounds which they mouthed aloud, for in their hearts they had no inkling of the truth."

Looking back, he wrote of their dualistic teaching, "I was gradually led to believe such nonsense as that a fig wept when it was plucked, and that the tree which bore it shed tears of mother's milk. But if some sanctified member of the sect were to eat the fig—someone else, of course, would have committed the sin of plucking it—he would digest it and breathe it out again in the form of angels or even as particles of God, retching them up as he groaned in prayer. These particles of the true and supreme God were supposed to be imprisoned in the fruit and could only be released by means of the stomach and teeth of one of the elect."

Manichaeans were indeed scrupulous vegetarians, believing that vegetables wept when being harvested. They preferred to grow melons and other fruit that separated itself naturally from its parent plants when ripe. They saw Jesus's agony repeated in the ripening of every fruit on every tree; thus his suffering would be prolonged until the world ended. A third-century anti-Manichaean writing accused them of apologizing to bread before eating it.

Science initially helped turn Augustine from Manichaeism. He compared the astronomical knowledge of his day, which was sufficient to forecast total and partial eclipses of the sun and moon, with the cosmology of Mani and found Mani to be lacking. In Book V of *Confessions* he wrote, "In all [Mani's] writings I could find no reasonable explanation of the solstices and the equinoxes or of eclipses and similar phenomena such as I had read about in books written by secular scientists. Yet I was expected to believe what he had written although it was entirely at variance and out of keeping with the principles of mathematics and the evidence of my own eyes. . . . [Mani] wrote at great length on scientific subjects, only to be proved wrong by genuine scientists, thereby making perfectly clear the true nature of his insight into more abstruse matters."

Trained as a teacher of literature and public speaking, skilled at preparing young would-be Roman lawyers and politicians for their work, Augustine—even though he shied away from taking the more serious Manichaean vows—wanted more than beginner's teachings. He described how he awaited the arrival of Faustus, a high-ranking Manichaean leader who could answer all his difficult questions. When he was able to talk privately with Faustus, however, he found him to be well-spoken and pleasant but uninformed on astronomical matters. Faustus, however, "was not entirely unaware of his limitations and did not want to enter rashly into an argument which might force him into a position which he could not possibly maintain and from which he could not easily withdraw." This honesty impressed Augustine even as his confidence in Manichaeism began to ebb. Indeed, Augustine credited Faustus, "who had been a deadly snare to many," with being the person who released him from the spiritual trap in which he later reckoned himself to have been caught.

Against the Manichaeans Augustine used an argument he had heard in his youth from a Carthaginian Christian named Nebridius: What would the cosmic forces of evil have done if God had refused to battle them? If the evil could have harmed the good, Nebridius argued, that was the same as saying that God was subject to

corruption. On the other hand, if evil could not harm good, how had the battle arisen in which some particles of God had become enmeshed in matter? If the particles—which formed human souls—were capable of being trapped and corrupted, then did not the god from whom they came share their weakness? Later in his life, Augustine wished he had been more impressed at the time by Nebridius's paradoxical rebuttal of the corruptibility/incorruptibility of the divine and "disgorged these men like vomit from my overladen system." Undoubtedly the popularity of Augustine's *Confessions,* with its many anti-Manichaean passages, contributed to the term *Manichaean* being used to describe other dualists who saw the world as the battleground of cosmic good and evil forces. Some continue to employ the term to this day.

Marcion   Born in 85 in Pontus, the area colonized by the Greeks along the southern shore of the Black Sea (now part of Turkey), Marcion was the son of a Christian bishop. Perhaps his upbringing engendered ecclesiastical organizing skills, for he became one of the few *GNOSTIC* teachers to create a viable church of his own, one that rivaled orthodox Christianity in the eastern Mediterranean.

Because he so thoroughly rejected the Old Testament, Mosaic law, and the Jewish heritage of Christianity, Marcion has been compared to Martin Luther, who lived 1,500 years later. But whereas Luther emphasized salvation by faith over salvation through good works people do, Marcion was a Docetist (see *DOCETISM*). *Docetist* is a general term for those who believed that Jesus only appeared to have a physical human body and therefore did not suffer at his crucifixion (*docere* is Latin, meaning "to show"). Like most Gnostics, he taught that Christ was sent by the true God to rescue humanity from the physical word, which was ruled by a false god (whom Marcion called the Cosmocrator, or "world ruler"—also known as the *DEMIURGE*), who was equated with Yahweh, the God of the Hebrews. Christ brought love; the God of the Jews stood merely for justice.

According to Marcion, Christ's teachings—as contained chiefly in Luke's gospel and Paul's epistles—completely superseded the Law of Moses. "The separation of the Law and the Gospel is the fundamental work of Marcion," wrote *TERTULLIAN,* a second-century theologian.

About 144, Marcion was rejected as an episcopal candidate by the Christian leadership in Rome and excommunicated for his teachings, which were summarized in a book called *Antitheses,* which listed contradictions between the Old Testament and the Gospels. After his excommunication, he turned to organizing his own congregations, which persisted into the third century. Orthodox writers later said that he had been excommunicated for immorality—a common accusation against heretics. But as Tertullian also commented, Marcion had a reputation for "imposing sanctity on the flesh," and like many Gnostics he rejected the institution of marriage as contributing to the imprisonment of more souls in the material world. Married people had to be separated from their spouses before being baptized in Marcionite congregations, and strict rules were imposed regarding what constituted proper food and drink for his followers. Women were allowed equal authority with men in Marcionite congregations, but their sexual nature was denied: A woman is "a temple built over a sewer," Marcion reportedly said. (A general term for Gnostics who taught that marriage was evil and imprisoned souls in matter was *Encratites,* or "self-controlled.")

According to the heresy hunter *IRENAEUS,* Marcion followed the teachings of a lesser-known Gnostic, *CERDO.* Both taught that Yahweh, the Hebrew God, learned that he was not absolute and that he was a creation of the true God only after Jesus preached his own message. This so angered the Demiurge that he arranged events so that Jesus would be persecuted and crucified—although the crucifixion itself was only a collective hallucination of the onlookers, since Christ had no physical body capable of suffering. Yahweh and his followers (the catholic, mainstream church) would continue to hate the true (Gnostic) Christians forever. At the end of time, however, those who truly understood Christ's message would be gathered to the true God, while Yahweh and his material world would be destroyed. This event, in Marcion's view, was not quite the same as the Second Coming, since strictly speaking there was no First Coming—that is, no incarnation of Christ in a human body.

Although he incorporated the Gnostic idea of the false god or Demiurge, Marcion, unlike some Gnostics, relied more on biblical materials than on Greek philosophy. In particular, he emphasized Paul's teachings, asserting that the original twelve apostles had misunderstood Christ's message by thinking him to be the messiah prophesied by the Old Testament rather than understanding him to be sent by the true God. Because of this misunderstanding, it was therefore necessary for Paul to receive a special revelation to correct it.

The orthodox church condemned Marcion on several points, including elevating the god of love above the god of creation and preaching that this good god would deliver only the souls of the believers, as opposed to the Christian doctrine of bodily resurrection.

"He mutilates the Gospel which is according to Luke . . . setting aside a great deal of the teaching of the Lord, in which the Lord is recorded as most clearly confessing that the Maker of this universe is His Father," Irenaeus wrote. "In a like manner, too, he dismembered the epistles of Paul, removing all that is said by the apostle respecting the God who made the world."

Irenaeus lambasted Marcion for teaching that Cain, the Sodomites, and the Egyptians had been saved by Jesus because they welcomed him when he descended into hell, whereas Abel, Enoch, Noah, Abraham, and the other Jewish patriarchs were not saved. "For since these men, he says, knew that their God [i.e., the Demiurge or Cosmocrator] was constantly tempting them, so now they suspected that He was tempting them, and did not run to Jesus, or believe His announcement: and for this reason he declared that their souls remained in Hades." Marcion, Irenaeus declared, was a spiritual descendant of *SIMON MAGUS,* first Gnostic and arch-heretic.

Marcion's teachings have points of similarity with the doctrine of dispensationalism, as taught by some later Protestants such as J. N. Darby (1800–1882). Both saw the true church, as they defined it, as being outside world history in a sense; both saw that one law had been made for the Jews, and that Christians lived under a different law (of dispensation), that of grace.

Marcus A *GNOSTIC* teacher active in southern Gaul (the Rhône Valley) during the time of *IRENAEUS* (the late second century), Marcus was denounced by that churchman as a self-proclaimed prophet and magician whose chief aim was having sex with his female followers. Marcus "concerns himself in particular with women," Irenaeus wrote, "especially those of high rank, the elegantly attired and wealthy, whom he frequently attempts to lead astray by flattering them and saying, 'I desire to make thee a partaker of my Grace [in Greek, *charis*]. . . . Adorn thyself as a bride who expects her bridegroom, that thou mayest be what I am, and I what thou art. Receive in thy bedchamber the seed of light. Receive from me the bridegroom and give him a place, and have a place in him. Behold, Grace has descended upon thee; open thy mouth and prophesy.'"

According to Irenaeus, Marcus performed a sacrament that involved mixing a purple liquid that he said was the "blood of Grace" with wine. By analogy with some other Gnostic groups' practices, as reported by the anti-Gnostic writer *EPIPHANIUS,* Marcus and his followers may have been mixing wine with small amounts of male semen and female menstrual blood, viewed as the essence of each gender. (Other Gnostics condemned the practice.) This ceremony would have been particularly abhorrent to Jewish Christians, since Jewish dietary law forbade the consumption of blood. Such a ceremony was more literal than the Eucharistic consumption of the body and blood of Jesus. Morton Smith of Columbia University, a historian of magic, has suggested that various Gnostics carried out such literal reenactments of Jesus's "This is my body; this is my blood," thus demonstrating further freedom from the restrictive law of the Old Testament.

After the women had been persuaded of their prophetic abilities, Irenaeus continued, they would utter "ridiculous nonsense" and compensate Marcus by offering him gifts of money and themselves.

Marguerite of Porete   See *BEGUINES*.

Mary, Mother of Jesus
See *COLLYRIDIANS*.

Mary Magdalene   Although a minor character in the orthodox New Testament, Mary Magdalene played a larger part in some of the noncanonical early Christian writings discovered buried in Egypt in 1945 (see *NAG HAMMADI*). In such works as the *Gospel of Philip* and (possibly) the *Gospel of Mary,* she is portrayed as one of Jesus's favored disciples and perhaps his wife or lover.

Mary Magdalene (or Magdalen or Magdala—her second name is derived from the name of her village, Mejdel) is mentioned as one of Jesus's followers in Luke 8:1–3: "With [Jesus] were the Twelve and a number of women who had been set free from evil spirits and infirmities: Mary, known as Mary of Magdala, from whom seven devils had come out; Joanna, the wife of Chuza, a steward of Herod's; Susanna, and many others. These women provided for them out of their own resources." Considering that Joanna was the wife of a royal official and that these women were financing the ministry, perhaps they were all from prosperous families.

For centuries, Christian tradition has persistently but perhaps erroneously identified a woman mentioned just earlier in the text (Luke 7:36–50) with Mary Magdalene. The scene is a Pharisee's home in the town of Nain in Galilee; although many of the Pharisees (Jews who strictly followed Mosaic law) mistrusted Jesus, this one had invited him to dinner. According to the gospel account, "A woman who was living an immoral life in the town had learned that Jesus was at table in the Pharisee's house and had brought oil of myrrh in a small flask. She took her place behind him, by his feet, weeping. His feet were wetted with her tears, and she wiped them with her hair, kissing them and anointing them with the myrrh." When the Pharisee, Simon, objects to her presence because she is an immoral woman, Jesus counters his objection with a parable, adding, "You see this woman? I came to your house: you provided no water for my feet, but this woman has made my feet wet with her tears and wiped them with her hair. You gave me no kiss, but she has been kissing my feet ever since I came in. You did not anoint my head with oil, but she has anointed my feet with myrrh. And so, I tell you, her great love proves that her many sins have been forgiven; where little has been forgiven, little love is shown." Because of the juxtaposition of these two passages, the identity of the (presumed) prostitute was merged in tradition with that of Mary Magdalene.

A second traditional merger sometimes occurred between Mary Magdalene and Mary of Bethany, sister of Martha and of Lazarus, whom Jesus raised from the dead in John 11. "This Mary, whose brother Lazarus had fallen ill, was the woman who anointed the Lord with ointment and wiped his feet with her hair." Contributing to the confusion were not only the two acts of anointing Jesus, but two Simons as well. In the Gospel of Mark, an unidentified woman comes into the house of "Simon the leper," where Jesus and his disciples are eating two days before his arrest at Passover, and pours oil of nard, an expensive perfume, over his head.

Mary Magdalene, however, is placed at the crucifixion and at Jesus's tomb in several gospel accounts. In Luke she is one of the group of women who go to the tomb offered to the disciples by Joseph of Arimathaea in order to prepare Jesus's body for burial, only to be told by "two men in dazzling garments" that Jesus has risen from the dead and is no longer there. When they tell the male disciples, however, they are not believed. (A similar story is told in Matthew.) Mark lists her among the group of women (including Salome) who witness Jesus's crucifixion. Here again the "seven devils" appear in the resurrection account in Mark 16: "When [Jesus] had risen from the dead early on Sunday morning, he appeared first to Mary of Magdala, from whom he had formerly cast out seven devils."

The Gospel of John describes Mary Magdalene coming to the tomb, seeing that the stone blocking its entrance has been moved away, and running back to the disciples saying, "They have taken the Lord out of his tomb, and we do not know where they have laid him." Later, weeping outside the tomb while Simon Peter and another disciple are investigating its interior, she sees Jesus but at first does not recognize him. At his command she goes to the other disciples and tells them that Jesus said that he is returning to the Father.

Hetcrodox Christians, later referred to as *GNOSTICS* because of their professed possession of secret knowledge (in Greek, *gnosis*) about Christ, made something more out of Mary Magdalene's being the first person Jesus spoke to after the crucifixion. Her status—one of Jesus's close disciples, yet not one of the all-male Twelve—made her a fitting channel for secret teachings, particularly those that showed how women as well as men could achieve salvation or that dealt with a feminine aspect of the divine. And if Mary Magdalene was indeed identified as a prostitute, her elevation to a source of spiritual truth was an attempt to overcome the virgin-or-whore dichotomy so common in the Judeo-Christian treatment of women.

Some Gnostic gospels show Mary Magdalene in doctrinal conflict with Simon Peter, who, as founder of the papacy in Catholic tradition, represents the voice of orthodoxy in contrast to her voice of heterodoxy. The two disciples clash in the *Gospel according to Thomas,* perhaps the best known of the Nag Hammadi texts. In *logion* (saying) number 114, Simon Peter says, "Let Mary go out from us, because women are not worthy of the Life." But Jesus replies, "See, I shall lead her, so that I will make her male that she too may become a living spirit [in Greek, *pneuma*], resembling you males. For every woman who makes herself male will enter the Kingdom of Heaven." The *logion,* which is believed to be a later addition to the text, must be interpreted symbolically. As Elaine Pagels wrote in *The Gnostic Gospels,* "female" may be equated with "human," and "male" equals "divine." In other words, disciples must overcome their human natures, and for women that probably meant avoiding what another text called "the works of femaleness"—sexual intercourse and childbearing.

Similarly, in the *Gospel of Mary,* set when the disciples are gathered immediately after the resurrection, Peter asks Mary Magdalene to tell the other disciples what she learned from Jesus, for "we know that the Savior loved you more than the rest of the women." After Mary describes a typically Gnostic ascent of the soul through seven levels, Peter scoffs, asking how Jesus could have taught Mary this without the male disciples knowing about it. Weeping, Mary replies, "Do you think that I thought this up myself in my heart or that I am lying about the Savior?" At this point, Levi, another disciple, defends her, telling Peter to control his temper and reminding him that Jesus "loved her more than us." In this version, Mary has not seen the resurrected Jesus in the flesh, but in a vision that Peter and some male disciples question. To Pagels, this distinction is critical in reinforcing the Gnostics' claim that anyone could experience the Savior directly—as Mary did—without going through the hierarchy symbolized by Peter.

Although its first six pages are missing, the *Gospel of Mary* as it survives is remarkably parallel in structure to the *Poimandres,* a Greco-Egyptian mystical work of the late Roman period but without Christian overtones. Both use a question-and-answer format, and both connect sexual desire with human mortality and offer a description of the soul's ascent through higher and higher levels until it reaches its final rest.

The *Gospel of Philip,* another Nag Hammadi text that some scholars ascribe to the tradition of the Gnostic teacher *VALENTINUS,* describes Mary Magdalene as one of three women "who always walked with the Lord" and as the "companion of the Savior," whom Christ loved more than all the disciples, thereby making the men jealous.

On the other hand, Mary of Bethany, Martha's sister, serves as a "bad example" in a text called *The Apostolic Church Order,* which circulated among orthodox third-century congregations. The *Order,* like the epistles written by or attributed to Paul, puts women in a definitely subordinate place. In it the apostle John recalls how "When the Master blessed the bread and the cup and signed them with the words, 'This is my body and blood,' he did not offer it to the women who are with us." Martha adds, "He did not offer it to Mary, because he saw her laugh," and Mary says, "I no longer laugh; he said to us before, as he taught, 'Your weakness is redeemed through strength.'" Despite Mary's efforts, the *Order* states clearly that only men may be priests and bishops. Whereas in Luke 10 Jesus gently reproves Martha for asking him to tell Mary to stop listening to him and help her sister with the housework, in the later *Order* Martha, who stayed in the kitchen, gains approval while Mary, who sat at Jesus's feet, is suspect.

Mary Magdalene's special role in nonmainstream Christianity did not cease with the early Gnostics, however. As mentioned above, some legends make her Jesus's wife—the marriage at Cana during which he turned water into sufficient wine for a large crowd is interpreted as being their wedding. This reading of her story is based partly on the question of how an apparently healthy and normal Jewish man could have lived until age 30 (the age at which Jesus traditionally is said to have begun his ministry) without being married. All Jewish men were expected to learn a trade and to have families, the skeptics argued; consequently, Jesus must have done likewise upon reaching adulthood, and Mary Magdalene's ambiguous character in both the canonical and Gnostic gospels derives from her special status as his wife.

A related story brings her from Palestine to southern France, carrying with her either the cup or dish used at the Last Supper—conventionally, the Holy Grail—or, in the most far-reaching speculations, her child fathered by Jesus, who then becomes a progenitor of the royal family of France. In that interpretation, the Holy Grail becomes a metaphor for her womb, which carried "the blood of Jesus." This interpretation makes the various Black Madonnas of Mediterranean France and Spain into a representation of her carrying Jesus's son rather than of the Virgin Mary carrying the infant Jesus.

Because the Gospels say that Mary Magdalene went to the tomb to prepare Jesus's body for burial, she is also associated with the Shroud of Turin (in Italian, *Santa Sindone*), the piece of linen cloth (14 feet 3 inches by 3 feet 7 inches) marked with images of a man's front and back sides and believed by some to be Jesus's actual burial wrapping.

Maximus   A fourth-century Neoplatonist (see *NEOPLATONISM*) mystic, Maximus was a major intellectual influence on the emperor *JULIAN THE APOSTATE,* who attempted to stop Christianity's growing power in the Roman Empire. Following the philosophical tradition of *IAMBLICHUS,* Maximus was teaching in the city of Pergamum in Asia Minor (present-day Bergama in western Turkey) when the future emperor heard of him and became his student. Maximus undoubtedly influenced Julian's conversion from the Christianity in which he had been raised to "reformed" Paganism, which he followed for the rest of his life. Essentially, this reformed Paganism was an attempt to blend Neoplatonic philosophy (Hellenism to its adherents) with a practical religious system based on the ancient Greek and Egyptian gods.

After Julian's death in 363, Maximus suffered during the resurgent Christian party's attempts to purge Julian's former advisers. The philosopher, who had been with Julian when he died after suffering a mortal wound in combat with a Persian army, was arrested on trumped-up charges of misconduct but freed thanks to the influence of powerful friends. He returned to teaching but was later arrested again and charged with attempting to divine the future of the emperor Valens. (Using divination to attempt to learn how long an emperor would rule was considered treason by both Pagan and Christian Roman emperors.) He was executed sometime in the late fourth century.

Men of Intelligence   The movement referred to as the Men of Intelligence represents another manifestation of the *FREE SPIRIT* heresy, but it occurred outside the communal houses of the *BEGUINES* and *BEGHARDS*. It apparently originated in Brussels in the 1300s and may be connected with a locally famous female heretic named Bloemardinne, a figure in the Free Spirit. Like other followers of the Free Spirit, she preached that people could achieve a state of grace in which none of their actions could be accounted as sinful; they would then be "free in spirit" and outside all human law. Bloemardinne preached a doctrine of free love, which she called "seraphic [i.e., angelic] love." Her followers honored her as a mystic and as a source of healing power even after her death.

In 1411, two leaders of the Men of Intelligence, Giles Cantor and William Hilderniss, were condemned by the bishop of Cambrai. The bishop's language included references to "seraphic love," suggesting a connection between these two men and Bloemardinne; an inquisitor operating at the same time also referred to the earlier heretic.

Giles stated that he had been visited by the Holy Spirit, who ordered him not to observe Lent or other fast days. William is said to have stated that Christ's death on the cross negated the need for confession, penance, and absolution for the rest of mankind; consequently, those sacraments were worthless. He asserted that persons like himself who were filled with the Holy Spirit could interpret the Bible more accurately than could the clergy and could preach "beyond human understanding."

According to Bishop Pierre d'Ailly's list of the Men of Intelligence's deeds and doctrines, women in the group who refused sexual intercourse were abused by the others, because the group regarded sexual union as the spiritual equivalent of prayer—although William cautioned his followers not to reveal the group's promiscuity.

Menander the Samaritan   A first-century successor of the *GNOSTIC* teacher *SIMON MAGUS,* Menander taught that he had been sent forth by heaven as a savior. He claimed that through the magic he taught, people could overcome the evil angels who ruled the world and become immortal.

Messalians   Cataloging—and thereby defining—the heresies of Christianity's first three centuries, Bishop *EPIPHANIUS* of Salamis mentioned two groups of Messalians, a name he defined as meaning "those who pray." The earlier sect he described as deriving from neither Christian nor Jewish roots: "They are simply Pagans who admit the existence of gods but worship none [of them]; they adore one God only, whom they call the Almighty." Some of these Messalians, he continued, prayed outdoors in the morning and evening, but others "have built for themselves something like proper churches where they gather at evening and morning with much lighting of lamps and torches and lengthy singing of hymns and acclamations to God by the zealous among them, [through] which hymns are acclamations they fondly think to conciliate God." By going out into the open air, he added, they "departed from the truth."

Epiphanius also described a contemporary (mid–fourth century) group of Christian Messalians, "people who have renounced the world and withdrawn from what is theirs, and sleep in the same place together, men with women and women with men, in the public squares when it is summer, because, they say, they have no possessions on earth." (In this life style, for which the Messalians claim the model of Christ and his disciples, we may see a prefiguring of such later heresies as the *FREE SPIRIT*.) The Messalians beg for their needs, he added, and preach nonsense: "Whichever of them you ask will say that he is whoever you want. If you say 'prophet,' they will say: I am a prophet. If you say 'Christ,' he will say: I am Christ, and if you say 'patriarch,' he will not hesitate to say that that is who he is, or 'angel,' he will say that too. O the frivolity of the human mind!"

In Mesopotamia some Messalians lived in monasteries or "folds," he wrote; "they wear their hair in feminine fashion and wear sackcloth for all to see." Even worse, they cut off their beards. These Messalians reminded Epiphanius of the Manichaean (see *MANI*) elect who did no work and lived on fruit. He argued that they should follow instead the words of the apostle Paul in 2 Thessalonians 3:10: "For even during our stay with you we laid down the rule: the man who will not work shall not eat."

Some historians perceive a connection between these Messalians and *MONTANISM* or the New Prophecy movement.

The term *Messalian* was also applied in the eleventh century to some heretics in the Byzantine Empire who were accused of worshiping Satanael (an angel fallen from heaven), practicing sexual orgies, and otherwise acting as Epiphanius described the Gnostics.

Michaelists   Named after a *FRANCISCAN* monk known as Michael of Cesena, the Michaelists were one segment of the *FRATICELLI,* purist Franciscans who upheld the ideal of holy poverty in imitation of the Twelve Apostles even in the face of papal disapproval. The dispute over whether Christ and the apostles held private or common property had split the Franciscan order since before Francis of Assisi's death, although a papal bull issued in 1323 had condemned the idea of "apostolic" poverty.

After that point, Franciscans debated one another and papal representatives over whether goods could be used without being "owned." Bonagratia of Bergamo, a supporter of Michael's, said that the order's relation to its possessions should be like that of a horse and its oats: It consumed them, but did not own them. He also argued that Jesus and the disciples had returned to a state of innocence and therefore needed no possessions.

The papal representatives, on the other hand, pointed out that in the days before his betrayal of Jesus, Judas Iscariot had been the disciples' treasurer and carried the common purse. Nor had Jesus made poverty a condition of discipleship, although he recommended it at certain times and places, they argued.

Michael, one of the leading spokesmen for what he saw as Francis's original teaching of holy poverty, was denounced and excommunicated in 1328 by Pope John XXII, but he went on trading arguments with him, even declaring the pope to be a heretic. John XXII replied with a lengthy defense of private property, arguing that there was no particular holiness to poverty and that since God had given Adam dominion over the earth, private property was divinely ordained. Even after Adam and Eve's expulsion from the Garden of Eden, God had told Adam, "You shall gain your bread by the sweat of your brow" (Genesis 3:19); therefore, whatever a man got or earned honestly was his own.

Many of Michael's arguments were carried on by the theologian William of Ockham; on both sides, the discussion became exceedingly dense and legalistic. Michael and his associates fled the French and papal dominions to live under the protection of the German emperor, although they continued to have some supporters in Italy. With the passing of its principals, however, the debate faded by the following century.

Mithras, Mithraism   Commonly regarded as one of Christianity's chief rivals during the Roman Empire, Mithraism, together with the cult of *SOL INVICTUS,* furnished Christianity with certain symbols and practices that remain alive today.

Mithras (or Mithra) was a Persian god, usually depicted straddling a bull and killing it with a sword. From the dying bull issued the seed of life for the world, and hence the god's act became the symbol of regeneration. Before his religion spread into the Roman world in the first century B.C., Mithras had been worshiped throughout the Persian Empire, where he represented a savior-king with solar symbolism similar to Apollo's. A Persian prophecy placed him as reigning last in a series of 7,000-year periods (each symbolized by one of the seven visible planets), followed by an apocalypse and renewal of the world. In some inscriptions he was referred to as *Sol invictus* (unconquered sun). Not surprisingly, this prophecy became blended with early Christians' views of the Second Coming of Christ.

In the Roman world, Mithras-worship was closed and initiatory rather than public as in Persia. Only men could become initiates: Following a baptism of some type, they passed through the grades of Crow, Bride, Soldier, Lion, Persian, Courier of the Sun, and finally Father, through a series of dramatic reenactments. Each grade was associated with a planet by means of astrological symbolism. Boys as young as seven could receive the initiation as Crow. The Mithraic religion was particularly popular in the Roman legions. Mithras-worshipers were considered to be disciplined and temperate men. Since legionnaires often served far from their homelands (the better to keep them from feeling too sympathetic to the local populace), the Mithraic religion formed a bond that at its best transcended regional or class loyalties, similar to Freemasonry in the imperial British army.

Temples to Mithras were built wherever the Romans ruled; for instance, one was built in what is now London. Most were small, holding no more than a hundred men at a time.

Because of its baptismal ritual and the initiates' communal meal, which resembled the Christian Eucharist, some early Christians perceived Mithraism as a threat. Justin said that the Mithraic ceremonial meal of bread and water was inspired by demons, and *TERTULLIAN* also commented on it. Nevertheless, it is not coincidental that Christ's birth is celebrated on 25 December, first celebrated as the birthday of Mithras.

Mithraic religion faded after the time of *CONSTANTINE* the Great, although it enjoyed a brief revival during the time of the Pagan emperor *JULIAN THE APOSTATE* before his death in 363. After he abandoned Christianity, Julian underwent a Mithraic initiation.

Modalism   During the first three centuries of Christianity, various explanations of the doctrine of the Trinity arose. One of these, which came to be considered heretical, was modalism, which characterized God the Father, God the Son, and God the Holy Spirit as the same divine person appearing in different modes of existence.

Although this view rejected the heresy of subordinationism—the teaching that the Son and the Holy Spirit were somehow inferior to the Father—it was criticized for failing to emphasize Christ's human nature and for fail-ing to treat the Trinity as three distinct divine persons. (Compare *MONARCHIANISM* and *PATRIPASSIANISM*.)

Modalism is associated with the teachings of Praxeas, who was attacked by the theologian *TERTULLIAN* in his work *Adversus Praxean* (Against Praxeas), written around 213. According to Tertullian, Praxeas taught that "the Father Himself came down into the Virgin, was Himself born of her, Himself suffered, indeed was Himself Jesus Christ."

Monarchianism   Derived from its adherents' statement that "we allow only the monarchy [of God]," this school arose during the late second century, as catholic theologians were developing the concept of the Trinity—one god in three persons. Advocated primarily by Sabellius (Monarchian Christians were frequently called Sabellians), Monarchianism declared that God the Father was incarnated and carried out his earthly ministry under the name of God the Son. For this reason, Trinitarian Christians were sometimes called Monarchians Patripassians (see *PATRIPASSIANISM*), from the Latin for "Father suffering." Monarchianism is frequently blended with *MODALISM*, the concept that there is only one god whose essence is expressed through the three modes of Father, Son, and Holy Ghost—not three distinct divine persons as in orthodox dogma.

In addition, the Arian heresy (see *ARIANISM*) is frequently seen as a form of Monarchianism insofar as Arius saw the Son as created after the Father, the only divine person who could be called "uncreated."

Monarchian ideas were attractive to many early Christians, including the noted theologian *ORIGEN*, who conceived of God the Father as beyond human comprehension. This view of the Father's remoteness from human comprehension made it hard for people to completely accept the idea of the Trinity without subordinating the Son and Holy Spirit to the Father to some extent.

Moneta of Cremona   A Dominican monk who lived in the thirteenth century, Moneta wrote a book on the doctrines of the *ALBIGENSIAN* or Cathar heresy. Many of the sources he relied on were subsequently destroyed; consequently, his writings are a rare contemporary, if biased, view of the notable medieval heretics.

Monophysites, Monophysitism   From the Greek for "one nature," Monophysitism arose in the Eastern Roman Empire in the fifth century, another of the numerous controversies over the nature of Christ. In contrast to the Catholic doctrine that Jesus had both a divine and a human nature, Monophysites argued that he had only one nature that combined divine and human elements. Monophysitism is associated with the teachings of *EUTYCHES,* who headed a monastery near Constantinople (modern Istanbul, Turkey). Its adherents claimed, for example, that when Jesus performed the miracles recounted in the Gospels, he acted as a mortal man but transcended the laws governing other people. His nature, they said, could not be divided into human and divine elements as a woodsman splits firewood with an ax.

This controversy over Christ's nature may be compared to the previous disagreement between orthodox and Arian (see *ARIANISM*) Christians over whether Christ was eternal or created. Like the Arians, the Monophysites were formally condemned at a church council convened to enforce doctrinal uniformity. Called the Council of Chalcedon, it was convened in 451 by Pope Leo I in Chalcedon, a city across the Bosporus Strait from Constantinople. This council is also referred to as the Fourth Ecumenical Council. Subsequent support for Monophysitism by some emperors, however, counteracted the papacy's opposition.

Indeed, Monophysitism exacerbated the growing division between the eastern and western branches of Christianity, a division that was partly patched up by the emperor Justinian I (reigned 527–565). But despite the eclipse of Monophysitism, there was an enduring split between the Eastern Orthodox and the Roman Catholic churches. Justinian and the other emperors of the fifth and sixth centuries were faced with a dilemma that combined theological and political questions. The popes, based in barbarian-beset Rome, were anti-Monophysite, but Monophysitism was strong among the peoples of Egypt, Palestine, Syria, and Asia Minor, who supplied the emperors at Constantinople with tax revenues, army recruits, and foodstuffs.

Some eastern churches retained Monophysite ideas, but they were mainly located in areas such as Syria and Egypt, which were conquered by Muslim armies in the 600s. More effective than church councils and theological pronouncements, the tide of Islam removed Monophysitism from the arena of Christian controversy. The doctrine lingers in the Coptic Christian churches of Egypt and Ethiopia and elsewhere in the Middle East among those churches tracing their founding to the apostle James.

In the era between the Council of Chalcedon and the Arab conquests, however, the Monophysite issue colored even sports and local politics in the Eastern Roman Empire. Chariot racing was a major urban spectator sport in Constantinople and other major cities such as Antioch and Salonika. The chariot teams represented two sides, the Blues and the Greens, whose fans also tended to divide themselves on religious issues (the Greens were Monophysites, the Blues orthodox Christians) and at times on political issues. With these volatile subjects separating them, it is no wonder that Greens and Blues sometimes rioted in the streets.

Montanism, Montanus   The New Prophecy movement, as called by its adherents, this prophecy-oriented early Christian heresy was begun by Montanus, a native of Phrygia (a country that is part of modern Turkey), who taught in the mid-second century.

Influenced by the Gospel of John's description of how Jesus would send the Holy Spirit, Montanus declared that he himself was the spokesman of the Holy Spirit promised by Christ. With him, therefore, a new era would begin. Speaking in prophetic ecstasy as a channel for the Holy Spirit, he proclaimed, "Behold, man is as a lyre [stringed instrument] and I play upon him as with a plectrum; man sleeps and I arouse him; behold, it is the Lord who throws men's souls into ecstasy and gives them a heart."

Two women, Maximilla and Prisca (or Priscilla), served as his assistants and led the movement after his death. They and other followers also delivered ecstatic prophecies; women more than men proclaimed prophecies and new Montanist teachings. This upwelling of nonaccepted new religious material alarmed church officials. After exorcisms by bishops did not sway the Montanists, they were excommunicated. The contemporary orthodox writer *HIPPOLYTUS* denounced Priscilla and Maximilla: "[The Montanists] allege that they have learned more from these [women] than from law and prophets and the gospels. But they magnify these wretched women above the Apostles and every gift of Grace, so that some of them presume to assert that there is in them something superior to Christ."

Eusebius, a fourth-century church historian writing with the advantage of hindsight, disparaged Maximilla for predicting a universal war that never came.

The antiheretical writer *EPIPHANIUS* cited the Montanists' special reverence for Eve because she first ate from the tree of knowledge in the Garden of Eden. In addition, he wrote, "They acknowledge the sister of Moses as a prophetess in support of their practice of appointing women to the clergy. . . . Women among them are bishops, presbyters, and the rest, as if there were no difference of nature."

Convinced that the end of the world was at hand and that the millennium—Christ's thousand-year reign—would soon begin, Montanus told his followers to abstain from marriage and separate from their spouses if they were married. Other rules about appropriate food and conduct were announced. Hippolytus, quoted above, wrote that the Montanists introduced "the novelties of fasts, and feasts, and meals of parched food and repasts of radishes, alleging that they have been instructed by women." The Montanists' strict life styles, combined with their willingness to accept martyrdom at the hands of Roman authorities, made it difficult for other Christians to condemn them. Indeed, they attracted many followers, including *TERTULLIAN,* one of the first important theologians, who joined a Montanist congregation in Roman North Africa, his homeland, and who wrote approvingly of at least one Montanist prophetess.

But like many prophetic groups since, the Montanists saw that the Second Coming did not arrive as foreseen; still, they remained convinced that they were living in the Last Days.

In their use of trance and prophecy, the Montanists resemble later pentecostal and char-

ismatic Christians. Because they added new material to the accepted canon, they have also been compared to Mormons, Christian Scientists, or Jehovah's Witnesses.

Montanus, who added to Scripture, may be contrasted with *MARCION,* who removed the Old Testament and part of the New from his list of acceptable books. The Montanists' temporary success shows how fluid the boundaries of Scripture were for early Christians; after their time the church found it necessary to declare that there were no new divine revelations. The Age of the Apostles was over; the Age of Scripture (and for the Catholic church, the Age of Tradition) had begun. By roughly 200 the New Testament canon (list of approved books) was fairly well established, although it would take roughly another 125 years to settle differences over the doctrine of the Trinity. (See also *ARIANISM; NICAEA, COUNCILS OF*.)

Müntzer, Thomas   A warlike leader of the *ANABAPTISTS,* Thomas Müntzer (or Münzer) was born around 1488, educated at the University of Leipzig, and ordained a priest around 1513. He was influenced by the thinking of Martin Luther, who helped him when he sought to be assigned to a parish in Zwickau, a town in Saxony in the midst of a silver-mining boom.

In Zwickau, Müntzer began to organize groups of *WEAVERS* and other craftsmen who faced hard times due to the inflation caused by the silver boom. Here he fell in with a radical group known as the Zwickau Prophets. One of their leaders, a weaver named Niklas Storch, had revived the millenarian doctrines popular among some of the *HUSSITES*: the Last Days were at hand, the Turks would conquer the rest of Europe, and the Antichrist would rule, followed by the Second Coming of Christ and his thousand-year rule over the earth—the millennium.

Convinced more and more that the Holy Spirit spoke through him—and possibly influenced by the old *FREE SPIRIT* ideas—Müntzer castigated the rich, other clergy, and the economic system that had made the silver miners rich and everyone else the victim of galloping inflation. Following an unsuccessful rising spearheaded by Storch's weavers, Müntzer's sixteenth-century version of liberation theology caused him to lose his pastorate, and he went to Prague, where he unsuccessfully sought the support of the Hussites in his attacks on the status quo and his call for a "renewed apostolic church."

Ejected from Prague, he entered a period of wandering, followed by marriage to a former nun. In 1523, Müntzer was offered a pastorate in the Saxon town of Allstedt. Here he set out to reform both church and society, creating a German Mass, a new church organization, and the German Order of Allstedt. He wrote revolutionary pamphlets, calling upon the people to overthrow the princes, clergy, and capitalists and to establish a "refined society" in which all things were to be in common. He, Thomas Müntzer, was the "new Daniel" who would lead his army against the opponents of the Holy Spirit.

Müntzer turned increasingly violent. Both corrupt rulers and clergy must die, he wrote: "The sword is necessary to exterminate them." If the existing authorities would not do the job, then "the sword shall be taken from them. . . . If they resist, let them be slaughtered without mercy. . . . At the harvest-time one must pluck the weeds out of God's vineyard. . . . For the ungodly have no right to live, save what the Elect choose to allow them."

His small band started out by destroying a nearby Catholic chapel. Müntzer continued peppering Martin Luther and other reformers with his manifestos without much positive response. Alarmed by the destruction of the chapel and by his treatises, Saxon authorities strongly suggested that the reformer of Allstedt keep quiet, but he had other ideas.

After seeking support elsewhere in Germany and in Switzerland, Müntzer joined an army of rebellious German peasants in what became known as the Peasant War of 1525, serving as their chaplain and leader. The peasants' uprising against their feudal overlords was sparked by their sense of growing economic, religious, and judicial oppression; uncoordinated revolts broke out in much of southern and eastern Germany (except Bavaria) as well as in Austria. The peasants' demands included the right to choose their own ministers, the abolition of serfdom, the right to hunt and fish on their overlords' lands, and better treatment in courts dominated by aristocrats.

In Thuringia, where Müntzer became involved, rebellious peasants temporarily formed a communal state with all property owned in common. Militarily, however, the peasants could not stand against the forces of the nobles and their mercenaries; after bloody fighting and atrocities on both sides, the revolt was smashed. Müntzer himself was captured, tortured, and beheaded. Martin Luther, his former supporter, wrote approvingly that Müntzer's execution was the judgment of God. "Whoever has seen Müntzer can say that he has seen the devil incarnate in his fiercest fury," Luther said. Other leading reformers also castigated him, giving Müntzer the distinction of having been condemned by both Catholics and Protestants.

Nag Hammadi   In December 1945 an Egyptian peasant, Muhammad Ali al-Samman, went with his brother to an eroded cliff near the village of Nag Hammadi to dig a type of nitrate-rich earth used as fertilizer. His mattock struck something hard, which turned out to be a large clay jar. At first the men were leery of opening it, lest in true Arabian Nights manner it contain a djinn, or evil spirit. But Egypt has a millennia-old tradition of grave robbing and treasure hunting, and once again curiosity overcame the fear of evil powers. Muhammad smashed the jar with his tool.

The "treasure" turned out to be a dozen ancient books, made from papyrus paper and bound with leather. All the same, Muhammad wrapped them in his clothes and took them home, where his mother burned a few pages to light a cooking fire. From there, the books were dispersed, given away or sold for small amounts to neighbors. In time, however, their owners took them to Cairo to peddle to antiquities dealers.

From Cairo, the books took different routes. One ended up in the hands of a Belgian dealer who offered it for sale in various places before selling it to the Jung Institute in Zurich, and it became known as the *Jung Codex*. It was eventually returned to the Egyptian government. Other portions of the collection never made it out of Egypt, but were seized as government-protected antiquities and placed in the Coptic Museum. Like the better-known Dead Sea Scrolls (copies of Jewish books also discovered by accident in the same decade), the Nag Hammadi Library took decades to be completely published, a period marked not only by wars and political upheavals in Egypt, but by scholarly jealousies over access to these textual treasures. One book, the *Gospel of Thomas,* became available in English translation in the late 1960s; the rest eventually followed in the 1970s.

The buried books contained 52 tractates, or individual works, written in Coptic, the language spoken in Egypt before the Muslim conquest generally replaced it with Arabic. Apparently, they had been translated from Greek originals. They included a variety of *GNOSTIC* texts, including the *Gospel of Truth,* possibly written by *VALENTINUS* himself, as well as translations of the works of Plato and of Jewish and non-Christian Gnostics. The existence of several works in the collection had been known previously only through passing references made by some early Christian or *NEOPLATONIC* writers.

It is significant that unlike the Dead Sea Scrolls, the Nag Hammadi find was made up of actual books, or codices, which in the fourth century were replacing the older rolled-up scrolls. To make them stiff, the leather covers were lined with used papyrus-based paper layered to form cardboards. When separated, these recycled papers conveniently turned out to include dated letters and business documents from the mid-300s. Examination of the covers and the handwriting has shown that a single scribe worked on more than one codex, and that three scribes worked on parts of different codices. Since there are some duplications among the tractates (although never in the same codex), some experts believe that the cached books came from two or three different collections.

Nag Hammadi is less than six miles from two early monasteries of the Pachomian order, and scholars have wondered whether the books came from their libraries. (The order's founder, Pachomius, who lived from about 290 to 346, is credited with founding the first communal or cenobitic monasteries in Egypt.) If the books were from monastic libraries, then the monks may not have been as orthodox as later historians presented them since they were studying a variety of Christian and non-Christian texts. Perhaps this is why in the 360s Theodore, head of the Pachomian order, circulated to all monasteries under his jurisdiction a letter from Archbishop Athanasius of Alexandria condemning heretics and their "apocryphal books to which they attribute antiquity and give the names of saints."

Why the books were hidden away remains a mystery. Someone rooting out heresies probably would have burned them; therefore, their burial suggests that they were being stored until danger had passed. Was the danger from the now-Christianized Roman authorities, flushing out suspected Gnostics or heretics in local monasteries? Or was it from ecclesiastical authorities on a similar mission? Roughly a decade after Theodore's letter, another bishop, *EPIPHANIUS,* assembled his own encyclopedia of heresies. Heresy hunting was in the air. Thus far, no one knows exactly why the Nag Hammadi codices were hidden, but clearly one feared for his safety if these books were found in his possession.

Neoplatonism   During the third and fourth centuries, the Greek philosophical tradition established by Socrates (circa 470–399 B.C.) and Plato (circa 427–347 B.C.) was revived by a new series of thinkers who, if not of Greek birth themselves, partook of the Greek-language (Hellenistic) intellectual culture of the eastern Mediterranean world.

The philosopher *PLOTINUS* is considered the father of Neoplatonism. His distinctive contribution was the idea that the One, the source of reality, Plato's "the Good," was unknowable by human intellects. Such successors as *IAMBLICHUS* elaborated this doctrine by teaching that humans could approach the One not only through pure contemplation but through magical and religious rites, thus moving Neoplatonism (or Hellenism as it was known at the time) toward religion and away from pure philosophy. (See *AMMONIUS SACCUS; HYPATIA; PORPHYRY.*) Plotinus and his successors exerted an irresistible influence on Christian theology. It was, for example, the Neoplatonic component of *ORIGEN*'s writing that led him

to be branded a heretic by some of his contemporaries, even though he is now recognized as a major church father.

The Neoplatonic cosmos developed as a structured hierarchy whose different levels of reality emanated from the One, its unknowable divine source. These emanations were not seen as occurring in a chronological sequence like the days of Genesis but were more in a sequence of concepts. Our material world, although far from its source, was still pervaded with the spiritual archetypes of everything in it: For example, the visible sun was a reflection of the One. (See *SOL INVICTUS.*)

Human souls came from the One and sought to be reunited with it, drawn by the power of eros or love. The task of the philosopher—or, in Iamblichus's view, the ritualist—was to guide this process. The soul's efforts at reunion with the One did not happen through grace, but through moral and intellectual effort as well.

As a religion, Neoplatonism appealed to the late Classical intellectuals, epitomized by the emperor *JULIAN.* Julian was raised a Christian, but as a young man he switched to religious Neoplatonism and, upon gaining the throne, attempted to destroy Christianity's prestige and put the empire back under an official state Paganism. The later Neoplatonists were, in a sense, monotheists, for they saw all peoples' deities as derived from a single, unknowable source. They were thus able to say that all gods and goddesses were real and worthy of worship and respect. Since there was no Neoplatonic cult per se, they argued that all people should follow their traditional religions or those new religions that accorded with Neoplatonic teachings, such as those of *MITHRAS* or Sol Invictus. Julian, for example, was an initiate of Mithra and served as priest at revived sacrificial rites in honor of the Olympian deities—Zeus, Apollo, and the rest.

Some early Christians, meanwhile, saw this Greek philosophy as a valid precursor to Christianity and a means by which difficult passages of the Bible could be understood. Although catholic Christianity insisted on the very un-Platonic concept of the Incarnation, Neoplatonism and the example of its proponents helped maintain the ideal of the contemplative monastic life as opposed to the worldly life, for example. It also provided the basis of the teaching that the material world was the outward manifestation of divine unity, a theme developed by a number of later theologians such as Duns Scotus Erigena. Neoplatonic philosophy was rediscovered during the Italian Renaissance; it was also carried into the Islamic world from the philosophical academies of Alexandria. Neoplatonic ideas influenced some medieval Jewish thinkers as well.

Nestorian Christians, Nestorianism   As a fifth-century heresy, beginning in Constantinople, Nestorianism became a significant Asian form of Christianity whose missionary activity stretched from the Mediterranean Sea to China.

It is named for Nestorius, Patriarch of Constantinople from 428 to 431. At its center lies a disagreement over the divine and human natures of Christ (compare *MONOPHYSITISM*). Nestorius and his followers taught that Christ's human nature came from his mother, Mary, and his divine nature from God the Father; therefore, Mary could not be called the Mother of God as she was in the Catholic church. They believed that the two natures were entirely separate, although they acted as one.

Condemned by the Council of Ephesus in 431, Nestorius was deposed as patriarch and exiled from Constantinople, the imperial capital. His followers crossed the border into Persia, where some Christian congregations survived despite opposition from the official religion of Zoroastrianism. The Persian church officially adopted Nestorian doctrines in 486, making a complete break with the West that mirrored the political differences between the Byzantine Empire and the Persian. The Nestorian church survived the introduction of Islam and the conquests of Tamerlane (1380) and other warlords. It was carried to China during the T'ang dynasty and to India, where it was known as the Church of St. Thomas after its legendary founding by the apostle Thomas.

Rumors of this far-off Christian church reached Western Europe and contributed to the legend of "Prester John" (a corruption of the Greek word *presbyter,* meaning "elder"), a fabled monarch ruling a Christian kingdom in either Asia or Africa. A letter from this king to the Byzantine emperor was circulated in the Middle Ages as a genuine document. Later stories shifted the location of Prester John's kingdom more definitely to Africa; these stories were probably influenced by tales of Coptic Christians in Abyssinia, present-day Ethiopia.

Beginning in the fifteenth century, the Nestorian church and the Roman Catholic church were gradually reconciled, although the Nestorians retained their own liturgy. Congregations remain in India, the Middle East, and, through immigration, in North America.

Nicaea, Councils of   In 325, a major church council in the Bithynian city of Nicaea (now the Turkish city of Iznik) produced the Nicene Creed, a statement of belief for Christians designed to refute the teachings of *ARIANISM* in particular as well as *GNOSTICISM* and *DOCETISM*. The council was convened at the order of the Roman emperor Constantine I, and some 318 of the roughly 1,800 bishops within the empire attended. The core of the creed that was produced is still used, with modifications, in the Eastern Orthodox, Roman Catholic, Anglican, and many Protestant churches.

At the heart of the Nicene Creed was a phrase asserting that Jesus was "of one substance with the Father," in contrast with the Arians' contention that the Son was created and only the Father was eternal. This contrasted to the simpler language of the older Roman Creed (often called the Apostles' Creed), which merely said that Jesus was the Son of God the Father, conceived by the Holy Spirit and born of the Virgin Mary.

Later, during the third Council of Toledo (Spain), in 589, the Western church added what is called the Filioque Clause, from the Latin words meaning "And from the Son." This caused the Creed to read in Latin, *Et in Spiritum Sanctum, Dominum, et vivificantem: Qui ex Patre, Filioque procedit* (And in the Holy Ghost, the Lord and Giver of Life, who proceeds from the Father and the Son). The Eastern church, on the other hand, taught that the Holy Spirit proceeded (conceptually rather than chronologically) only from the Father and said that the added clause put the Holy Spirit in an inferior position to the other two persons of the Trinity. A compromise position adopted in 1439, that the Holy Ghost proceeded from the Father through the Son, was repudiated in 1472 by the Eastern church. This difference in dogma has remained a key difference between Western and Eastern Christianity until the present time.

A second Council of Nicaea was convened in 787 by Irene, empress of the Eastern (Byzantine) Roman Empire, during the controversy over *ICONOCLASM,* the destruction of sacred images (icons). The Eastern Orthodox church said that icons could be venerated—as opposed to worshiped—directly. (Members of the pro-icon party were called iconodules, or servants of the icons.) The 375 bishops present at the council adopted an anti-iconoclastic position and ordered the return of icons that had been removed from churches. (The Western church believed that pictures and statues were only for instructional purposes and could not even be venerated.) From the Eastern Orthodox viewpoint, the second Nicene Council was the last true "ecumenical" church council. See also *BOGOMILS.*

Nicolaites, Nicolaitans   Nicolas of Antioch was one of the seven deacons chosen by the apostles to administer the affairs of Jesus's followers while they were attempting to live communally, as described in Acts 6. However, in the account given in the *Panarion* (Medicine chest against heresies) of *EPIPHANIUS,* written in the 370s, Nicolas is regarded as a father of *GNOSTIC* heresy—a misguided heir to *SIMON MAGUS.* Epiphanius, a former monk interested in sexual sins, wrote that Nicolas, who was married to a beautiful woman, had given up sexual relations in imitation of some of the apostles. When he found himself unable to conquer sexual desire, however, he was misled by the devil into declaring that daily sexual intercourse was a prerequisite of salvation. He would have done better to simply admit that he was unable to be celibate and resume marital relations, Epiphanius commented. In his account, Nicolas became unreasonably jealous of his wife and somehow turned to the elaborate cosmology and sacramental sexual practices endorsed by some of the Gnostics.

Other church fathers such as *IRENAEUS* also regarded the Nicolaite sect as connected with Nicolas, but modern scholars see no reason for the connection. Apparently the term *Nicolaite* was attached to certain Antinomian Gnostics (see *ANTINOMIANISM*); it may be connected with the denunciation of the church at Thyatira for harboring "the woman who claims to be a prophetess, who by her teaching lures my servants into fornication and into eating food sacrificed to idols" (Revelation 2:20).

The term *Nicolaite* was revived in the Middle Ages as an epithet for someone holding a lax position on the issue of clerical celibacy.

Novatians, Novatus   A late third-century Roman bishop, Novatus advocated a radically strict form of Christianity, and his followers were among the first to be described as *CATHARI,* in other words, pure ones. Like the Donatists (see *DONATISM*) of North Africa, the followers of Novatus denounced Christians who had lapsed during Roman persecution—for example, by procuring an affidavit stating that they had sacrificed to the Roman emperor—and rebaptized those who joined their congregations, making them in a sense among the first *ANABAPTISTS.*

Spreading through the Roman world, the Novatians were sometimes identified with another puritanical sect, the Montanists (see *MONTANISM*). During the early 400s, the bishop of Rome took over Novatian churches there, but separate Novatian congregations remained in the eastern Mediterranean for another century.

Oldcastle, Sir John   See *LOLLARDS*.

Ophites   The Ophites were a second-century *GNOSTIC* sect that worshiped the serpent of Paradise, honoring him as the first rebel against the evil *DEMIURGE,* who was the creator of this world but not the true God. Scholars today generally use the term *Ophite* as synonymous with *SETHIAN*. In Ophite teaching, the serpent of Genesis 3 was humanity's helper. It was typical of Gnostics to identify Eve (Hebrew for "life") with wisdom and thus to read that chapter as a story of how humanity almost escaped the rule of the Demiurge. Ophites were said to use live snakes in their rituals.

Origen   A leading figure of the early church, Origen was judged heretical by the Fifth Ecumenical Council in 553. Today, however, he is considered a significant theologian.

Born in or about the year 184 in the Egyptian city of Alexandria and the son of a Christian martyr, he studied philosophy under *AMMONIUS SACCUS,* taught and lectured, traveled widely, and wrote more than 2,000 works, less than half of which survive. (One set out to rebut the anti-Christian arguments of the Pagan philosopher *CELSUS*.) Despite his grounding in Greek philosophy, which generally urged a life lived according to the principle of moderation, Origen literally made himself a eunuch for the sake of the kingdom of heaven (one translation of Matthew 19:12). In Alexandria, however, that was not an entirely original idea: Priests of the Pagan goddess Cybele, among others, also castrated themselves, as did some other enthusiastic Christians.

Throughout his life, Origen found himself in conflict with *GNOSTIC* Christians. When he was left fatherless at the age of 19 or so, he lived in the home of a rich Christian woman but moved out rather than stay under the same roof with her resident Gnostic chaplain. His best-known work, *On First Principles,* rebutted Gnosticism at length, but after his death it caused some catholic Christians to consider him a heretic for having taught the doctrine of the preexistence of souls (also interpreted by some readers as a teaching of reincarnation). In addition, in the centuries following his death in 254, Origen was sometimes condemned for teaching that any of God's creations, even the fallen angels, could be redeemed. To deny that possibility, he felt, was to fall into Gnostic dualism.

Origen's philosophical background showed in how he handled objections to scriptural inconsistencies. Even as Plato and his followers had divided the universe into the realms of body, soul, and spirit (or mind), so biblical texts had three levels of meaning. They could be understood literally or historically, morally, and finally as allegories.

Orléans Heretics   The case of the Orléans heretics of 1022, who included priests, nuns, and laypeople, is significant because of the range of participants. It may be the first instance in the Middle Ages of charges of devil worship leveled against so-called heretics. The heretics were also charged with being Manichaeans, but this should not be taken literally to mean "followers of *MANI*"; it simply implied heretics with tendencies toward *DUALISM*.

At the core of the heretical group were ten canons—priests attached to the Cathedral of Sainte Croix (Holy Cross) in the French city of Orléans. According to Paul of Chartres, a monastic chronicler of the time, the heresy was unwittingly disclosed by a priest named Héribert, who was the private chaplain of a northern French nobleman named Aréfast. In 1022, Héribert journeyed to Orléans and met two of the canons, priests named Étienne (or Stephen) and Lisoius, who were "in popular repute distinguished above all others in wisdom, eminent in holiness and piety, bountiful in charity." Héribert began to take instruction from them, or, in the words of the monastic chronicler, "he was made drunken by them with deadly draughts of evil." When he attempted to convey the same doctrines to Aréfast—a knight who, unlike most of his fellow feudal nobles, apparently took a serious interest in theology—Aréfast realized that his chaplain "had strayed from the path of righteousness." He informed his feudal lord, Duke Richard of Normandy, of the spread of heresy in Orléans, and the duke informed King Robert. The king asked Aréfast to go and investigate in person. Another priest, Evrard, sacristan of the church at Chartres, suggested that Aréfast take communion every day for spiritual protection against the false doctrines he was about to hear.

Pretending to be an earnest seeker, Aréfast sought out the heretical priests; that he was readily accepted by them suggests that they had already gained other upper-class disciples. According to the chronicler, they told him, "You [like a wild tree from the forest transplanted into a garden], being transferred from the evil world into our holy companionship, will be well supplied with the water of wisdom until you are instructed and are strong enough to be shorn of the thorns of evil by the sword of the Word of God, and when we have driven absurd teachings from the shelter of your heart, you can receive with purity of mind our teaching, bestowed by the Holy Spirit."

These teachings, Paul the chronicler recounted, included that the sacraments of baptism and Holy Communion were of no value and that Christ was not born of a virgin, nor had he risen from the dead—apparently a form of *DOCETISM*. Instead, the canons and their followers claimed to believe only what they could see with their own eyes and to be guided by the Holy Spirit. With true spiritual understanding, they told Aréfast, a person would no longer be misled by "fictions written on animal skins" (i.e., on parchment).

According to Paul of Chartres, however, their wickedness did not end with false doctrine. He also accused them of holding sexual orgies, summoning demons, and ritually cremating babies born as a result of their indiscriminate sexual intercourse. The heretics preserved the babies' ashes the way Catholics venerated the consecrated hosts that were the body of Christ, he said. "Indeed, such power of devilish fraud was in these ashes that whoever had been imbued with the aforesaid heresy and had partaken of no matter how small a portion of them was scarcely ever afterward able to direct the course of his thought from this heresy to the path of truth."

In making these accusations Paul—together with another contemporary chronicler, Adhémar—was repeating stock charges that have a long history in European and North American culture, as the British historian Norman Cohn ably argued in his work *Europe's Inner Demons*. The very same accusations of sexual orgies in the dark, baby killing, and cannibalism have been made by Pagan Romans against the followers of Middle Eastern mysteries (such as those of Dionysus—forbidden by law in ancient Rome), by the Romans against the early Christians, by orthodox Christians against Gnostics, by Eastern Christians against Bogomils in the Byzantine Empire, by Western Christians against assorted heretics in Western Europe, and against Satanists during the past two centuries. The substance of these accusations has changed very little, but reliable evidence has been elusive for all these centuries.

When the Orléans heretics were brought before King Robert, Queen Constance, and a group of bishops on Christmas Day in 1022 in the Cathedral of Sainte Croix, they were examined on their doctrine, not on charges of baby killing; this much is clear from Paul's own narrative. Aréfast was among them, chained like the rest. When the canons attempted to evade the bishops' questions, he spoke out, disclosing his role as informant. He accused them of retracting their doctrinal claims for fear of execution. He was released as planned, and the bishops bore down harder with their questioning.

Caught in their evasions, the heretics admitted that they had taught Aréfast and others that Christ did not truly suffer on the cross, that baptism by water was valueless, and so forth. "To us, however, who have the law written upon the heart by the Holy Spirit (and we recognize nothing but what we have learned from God, Creator of all), in vain you spin out superfluities and things inconsistent with the Divinity," they said.

After nine hours of cross-examination, only two heretics—one priest and one nun—abandoned their doctrines. Late in the day, a lynch mob of townspeople attempted to break into the cathedral, but the queen faced them down and barred the doors. And when the heretics were led to the execution site, she struck Étienne with her staff and blinded him in one eye, angered because he had been her confessor and she had trusted his spiritual guidance. The heretics were burned outside the city walls on 28 December 1022. Apparently, most of the heretical priests' lay followers had recanted; somewhere between 10 and 14 clerics

were executed. According to some chronicles, they went to the pyre laughing—until the flames rose around them, and then they screamed.

Not content with that, the king and the bishops ordered that the bones of Théodat, another clerical follower of the heretics who had died three years earlier, be dug up and scattered away from consecrated ground.

Despite the accusations of devil worship and Manichaeism made by some chroniclers at the time, the Orléans heretics appear to have been neither, wrote Jeffrey Burton Russell, a historian of the later medieval and Renaissance witch persecutions. Instead, Russell sees the heretical canons as skeptical intellectuals and their heresy as one of many early attempts at reforming what had already become a worldly and too frequently corrupted church.

Panarion A fourth-century encyclopedia of heresies, the *Panarion,* or Medicine chest, was written by Bishop *EPIPHANIUS* of Salamis (later canonized) to provide antidotes to the various diseases of heresy.

Panthera According to a variety of Jewish and Pagan traditions as old as the written books of the New Testament, a Roman soldier named Panthera or Pantera (the panther) was the actual father of Jesus as the result of Mary's adultery. The oldest of these stories deals with the famed rabbi Eliezer, who lived in the latter part of the first century, and speaks of him hearing a Galilean speak "in the name of Jesus the son of Panteri." This accusation was old enough in rabbinic circles that some Christians felt the need to refute it by arguing that what was meant was the Greek *parthenos* (virgin) and was a reference to Jesus's virgin birth. The Jewish references, however, predate the Christian emphasis on the virgin birth.

The historian Morton Smith, who compiled a number of non-Christian references to Jesus in *Jesus the Magician,* also noted that although Panthera was not a common name, the grave of a Roman soldier of Sidonian origins (i.e., from Sidon, a city located in today's Lebanon), one Tiberius Julius Abdes Pantera, has been found in Germany where his legion was stationed. "It is possible, though not likely, that his tombstone from Bingerbrück is our only genuine relic of the Holy Family." (But see *MARY MAGDALENE.*) This and other stories collected in the Babylonian Talmud make Jesus out to be a heretical Jewish magician, one of the type of free-lance messiahs referred to by the Pagan writer *CELSUS* in his work *Against the Christians.*

Interestingly, a medieval bestiary—a compilation of observations and allegories about different real and imaginary animals—from twelfth-century England (the Cistercian Abbey of Revesby in Lincolnshire) has this to say about the Panther: "The true Panther, Our Lord Jesus Christ, snatched us from the power of the dragon-devil on descending from the heavens. . . . And because it is a beautiful animal, the Lord God says of Christ, 'He is beautiful in form among the sons of men.'"

Passagians A group of twelfth-century heretics in Lombardy, part of northern Italy, the Passagians were contemporaries of *EUDO DE STELLA* and the *CATHARS.* Their leaders are unknown, and their doctrines can be learned only from a work written around 1200 to confute their teachers as well as others judged heretical.

This *Summa contra haereticos,* ascribed to Praepositinus of Cremona, describes the Passagians as retaining the Old Testament rules on circumcision, kosher foods, and the Jewish holy days. They were also accused of preaching a form of *SUBORDINATIONISM,* teaching that Christ was a created being and less than the Father.

Patarine Heresy, Patarini A group of radically puritan and anticlerical dissidents arose in eleventh-century Milan, led by a man named Erlembaldo. Milan at the time was ruled by an archbishop, and the Patarini claimed that this secular authority on the part of a high church official was part of a pattern of corruption and *SIMONY* throughout the local clergy. These early puritans went on to further question Catholic teaching, refusing to accept the sacraments from "unworthy" priests—a refusal that whenever advocated throughout the centuries has earned its advocates the title of heretics. From that refusal, some moved to question whether the sacraments themselves had any power. Although sharing a general early medieval reforming impulse, the Patarini also represent the growing social consciousness of the artisans and merchants of the Italian towns and their resentment of clerical and aristocratic overlords. One of them told a thirteenth-century writer, Yves of Narbonne, that they selected their brightest young men to send to Paris to study theology in order to refute the Catholics (compare the story of *ARNOLD OF BRESCIA*), and that the merchants among them attempted to spread their doctrines during trading fairs.

According to a literary debate between a fictitious Patarine and a Catholic written around 1250, the Patarines also taught that human bodies were created by the devil, putting them in the dualist (see *DUALISM*) or *CATHAR* camp. Indeed, part of the difficulty in describing the Patarines (or Patarini) is that like *Cathar* or *Manichaean,* the term was loosely employed by medieval writers on heresy and not restricted to any one group. See also *ALBANESES*.

Patripassianism   From a Latin phrase meaning "Father suffering," this heretical teaching said that God the Father himself became man (the incarnation) and suffered death by crucifixion. It arose in the mid-second century, contemporaneously with Marcionism (see *MARCION*). Embraced by some early Christians, patripassianism may also be seen as a complete contrast to the Gnostic idea of the unknowable, wholly spiritual Father who had not even created the material world, leaving that chore to one of his emanations. (See *BASILIDES; DOCETISM; GNOSTICISM; VALENTINUS*.) During this era, the doctrine of the Trinity—three divine persons who were One and yet were distinct from one another—had not been fully developed and articulated by such early Christian theologians as *ORIGEN*. But after Trinitarian doctrine had been formalized by theologians and by the first Council of *NICAEA* in 325, patripassianistic thinking became viewed as heretical, a variant of *MONARCHIANISM*.

Paul of Samosata   Paul of Samosata, who lived circa 200–275, was a bishop who followed

the heresy of *ADOPTIONISM*. Through his conflicts with the orthodox establishment, he wound up in a Roman court in a dispute over who controlled church land and buildings in Palmyra, a city in Syria, then part of the Roman Empire. Known as "wretched little Paul" to his catholic opponents, he was condemned by the Council of Antioch, circa 268.

Paul was apparently an innovator in other ways; for example, he is credited with being the first bishop to permit women to sing in church choirs, and he also encouraged audience participation in sermons. At the same time, he was attacked by other Christians for being too cozy with the Roman authorities. His ideas, however, were carried forth by a long-lived *PAULICIAN* church in Asia Minor.

Paulicians   The concept of *ADOPTIONISM*—that Jesus was not divine but was adopted by God at his baptism at age 30—combined with several other ideas current in Eastern Christianity to form the basis of the Paulician church. For a time, its members created a kingdom on the upper Euphrates River, becoming a border state between the Christian Byzantine Empire and the Muslim realms to the east. Led by Karbeas and his successor Chrysocheir, former officers of the Byzantine army, Paulician forces raided the eastern borders of the empire during the ninth century until they were defeated by the emperor Basil I in 872. The survivors fled into the mountains of Armenia or took refuge among the Arabs. One group, however, had been settled in Thrace by an earlier eighth-century emperor to serve as a frontier garrison; these Paulicians have been viewed by some historians as providing the seed of the later *BOGOMIL* dualist heresy among the Bulgarians. Indeed, some later Paulicians did move toward an extreme dualist position, rejecting the idea of Christ's humanity and treating the material world as having been created by Satan, who was equated with the God of the Jews. See also *ALBIGENSIANISM; DUALISM; GNOSTICISM*.

Pelagius   Branded a heretic by the bishop *AUGUSTINE OF HIPPO,* the fourth century's greatest theologian, Pelagius nonetheless opened a controversy that continues to this day: whether humans' free will and actions or God's grace are more important to salvation. In the name of moral reform and to stop people from blaming their failings on their weak flesh, Pelagius emphasized human freedom and will, urging people to stop seeking alibis and work for their salvation. Although he was condemned, his doctrines have survived, if only in modified form.

Born in either Ireland or Roman-ruled Celtic Britain around 360, Pelagius came to Rome in about 400 as a monk and missionary. No doubt the corruption he encountered in the former imperial capital (which would be sacked by the barbarian Goths ten years later), the theological disputes, and the backsliding of many professed Christians caused him to advocate a kind of practical Christianity focused on good works and moral choices. He attacked the practice of infant baptism and through it the idea of original sin, or sin carried by every newborn baby as part of its human condition.

"In the freedom to choose good or evil lies the preeminence of the rational soul," Pelagius wrote. "In this lies the honor of our nature and our dignity. . . . There would be no virtue in him who perseveres in the good if he had not the possibility of going over to evil." A just and merciful god, he thought, would not punish all humanity for Adam's sin.

This teaching brought him into conflict with Augustine, who believed that humans were born corrupted by original sin, passed from one generation to the next by the very pleasure of the parents in sexual intercourse. In Augustine's view, nature itself was spoiled by human sin: In the Garden of Eden, all was in harmony; had humans remained in that state, they would not have suffered pain or death. After Adam and Eve sinned, however, death and sickness entered the world; nature itself became hostile, something humans had to struggle against to survive. Human sin had corrupted nature. Ultimately, Augustine developed the idea of predestination, foreshadowed in the writings of Paul—namely, that God had chosen only some people for salvation for all eternity and that it was only through his divine grace that that group would be saved. Humanity otherwise tended toward corruption and evil, Augustine believed.

When the two men met face to face, they were unable to find a middle ground. Unable to withstand Augustine's intolerance and the charge of heresy leveled against himself and his followers (who, if they were monks or priests, were often forced from their positions), Pelagius visited the eastern portions of the Roman Empire. According to legend, he was eventually expelled from Jerusalem for his views. He is believed to have died around 420.

Some scholars see in Augustine's condemnation a realization that Pelagian ideas undercut church authority; the bishop's attack on Pelagius paralleled his earlier condemnation of the Donatists (see *DONATISM*), another group that challenged the orthodox establishment. In Augustine's view, humanity could be saved only through an alliance between a unified, hierarchical church and the imperial government. Only through church-directed government, he believed, could peace and order be imposed on a sinful humanity—even on baptized Christians. His pessimistic views on humanity and nature triumphed over Pelagian freedom and moral choice and continued to dominate Christianity for centuries afterwards.

Peter de Bruis   See *PETROBRUSIANS*.

Petrobrusians   Named after Peter de Bruis (or Bruys), a Frenchman who attacked the twelfth-century clergy for their corruption, the Petrobrusian heresy was apparently found in the Rhône Valley and Gascony. Peter himself was apparently burned at the stake around 1131. His ideas, however, were taken up by another heretical preacher, an ex-monk called Henry of Le Mans.

Peter's followers denied the efficacy of infant baptism and declared that church buildings were useless because, as the French abbot Peter the Venerable of Cluny put it, "God hears as well when invoked in a tavern as in a church, in a marketplace as in a temple, before an altar or in a stable, and He hearkens to those who are worthy."

Peter the Venerable also wrote that Peter de Bruis had ordered crosses to be "hacked to pieces by swords, burned by fire," because as the instruments of Christ's death they too should be destroyed. Likewise, the abbot continued, the Petrobrusians denied the value of the Eucharist and of prayers for the dead.

Henry of Le Mans in turn wandered the Rhône Valley, "irreverently disparaging the sacraments as well as the ministers of the

Church," as a biographer of the abbot St. Bernard of Clairvaux wrote in 1145.

Plotinus   An intellectual mystic and philosopher who lived circa 205–270, Plotinus is often considered the father of Neoplatonic philosophy (see *NEOPLATONISM*), which extended Plato's teachings (already six centuries old) in a religious direction. Possibly born in Egypt, Plotinus was a student of the Alexandrian philosopher *AMMONIUS SACCUS* (whose pupils included the Christian theologian *ORIGEN*). He advocated living an ascetic, moral, and self-disciplined life that would permit a person to raise his or her mind to a point of union with "the One," the indescribable highest level of being (also referred to in Platonic terms as "the Good"). All seeking for truth was ultimately a search for union with the One.

After eleven years' study with Ammonius, Plotinus joined the Roman emperor Gordian's expedition against the Persians in 242 as a non-combatant, hoping to have an opportunity to learn more of Persian and Indian philosophy. When the expedition ended with the emperor's defeat and assassination in Mesopotamia, Plotinus settled in Rome, teaching and writing. He considered the details of his own life to be unimportant: He would not let his portrait be painted (although a Roman artist did one from memory) and refused to celebrate his own birthday, but only those of the ancient philosophers Plato and Socrates. At one point he nearly succeeded in gaining imperial patronage for a utopian community modeled on that described in Plato's *Republic*.

The teachings of Plotinus were collected by his student *PORPHYRY* in six sets of nine treatises, referred to as *The Enneads* from the Greek word for "nine." In them, he describes the One in divine rather than abstract terms but at the same time makes it more impersonal than the god of Christianity. An enlightened and moral person can draw near the One but cannot address petitions to the One, for God cannot "come down." Here lay the objection Plotinus and other Platonists had against Christianity. In their view, the universe existed on a continuum from the highest good (which has no specific traits and cannot be described in human language) through the realms of intellect or ideas, of soul, and finally of the senses and matter.

This picture left no room for the incarnation of Christ to occur. At the same time, Plotinus condemned the *GNOSTIC* Christians for their teaching that the material world was an evil, inferior creation. This notion, he said, led to a rejection of morality and discouraged people from leading the good lives that would permit them to be drawn toward the Good. Splitting the universe into a good half and a bad half denied the Platonic teaching that it had developed "in accordance with intelligence" and "admits of a rational explanation." But like the Gnostics, he felt that not all people made the effort to comprehend the individual soul's unity with the higher realms.

Some historians see Plotinus's influence even in Latin American liberation theology, holding that Neoplatonic thinking underlies "the Latin American propensity to assume that will, consciousness, and mind-energy can always triumph over matter—or the illusion of matter," as Frederick Pike wrote.

Porphyry   Follower of the philosopher *PLOTINUS* and editor of his writings, Porphyry made an even sharper attack on Christianity than did his teacher.

Born around 234, Porphyry may have been raised a Christian; at the least, he had been extensively exposed to Christianity and was familiar with the Bible. He was probably a native of Tyre and studied at the famous philosophical school in Athens before moving to Rome and Plotinus's tutelage. Late in life (he died in 305) he married a widow named Marcella; his *Letter to His Wife Marcella,* describing the ideal philosophical life, is still extant.

During his time, however, he was also known for a work titled *Against the Christians,* which so enraged church leaders that all copies found were destroyed. Our knowledge of it is only through quotations embodied in Christian counterattacks. Some of the points Porphyry made in his rational criticism of the Bible have been upheld by later scholarship—for example, that the Book of Daniel was written during the Maccabean period, centuries later than the time it describes.

In other portions of the book, Porphyry listed other perceived discrepancies: the various accounts of Jesus's resurrection, for example. He questioned how Paul could tell his fellow Christians to "Bless and curse not" but so bitterly denounce his opponents in the early church.

In his own life, Porphyry was as ascetic as many Christians, however. He avoided gambling, the theater, horse racing and other public games, and, as mentioned, marriage until late in life. He was a vegetarian because he believed that the less-developed souls of animals entered those who ate their flesh; likewise, he apparently taught a form of reincarnation.

Prunicus   A name for the heavenly power in *GNOSTIC* cosmology more often referred to as *BARBELOS*.

Pseudo-Dionysius
See *DIONYSIUS THE AREOPAGITE*.

Raymond of Tarrega   A Spanish Dominican monk, Raymond of Tarrega swam against the current of medieval thinking on *WITCHCRAFT* and demonology when in about 1370 he wrote a book called *On the Invocation of Demons,* which reminded its readers that even demons were created by God.

Since they were so created, he continued, it was permissible to adore what was godlike in them. Like other theologians, he made a distinction between *dulia,* or "service" (from a Greek word meaning "servant"), and *latria,* or "worship." In other words, demons could be approached in the same way as saints: A Christian could adore them, pray to them, or make a special vow to them.

Not surprisingly, Raymond's book was not well received by the *INQUISITION.* Officials of the Inquisition in Christian Spain seized what copies they could and burned them. Raymond himself, however, escaped the same fate, perhaps because of the abstract and intellectual nature of his arguments.

The rack, a favored instrument of torturers employed by inquisitors such as Robert le Bougre. (From Joost Damhouder, Enchiridion, *1554.)*

Robert le Bougre   One of the first inquisitors in northern France, Robert le Bougre had a short but bloody official career, often compared with that of his contemporary, *CONRAD OF MARBURG.* A Dominican monk, Robert was evidently a former heretic himself, possibly an *ALBIGENSIAN,* because his nickname translates as "the Bulgarian." Rather than indicating ethnicity, the nickname demonstrates the transfer of the Bulgarian *BOGOMIL* label to the Italian or the French heretics believed to share the Bogomils' doctrines. (Through Norman French, the same word entered the English language as *bugger,* because such heretics were said to favor sodomy either to avoid conceiving children or out of heretical perversity. See *HOMOSEXUALITY.*)

In 1231, Pope Gregory IX empowered Robert to persecute heretics in the region of Burgundy, and the monk so distinguished himself that he became known to his clerical colleagues as *Malleus Haereticorum,* "the hammer of heretics." He survived an attempt by French bishops to have him removed in 1234. The pope was convinced that the spread of Albigensian doctrine was a greater threat than Robert's enthusiasm for large public trials and subsequent executions, and Gregory's method was to give more power to the Dominicans and Franciscans as opposed to local clergy with local ties. (See *INQUISITION*.)

Rather than hold private trials, Robert preferred to move quickly, bringing groups of suspected heretics before a public trial and giving them the alternative of recanting their heresy and performing penance or being swiftly handed to the executioner. In one of his more notable mass trials, he interrogated nearly 200 suspected *CATHARS* at Mont-Wimer in Champagne. On 13 May 1239, with a panel of bishops and royalty looking on, some 183 convicted heretics were burned at the stake. In the words of one chronicler, it was a "holocaust, very great and pleasing to God."

Despite playing to local church and government authorities, Robert made even powerful people nervous in his zeal to try and condemn suspected heretics. Eventually enough protests were made to the right individuals, and Robert was removed from office by the Dominican order itself and kept out of sight under virtual imprisonment for the rest of his life. A similar instance of Dominican zeal provoking a counterreaction may be seen in the careers of the German inquisitors Krämer and Sprenger, authors of the *MALLEUS MALEFICARUM*.

Sabellius, Sabellianism
See *MONARCHIANISM*.

Saturnilus   A Syrian exponent of *GNOSTICISM*, Saturnilus (or Saturninus) taught during the first years of the second century. Like some other Gnostic Christians, he sought to combine teachings about Christ the Savior (but not Jesus the Jewish messiah) with Platonic cosmology and the Platonic theory of archetypal ideas. According to his teaching, seven angels—one of whom was Yahweh (Jehovah)—created the material world.

Scholasticism   The chief medieval philosophical method, Scholasticism used philosophical logic and biblical revelation to construct what thinkers of the time believed would be a complete, all-encompassing system of knowledge. Unlike *GNOSTICISM*, Scholasticism required no special spiritual insight or revelation: All its conclusions could be arrived at intellectually. Scholastics, the greatest of whom was St. Thomas Aquinas (1225–1274), have been ridiculed for discussing such questions as how many angels could dance on the head of a pin. In their time, however, the question was a serious one: Were angels immaterial beings or merely made of a finer material than human beings? As the authorized way of handling knowledge in medieval Catholic universities, Scholasticism as a school was opposed to all heresies that depended on special revelations or radical reinterpretations of the Bible.

Servetus, Michael   A physician and theologian, Michael Servetus (in Spanish, Miguel Serveto) was born in Catholic Spain in 1511 and executed for heresy in Protestant Switzerland in 1553. After studying law and medicine at the universities of Toulouse, Paris, and Montpellier, he practiced medicine in Vienne, France. Around this time he began corresponding with the famed Protestant reformer John Calvin and shared with Calvin his unorthodox views on the Trinity, expressed in his book *De Trinitas Erroribus*. (He also published a ground-breaking work on the circulatory system.) In essence, Servetus denied the doctrine of the Trinity as being a form of polytheism and took a more Adoptionist view of Christ's nature, considering him to be a perfect man whom the Father "adopted" (see *ADOPTIONISM*).

Despite his views, Servetus requested and received permission to visit Geneva, the city Calvin controlled as a virtual dictator. While attending church he was arrested. He was then tried for heresy, convicted, and burned at the stake.

Seth, Sethians   Described in Genesis as Adam and Eve's third son, Seth was a divine personage, a forerunner or indeed a previous incarnation of Christ, in some traditions of *GNOSTICISM*.

Genesis 4:25 describes Seth briefly: "Adam lay with his wife again [after their first son, Cain, had killed Abel, their second son]. She bore a son, and named him Seth [granted], 'for,' she said, 'God has granted me another son in place of Abel, because Cain killed him.' Seth too had a son, whom he named Enosh."

The list of Adam's descendants in Genesis 5 reintroduces Seth: "Adam was one hundred and thirty years old when he begot a son in his likeness and image, and named him Seth. After the birth of Seth he lived eight hundred years, and had other sons and daughters. . . . Seth was one hundred and five years old when he begot Enosh. After the birth of Enosh he lived eight hundred and seven years, and had other sons and daughters.''

Based on these two slim references and the idea that with Abel dead and Cain ''a vagrant and a wanderer on earth,'' Seth was the *de facto* ''eldest son,'' Jewish tradition proceeded to flesh out the story considerably. He was portrayed as the faithful son whose many descendants prospered and produced many advances, including the discovery of astrology, according to the first-century Jewish historian Josephus.

The *NAG HAMMADI* texts include a group of books referring to Seth, possibly compiled by Jewish Gnostics. Scholars place ten texts in the Sethian group, including the *Three Steles of Seth,* the *Hypostasis of the Archons* (also translated as the *Reality of the Rulers*), the *Apocryphon of John,* the *Gospel of the Egyptians,* and the *Apocalypse of Adam.* Another writing, the *Second Treatise of the Seth,* mentions him only in its title and is otherwise devoted to Jesus.

The *Gospel of the Egyptians,* for example, describes him as ''the power which really truly lives,'' as ''the father of the immovable, incorruptible race,'' and as a participant in a Gnostic creation story. Seth himself prepares a ''logos-begotten body . . . secretly through the virgin,'' and Jesus is described as ''he whom the great Seth has put on.'' In it the three highest divine powers are described as the Father, the Mother, and the Son, who, in turn, created myriad lesser powers.

Seth also carries Gnostic teachings in the *Apocalypse of Adam.* Because this book has no overtly Christian content, some authorities believe that it represents a transitional stage from Jewish to Gnostic apocalyptic literature, describing how those with the true knowledge will triumph over the false powers at the end of history. In it, Adam reveals to Seth the future of the race, including Noah's division of the earth among his sons Shem, Ham, and Japheth and the conflicts between the followers of the eternal God and the false god of the world (the god of the powers, or archons). That god accuses Noah of deceiving him by creating another generation of humans besides those saved in the ark. When Noah disclaims responsibility, the other people, who have the *gnosis* or knowledge of the eternal true God, are rescued from the world and borne away ''into their proper (heavenly) land.''

Although little is heard of Sethian Gnostics after the second century, the Sethian books in the Nag Hammadi cache have provided ammunition for those scholars who argue that Gnosticism developed independently of Christianity rather than being a variant form of it.

Simon Magus   A flamboyant first-century *GNOSTIC* teacher and miracle worker, Simon was born in Samaria (*magus* simply means ''magician'' or ''miracle worker'' in this context). He is traditionally identified with the Simon described in Acts 8:9–13: ''A man named Simon had been in the city [Jerusalem] for some time, and had swept the Samaritans off their feet with his magical arts, claiming to be someone great. All of them, high and low, listened eagerly to him. 'This man,' they said, 'is that power of God which is called ''The Great Power''.' They listened because they had for long been carried away by his magic. But when they came to believe Philip with his good news about the kingdom of God and the name of Jesus Christ, they were baptized, men and women alike. Even Simon himself believed and was baptized, and thereupon was constantly in Philip's company. He was carried away when he saw the powerful signs and miracles that were taking place.''

Acts 8:18–24 records a confrontation between Peter and Simon in Samaria. After seeing the apostles Peter and John laying hands on converts so that they would receive the Holy Spirit, Simon approached them and said, ''Give me the same power too, so that when I lay my hands on anyone, he will receive the Holy Spirit.'' Peter responded, ''Your money go with you to damnation, because you thought God's gift was for sale!'' After Peter further rebuked him, Simon begged the apostle to pray for him ''and ask [the Lord] that none of the things you have spoken may fall upon me.'' From this story, the buying or selling of church offices and clerical bribe taking came to be called *SIMONY.*

Whether or not Simon Magus and the Simon described in Acts are one and the same, early Christian legend preferred to see him die during a confrontation with the apostle Peter rather than be converted to Christianity. In this story, Peter and Simon clashed in Rome, where

Simon announced he could "ascend to heaven" through his power. As he rose into the air, Peter's prayers caused him to fall to earth. According to some early Christians, Simon's magic was performed with the aid of a murdered boy's spirit that he had commanded to serve him.

Hans Jonas, a noted scholar of Gnosticism, points out that the Simon in Acts may not necessarily have been the same Simon Magus repeatedly denounced by later churchmen such as *EPIPHANIUS* because, as the prototypical Gnostic heretic, Simon Magus was still being denounced long after his death. Jonas suggests that the Simon Magus described as the father of heresies probably lived a generation or two later than the Simon of Acts and, rather than being

baptized a Christian, founded a separate non-Christian Gnostic religion whose teachings are summarized below. In Jonas's view, it is significant that Simon's teaching that the primal being was self-divided into light and darkness differed from the Iranian Gnosticism typified by *MANICHAEISM,* in which light (good) and darkness (evil) have always existed and will be locked in battle until a final climax at the end of the world. Simonian Gnosticism, however, was more typical of the schools of Alexandria or Syria.

Early Christian writers, meanwhile, dwelt on Simon's allegedly unsavory character and told a different story about his life. In the late 200s, *IRENAEUS* thundered that all people

A fifteenth-century depiction of Simon Magus and Saint Peter. (Tempera on wood painting by Benozzo Gozzoli. Courtesy of the Metropolitan Museum of Art.)

"who in any way corrupt the truth and harm the teaching of the church are the disciples and successors of Simon Magus of Samaria." In the 490s, Pope Gelasius I included him in a diatribe against heretics.

Irenaeus wrote that Simon's companion was a woman named Helen, whom he had found working as a prostitute in the Phoenician city of Tyre. According to this version, Simon's cosmology was essentially Gnostic, flavored by Platonism. In it, the godhead (the One) produced Thought (in Greek, *Ennoia*) as its first emanation; from Thought came the angels who bridged the pure world of spirit with the world of matter. But some of these powers and angels turned on Thought and forced her to become imprisoned in a human body through successive incarnations, including one as Helen of Troy. So Simon incarnated to save her from the false angels; his other followers would also be freed from the ruling spiritual powers of this world and permitted to rejoin the true, but distant, God. But Irenaeus believed that Simon's inner circle was sexually promiscuous and inclined to raise money by mixing potions and casting spells for money:

> Thus, then, the mystic priests belonging to this sect both lead profligate lives and practice magical arts, each one to the extent of his ability. They use exorcisms and incantations. Love potions, too, and charms, as well as those beings who are called "Paredri" (familiars) and "Oniropompi" (dream-senders). And whatever curious arts can be had recourse to, are eagerly pressed into their service. They have an image of Simon fashioned after the likeness of Jupiter, and another of Helen in the shape of Minerva; and these they worship. . . . The successor of [Simon] was Menander, also a Samaritan by birth, and he, too, was a perfect adept in the practice of magic. He affirms that the primary Power continues unknown to all, but that he himself is the person who has been sent forth from the presence of the invisible beings as a savior, for the deliverance of men.

According to the orthodox writer *HIPPOLYTUS,* Simon Magus taught that the Gar-

den of Eden was the womb, continuing the allegory by interpreting the "river that flowed forth from Eden" as the umbilical cord that feeds the fetus, the exodus from Egypt as the passage through the birth canal, and the crossing of the Red Sea as the blood and fluids accompanying birth. (Some *SETHIANS* and the Gnostic teacher *MARCUS* shared this view.)

Epiphanius, a fourth-century bishop and cataloger of heresies, wrote in his *Panarion* that "He came from Samaritan territory and was Christian in name only. He taught people to perform obscene acts, the defilement of promiscuity with women." The sect of Simon Magus was the first to spring up after the crucifixion of Jesus, he wrote. Like the followers of *CARPOCRATES,* whom he also denounced, the Simonians offered sexual sacraments according to Epiphanius, "rites of shamefulness and of fluxes from bodies, to speak with some decency: of men through effluence [semen], and from women through the usual menses, which were collected for the rites, a most shameful collection. And these he said were rites of life, knowledge [and] perfection."

Describing how Simon called his companion the reincarnation of Helen of Troy, Epiphanius wrote that he even allegorized the story of the Trojan horse as a Gnostic metaphor of ignorance. He quoted Simon as teaching that "As the Phrygians [Trojans] in pulling it unwittingly drew on their own destruction, so also the nations, that is human beings without the knowledge which I give draw on themselves perdition by their ignorance."

In addition, Simon Magus has been credited by both Jonas and religious historian Mircea Eliade with being the prototype of Faust, the legendary magician who made a pact with the devil, an observation possibly derived from Simon's Latin nickname, Faustus (favored).

Simony   Simony, the buying or selling of church offices by either clerical or lay authorities, was periodically denounced as a heresy during the Catholic church's first thousand years. The rationale was that because the sacraments, and the power to perform them, are gifts of the Holy Spirit, to say that they can be sold is to say that the Holy Spirit can be sold. Church pressure against the simoniac heresy increased during the papacy of Leo IX (1049–1054) and subsequent popes as part of clerical reformers' efforts to keep other rulers from interfering with church affairs. Later, Thomas Aquinas said that simony was indeed a heresy—as opposed to a sin—when the simonist thought that he was in fact buying or selling the Holy Spirit as opposed to merely buying or selling a bishopric or other church office.

Sol Invictus   Under the Emperor Aurelian, who ruled from 270 to 275, elements of the Roman state priesthood set up a cult of the Unconquerable (or Invincible) Sun, which would unify the empire religiously. All father or solar deities—such as the Roman Jupiter, the Greek Zeus, the Persian *MITHRAS,* the Egyptian Ra, or even the Judeo-Christian God—could in their view be seen as sharing the same "solar" characteristics. In a time when the empire was threatened externally by Persians, German tribes, and North African nomads, religious unification under the sun and a semidivine emperor was a component of political unity.

Although intellectually pleasing, the religion of Sol Invictus did not appeal to the common people, but it was successfully integrated with the all-male cult of Mithras, which was widespread in the Roman legions. The official emphasis on Sol Invictus was continued by later emperors. Even *CONSTANTINE* the Great, who favored Christianity and was baptized on his deathbed, used the image of the triumphant sun on some of his coins.

The major festival of Sol Invictus was of course the winter solstice, when the sun is "reborn." Although Christians resisted letting their religion be included under the syncretic sky of Sol Invictus, insisting that it was unique and true, the celebration of Jesus's birth (which probably occurred in the spring), did somehow migrate to the solstice, although later changes in the calendar have put them about four days apart.

Sophia   Perhaps the most haunting figure in the Gnostic cosmology, Sophia is seen variously as the personification of divine wisdom, as a female divinity equated with the Holy Spirit, as an allegory of the soul separated from its true home, and as the inspiration for every old story of a "damsel in distress."

Greek-speaking Jews of the Roman Empire translated the Hebrew word for "divine wisdom," *Hokhmah,* as "Sophia." (Both words are grammatically feminine in their respective tongues.) Although fundamentally monotheistic, some Jews, particularly those living in Alexandria and other areas away from Palestine and removed from the temple Judaism, developed what is called the "Wisdom Literature," a group of scriptures portraying Wisdom personified. In such biblical books as Proverbs and Ecclesiastes, as well as in the apocryphal books of The Wisdom of Solomon and Ecclesiasticus (Ben Sirach), long passages are devoted to Wisdom. The Wisdom of Solomon states, "Wisdom is radiant and unfading, and she is easily discerned by those who love her, and is found by those who seek her."

Proverbs 8 states:

> The Lord created me [Wisdom]
> > the beginning of his works,
> before all else that he made, long ago.
> Alone, I was fashioned in times long past,
> at the beginning, long before earth itself.
> . . . When he set the heavens in their place
> > I was there,
> when he girdled the ocean with the horizon,
> when he fixed the canopy of clouds
> > overhead
> and set the springs of ocean firm in their place,
> when he prescribed its limits for the sea
> and knit together earth's foundations.
> Then I was at his side each day,
> his darling and delight,
> playing in his presence continually,
> playing on the earth,
> when he had finished it,
> while my delight was in mankind.

Like the more-developed Gnostic Sophia, the Jewish Wisdom is depicted as having helped create the world and favoring humankind. Hokhmah, however, stays with Israel, her rightful home, whereas the Gnostic Sophia seeks to return to the highest heaven, the dwelling of the true God. In some Gnostic cosmologies, her "creation" of the world is shown as a terrible mistake that only Christ, her partner, can remedy by showing her as well as human souls how to escape it.

The parallels between Sophia and Hokhmah, however, have led some scholars to see Jewish roots in Gnosticism: In George MacRae's words, "some kind of (no doubt perverse) use of the Jewish Wisdom figure lies at the source of the Gnostic myth."

As Saint Sophia, divine wisdom was personified and canonized by the Eastern churches. The most famous church dedicated to her was Hagia Sophia (St. Sophia), built during the 530s in Constantinople, capital of the Byzantine (Eastern Roman) Empire (330–1453), and later converted to a Muslim mosque after the Turkish conquest of 1453. The large domed building, which influenced mosque design throughout the Ottoman Turkish Empire, was converted by the Turkish government into a museum in 1937.

Furthermore, by divinizing Sophia, the Hebrews may have perpetuated something of earlier Pagan pantheons, which paired a male god with a divine spouse; some early Hebrew inscriptions speak of "the Lord and his Ashera," the latter being a Canaanite goddess of war, love, and fertility. Replacing Ashera (or Ishtar or Astarte) with Sophia permitted the Middle Eastern great goddess to keep a toehold in Judaism. Indeed, in *Thunder, Perfect Mind,* among the *NAG HAMMADI* manuscripts striking for its absence of overtly Christian language, the speaker—evidently Sophia—speaks at one point in language reminiscent of a hymn to *ISIS*:

Why have you hated me, you Greeks?
Because I am a barbarian among
   [the] barbarians?
For I am the wisdom of [the] Greeks
and the knowledge of [the] barbarians.
I am the judgment of [the] Greeks
   and of the barbarians.
[I] am the one whose image is great in Egypt
and the one who has no image
   among the barbarians.

Other Gnostic writings combined the story of Sophia with that of Christ the redeemer. Different versions vary, but typically Sophia was one of the last of the heavenly beings created (or emanated). Through her pride (in Greek, *hubris*) or wantonness, she falls into the material cosmos. In some variations, she creates the *DEMIURGE,* but in others she fights him, struggling to return to her heavenly home. By some accounts, her emotions during this struggle (referred to as the passion of Sophia) took material form and became the material world, described disparagingly as an abortion or an incomplete creation. Ultimately she is saved by Christ as the prototype of all human souls.

The idea of Sophia/Wisdom separated from God and offering humanity its only consolation before the arrival of the Gnostic Christ may underlie some initial verses in the Gnostic Gospel of Philip: "Ever since Christ came the world is created, the cities adored, the dead carried out. When we were Hebrews we were orphans and had only our mother [Sophia?], but when we became Christians we had both father and mother."

Later, the Gospel of Philip evidently identifies Sophia with the Holy Spirit, for the author denounces the story of Jesus's virgin birth, arguing, "Some said, 'Mary conceived by the Holy Spirit.' They are in error. They do not know what they are saying. When did a woman ever conceive by a woman?"

Sophia was generally ignored by the Western church, which focused on the Virgin Mary as accumulator of the qualities formerly ascribed to Isis and other goddesses worshiped in the Roman Empire. In the seventeenth century, however, the German mystic Jakob Boehme and followers of pietist movements reacknowledged her, returning to the idea that a man must discover and unite with his inner Sophia, an idea echoing both the Gnostic ritual of the bridal chamber and the Jungian concept of the anima.

She continued to be honored in the Eastern churches; for example, to the influential Russian mystic Vladimir Solov'ev (1853–1900), she personified variously divine wisdom, the body of God, the universal church, the bride of Christ, and active love for the world and humanity.

In recent years, Sophia has received renewed attention among some Western Christians for her feminine image of divinity. For example, in the early 1990s, two United Methodist pastors proposed experimental Bible readings that replaced Jesus's name in passages about the crucifixion with Sophia's, thus returning to the idea of the passion of Sophia—her

Sophia, the goddess Heresy, depicted as an allegorical figure of only superficial beauty. (From a handbill designed by the sixteenth-century German artist Anton Eisen.)

attempt to extricate herself from the material world and be reunited with God.

Spanish Inquisition

See *INQUISITION; TORQUEMADA.*

Subordinationism

Not a specific movement, subordinationism stands as a general term for any doctrine that, in attempting to deal with the problem of explaining the Trinity, subordinates the Son and/or the Holy Spirit to the Father. For example, the Arians (see *ARIANISM*) saw Christ as created by and after the Father, but the Patripassians (see *PATRIPASSIANISM*) believed that the Father suffered through the crucifixion of the Son. For other approaches see *MODALISM; MONARCHIANISM.*

Taborites   See *HUS, JAN.*

Tanchelm   One of a series of reformers who tried to purify the medieval Catholic church and were labeled heretics, Tanchelm was born in the late eleventh century in the Low Countries, probably in what is today the Netherlands. Possibly a monk, he was recorded as living in the court of Count Robert of Flanders around 1109, where he aided the count in an unsuccessful scheme to redraw some diocesan boundaries. This maneuvering had to do with a power struggle between Count Robert's ally, Louis VI of France, and the current head of the Holy Roman Empire (chiefly a German empire), Henry V.

After the count's death, Tanchelm became an unauthorized preacher, traveling through Flanders (an area chiefly within present-day Belgium) between 1111 and his death in 1115. During those four years, he and his growing number of followers were perceived as such a threat by the clergy that he was murdered by a Catholic priest after one of his outdoor sermons. (He was, of course, not permitted to preach in the churches.)

Although no connection has been demonstrated between Tanchelm and the *ALBIGENSIAN* heretics far to the south, the similarity of some of their teachings indicates the same type of would-be reforms and purification of the church that cropped up again and again through these centuries. Tanchelm is said to have rejected the importance of the sacraments, saying (as did many others labeled heretics) that when the bread and wine were consecrated by a sinful priest, no valid Eucharist could be celebrated. Equally as threatening was his telling the people not to pay their tithes, thus undercutting a significant source of church funds.

The influence of his doctrines among the Flemish people and some clergy continued to cause ecclesiastical alarm for some years. Chroniclers wove fantastic stories—discounted by modern historians—about his thousands of bodyguards, his promiscuous sexual habits, his luxurious clothing, and so forth. He may indeed have encouraged a cult of personality; considering how the Middle Ages venerated saints' relics, the story in one account that his followers would solemnly drink his bathwater is almost believable; as is the notion that his followers gave him large gifts of money. That he also had intercourse with virgin girls in front of their mothers sounds more like propaganda.

A generation later, *EUDO DE STELLA* would follow a similar but more violent course until he was halted and some of his followers executed.

Tarot   Perhaps because its origins are genuinely mysterious, the Tarot deck has been connected with various heresies, particularly the *ALBIGENSIANS*, the *WALDENSIANS*, and the *GUGLIEMITES*. One reason may be that traditional interpretations of some cards' meanings suggest a dualistic outlook among the Tarot's originators. For example, the Devil card is usually interpreted as "bondage to the material world," and various dualistic heretics have considered the Christian devil the creator of the material world (see *DUALISM*). In addition, the card of the Female Pope (or Pope Joan), also called the High Priestess in nineteenth- and twentieth-century packs, is seen as symbolizing spiritual *gnosis,* whereas the Pope card stands for oppressive orthodoxy.

The Tarot combines the usual 52 playing cards with four more court cards—the knights—for a total of 56, then adds 22 distinct picture cards, also called the trumps, triumphs, or keys. This second group is frequently called the Major Arcana (Big Secrets) by occultists; the other cards are the Minor Arcana. One question that has vexed historians is whether the two groups of cards developed separately or together; at the present time, informed opinion suggests that the four suits of the Minor Arcana originated in the Islamic world, perhaps in the Muslim kingdoms of northern India or Egypt, and the Major Arcana took shape in Europe. Most Tarot decks known today, however, were "improved" by a series of nineteenth-century occultists.

Aside from the numbered trump cards of the Pope, the Last Judgment, and the Devil, the Tarot seems superficially devoid of Christian imagery. There are no Father, Son, or Holy Spirit, no saints, and no sacraments. Instead, the cards show a mixture of secular rulers (and in some decks, peasants and artisans), abstractions such as Justice and Temperance, and cosmic symbols such as the Sun and the Moon. Because of this, esoteric writers have fancifully placed the Tarot's origin in ancient Egypt or even further away—35,000 years ago in the mythical lands of Atlantis and Mu. Another cherished legend tells that in about 1200 a group of leading Arab occult philosophers met in the Moroccan city of Fez and decided to condense all their wisdom into a set of pictures. The ignorant masses would use these for card games and thus ensure their survival until worthy students of the future could absorb their true meanings.

However, references to games and gambling from Classical Roman, early Christian, and medieval Christian sources do not mention card games, and when it came to denouncing popular gambling games, the Christian polemicists rarely missed a trick. Furthermore, the fourteenth-century Arabian Nights and various early Sanskrit manuscripts on sports and games fail to mention playing cards. The prolific fourteenth-century poet and biographer Francesco Petrarch (or Petrarca), who lived from 1304 to 1374 in northern Italy and southern France, wrote a treatise on gambling without mentioning cards. But it may be significant that his last important work was a long allegorical poem called *I Trionfi* (the triumphs, or trumps).

The triumphs Petrarch celebrated are those of Love, *CHASTITY*, Death, Fame, Time, and Eternity, each one having its successive influence on the life of the ideal man. They do not exactly parallel Tarot trumps, but with slight effort could be equated with them, especially as the card called the Lovers in modern decks has also been drawn as Love. (The other trumps might be Temperance, Death, the Wheel of Fortune, and the World, depending on how one reads them.) More important, this work of the mid-1300s shows how one of the leading Italian literary artists of the time was wedded to the notion of allegory, and the greater trumps themselves are all allegories.

Petrarch himself survived one of the watershed events of European history, an event that left its mark on the Tarot: the Black Death. Between the years 1347 and 1351, most areas suffered one or more outbreaks of bubonic plague, a fast-acting bacterial disease spread by flea bites, droplets of saliva from infected persons, and, in some cases, direct contact between mucous membranes and contaminated body parts such as the fingers. Its nickname came from the purplish-black appearance of many victims after their deaths from respiratory failure.

Unable to understand where the plague came from or how it spread, Europeans frequently reacted in one of two ways. They became convinced that it was God's punishment for their sins, or they decided that since life was increasingly uncertain, they would enjoy themselves while they could. The first reaction produced a new kind of religious theater, and the second encouraged gambling and other pleasures. Under the influence of recurring waves of bubonic plague, a street sermon was developed on the theme of Death the Leveler. Groups of the faithful would enact the danse macabre (also used as the theme for woodcuts and paintings), showing Death leading away representatives of all classes of society: sturdy farmers, young mothers, proud knights, humble monks, wealthy bishops, and so on. Presentations might also include sermons urging repentance (see *FLAGELLANT SECTS*). The plague of 600 years ago gave us the image of Death as a grinning skeleton, wielding his scythe to harvest a field of body parts, the image seen on the thirteenth trump card of most traditional Tarot decks.

The image of the Death trump firmly anchors the Tarot in a definite historical past. It is in the post-plague decades that references to cards began to appear in European documents. Written sermons and city laws forbidding card playing on moral grounds began to appear in the late 1300s. One famous denunciation of playing cards that supposedly gave "a picture of the world" is attributed to Johannes von Rheinfelden, a German monk writing about 1377. Unfortunately, evidence for the date is shaky; the monk's sermon may have been written later. But cards are mentioned negatively in a Parisian decree of 1397, a Bernese legal document of 1367, and a Florentine decree of 1376.

It is not always possible to tell whether the cards denounced are the 52-card deck, the 56-card deck, or the trumps. These documents, however, predate the arrival of the Gypsies in Western Europe, and they do not mention the cards in any Gypsy connection. Most likely some medieval Gypsies practiced palmistry or other forms of fortune-telling, but the evidence suggests that they first encountered cards in Europe and adopted them rather than introducing them from their homeland.

A likely candidate for the place where the Major and Minor Trumps were combined was the ducal court of Este in Ferrara, a city near Bologna in northern Italy. The Este family's Renaissance court was noted for its love of literature and learning; one duke founded the University of Ferrara in 1391.

The original Italian trumps had a less esoteric flavor than those in many modern decks. What they suggest, rather, is the mixed mental universe of an educated upper-class person of the time: part Christian, part secular European, and partly flavored by the stirrings of interest in Classical Greece and Rome that gave the Renaissance its name. Consequently they contain religions notions (Death the Leveler, the Last Judgment) flavored by the medieval concern for the afterlife; secular rulers such as the Emperor and the Empress; astrology in the personified Sun and Moon; and the classical Pagan virtues of Strength, Temperance, and Justice.

The trump of the Female Pope, mentioned above, has also been identified with Sister Manfreda, a relative of the Visconti and Sforza families, Milanese aristocrats who commissioned one of the oldest surviving Tarot decks around 1450. Manfreda is said to have been elected pope by *GUGLIELMITE* heretics and burned at the stake around 1300. (These here-

tics followed *JOACHIM OF FLORIS*'s teaching that a new age of the Holy Spirit was at hand and believed that Manfreda incarnated the Holy Spirit.) Her presence in the deck was particularly infuriating to the heretic-hunting Dominicans, who denounced the cards in the 1400s.

In the mid or late 1300s, someone, whether in Ferrara, Milan, or elsewhere, was indeed trying to put "the world" into a deck of cards—a world of language, symbols, and bits and pieces of Christianity, *NEOPLATONISM*, and popular outlook. Most likely this person (or persons) was either a layperson or a rather worldly cleric who viewed the world in a philosophical and literary way—conscious of allegory, not impious, but no longer orthodox in the medieval way either.

Somehow the greater trumps became melded with the Minor Arcana. In Europe this was codified into a fourfold division (although some non-European decks had five suits, for example). That fourfold division reflected the exceedingly ancient Indo-European division of society into priests, warrior aristocrats, and stockbreeders/farmers, to which was added the newer class of merchants. In modern Tarot card terms, these are swords (aristocrats), cups (priests), wands (farmers), and coins (merchants).

Templars   See *KNIGHTS TEMPLAR*.

Tertullian   Born in the Roman colonial city of Carthage (in present-day Libya), Quintus Septimus Florens Tertullianus was the son of a Roman centurion and lived from approximately 155 to 222. He became a lawyer and later one of the most influential Christian theologians. Sometime between 190 and 195, Tertullian became a Christian while living in Rome; around 207, having returned to Carthage and become a presbyter (leader of a congregation, priest), he joined the Montanist (see *MONTANISM*) or New Prophecy sect, which was later declared heretical.

Shortly after his initial conversion, Tertullian drew upon his legal training to write the *Apologeticus* (Defense of Christianity), which defended Christians against charges of cannibalism, sexual promiscuity, and other slanders and argued that the persecution of Christians was illegal under Roman law. Yes, Christian congregations collect money from their members, he wrote, but "no one is compelled and the offering is voluntary. This is as it were the deposit fund of kindness. For we do not pay out money from this fund to spend on feasts or drinking parties or inelegant 'blow-outs,' but to pay for the nourishment and burial of the poor, to support boys and girls who are orphan and destitute [and other people in dire financial straits]. . . . You jeer at our humble meals as being extravagant as well as infamously criminal. . . . The name of the feast explains the reason for it; it is called by the Greek name for love [*agape*]. . . . Before reclining they taste first of prayer to God; enough is eaten to satisfy hunger; as much is drunk as befits the temperate." Christians were everywhere in Roman society, he wrote: "We sail with you, we serve in the army with you, and till the ground with you." (Later, however, Tertullian would write that no Christian should serve in the Roman legions: "There is no congruity between . . . the standard of Christ and the standard of the devil, the camp of light and the camp of darkness . . . the Lord in disarming Peter unbelted every soldier from that time forth.")

Despite his Montanist affiliation, Tertullian remains an influential early Christian writer today. He vigorously defended Christianity against Pagan and Jewish critics as well as attacked other heresies. As part of the ongoing debate over the nature of Christ, he began to develop the concept of the Trinity, that God was both unified and yet three persons: Father, Son, and Holy Spirit.

Tertullian's work is especially significant in Catholic church history for being written in Latin, the language of the Western Roman Empire, rather than in Greek. In his writing he frequently borrowed Roman legal terms, giving his theology a legalistic character. His major works included *Apologeticus* and also *De Praescriptione Hereticorum,* which argues that the church has authority to declare what is orthodox and what is heresy. Other works urged his fellow Christians to live modestly, avoid second marriages, shun the Roman theater and gladiatorial matches, dress simply, and fast often.

Tertullian's ascetic tendencies may have helped move him in the direction of the Montanists, who combined asceticism with a belief that new prophecies and teachings were still being revealed to the faithful. After becoming a Montanist, he turned his vigorous literary skills to criticizing orthodox Christians for failing to meet the standards he set forth.

Torquemada, Tomás de   Born in the year 1420, Tomás de Torquemada entered the Dominican order and rose to become prior of a monastery in Segovia. While prior, he gained the assistance of King Ferdinand and Queen Isabella in securing papal appointment as the *INQUISITION*'s leading officer in Spain, the grand inquisitor for the kingdoms of Castille and Aragón, in 1483. His conduct caused his name to become a byword for cruelty.

Although the Inquisition had operated in Christian-controlled areas of Spain (particularly the kingdom of Aragón) for several centuries, Torquemada's appointment coincided with its restructuring into a separate organization under royal rather than papal control. It had its own ministry, el Consejo de la Suprema y General Inquisición, its own courts, and its own prisons, all operated in an atmosphere of total secrecy. As the Spanish Empire grew, the Spanish Inquisition's jurisdiction grew as well, until it extended from Spain to Mexico, Peru, and the Philippines. Its mission was to guard Spanish Catholicism from all corruption by mystics (*alumbrados,* or illuminated ones), Jews, or Muslims who only feigned conversion but practiced their religion in secret, other heretics, and eventually also Protestants.

As first head of this regenerated Spanish Inquisition, which exceeded any of its counterparts in other countries in power and in secrecy, Torquemada, who died in 1498, commenced one of the darker chapters of the long history of the Roman Catholic church. Although he was not personally accused of corruption, the austere and rigid character he passed on to the Inquisition would come to horrify outside observers.

The Spanish Inquisition was suppressed by French military authorities after Napoleon I's conquest of Spain in 1808. It was revived briefly by a subsequent royal Spanish government, then it was permanently shut down in 1834.

Valentinus An Egyptian-born poet and religious leader who traveled to Rome in about 140 and later lived in Cyprus, Valentinus (or Valentine) was the progenitor of an important school of *GNOSTIC* Christians. A significant difference between Valentinian Gnostics and orthodox Christians is that the former group—perhaps influenced by their teacher's love of literature—believed that anyone who had received the illumination, or *gnosis,* should demonstrate it by producing written works of prophecy, accounts of their religious visions, or other creations such as poems or dialogs between the Gnostic Christian and Christ, who was seen as the offspring of *SOPHIA,* or Divine Wisdom. Sometimes their titles indicated that they were "in the spirit" of *MARY MAGDALENE* or one of the apostles. Valentinians often considered these works to be as important as the gospels and epistles shared with all Christians.

Valentinus, who may have been a Christian presbyter (elder or priest) and possibly a bishop, was, according to some accounts, candidate for the bishopric of Rome, which in his time had not yet evolved into the powerful papacy it later became. The theologian *TERTULLIAN,* writing much later, said that Valentinus's bitterness after losing the election precipitated his heresy, but this is doubtful. Neither Valentinus nor his followers withdrew from the catholic church; if anything, the Valentinians were forced out by increasingly strict definitions of orthodoxy. Tertullian also said Valentinus was acquainted with the theologian *ORIGEN*—both were Alexandrians.

Following upon the work of such Gnostic leaders as *BASILIDES,* Valentinus offered a form of Christianity in which Christ came to offer truth and spiritual health that was lost in the material world, a world created by an inferior deity. Neither the piling up of material goods nor the emotional and moral life of the psyche, or soul, offered steps to salvation, but only knowledge of the spirit's ultimate union with a higher realm. Even the average Christian mistook images of a heavenly ruler or judge for the true God, the indescribable source of the universe.

Between that source and this world Valentinus described a series of eternal principles, removed in degrees of logic but not in chronological time from God. These principles, totalities, or aeons, were described in pairs; together they made up the fullness or *pleroma* of the godhead. In the words of the Valentinian author of *The Tripartite Tractate,* one of the Gnostic texts from *NAG HAMMADI,* "The emanation of the Totalities, which exist from the one who exists, did not occur according to a separation from one another, as something cast off from the one who begets them. Rather, their begetting is like a process of extension, as the Father extends himself to those he loves, so that those who have come forth from him might become him as well." The first group of aeons—known from the Greek word for "eight" as the Ogoad— are Depth, Silence, Mind, Truth, Word, Life, Man, and Church. Of the last, *The Tripartite Tractate* says, "The Church, too, existed from the beginning. . . . it is the Church consisting of many men that existed before the aeons, which is called, in the proper sense, the 'aeons of the aeons.'"

Two more groups of aeons proceeded from the Ogoad: the Decad (ten) and the Dodecad (twelve). Last of the Dodecad was Wisdom, *SOPHIA,* who, frustrated in her attempt to know the Father, produced an amorphous substance later referred to as the "abortion." From her grief over this imperfect creation was born the *DEMIURGE,* the false God of Israel, who made this world and whom humans falsely worship. Sophia's action so upset the harmony of the aeons that Mind brought forth several more, including Christ, Holy Spirit, the angels, and Jesus; comforted by these, Sophia brought forth the pneumatic or spiritual race, those capable of learning the truth about the material universe.

Of all Gnostic theologians, Valentinus represented the greatest threat to the catholic church: The apparent similarity of portions of his teaching to orthodoxy motivated *IRENAEUS* to write his *Adversus Haereses,* the "refutation of Gnosis, falsely so-called." Among the other church fathers, Jerome (circa 340–420) admitted that Valentinus possessed an outstanding and God-given intellect, and *TERTULLIAN,*

coming a generation later, cited Valentinus's eloquence—high praise from a lawyer. Under the pressures of orthodoxy and heresy hunting, Valentinian Gnosticism apparently died out in the late fourth century. The Nag Hammadi collection of books, many of them of Valentinian origin, were hidden away and forgotten about the same time.

Vaudois   Literally meaning *WALDENSIAN,* the French term *Vaudois* was also applied in the late Middle Ages to alleged witches. When the *INQUISITION* began to persecute *WITCH-CRAFT* as heresy in the fifteenth century, the term was often misleadingly applied to the accused, just as earlier heretics were called Manichaeans (see *MANI*) even though they had no direct connection with that religion.

Waldensians Unlike many medieval attempts to return to a "purer" form of Christianity, the Waldensian movement was not started by a priest or monk, but by a layman. Its founder, Peter Waldo (Valdes or Waldes in some spellings, also Latinized as Petrus Waldus), did not envision a monastic order as did Francis of Assisi (see *FRANCISCANS*). Instead, he sought to lead other laypeople to the Gospels, which were then available only in Latin or Greek and consequently had to be translated and explained by the clergy.

A rich merchant in the Rhône Valley city of Lyons, Peter Waldo was born some time in the mid–twelfth century. (Some authorities are not certain whether his given name was indeed Peter or whether that name was added by followers comparing him to the apostle.) Around 1170 he experienced a spiritual crisis, becoming convinced that his prosperity had been gained at the expense of his soul; for instance, he had loaned money out at interest—a practice that the Catholic church at the time condemned as usury. (Medieval interest rates were quite

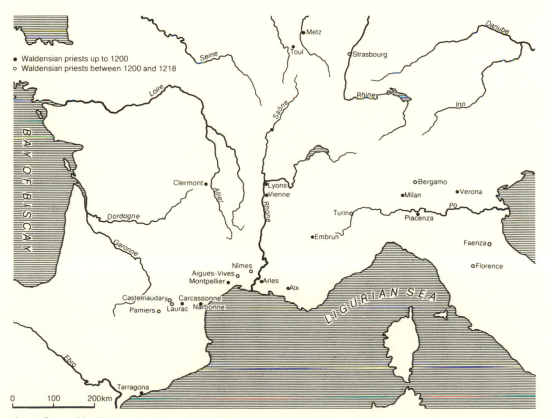

Areas first influenced by Waldensian ideas (1177–1218). (Map by Matthias Weis, reprinted, by permission of the publisher, from Erbstösser, Heretics in the Middle Ages, Edition Leipzig, 1984.)

high by modern standards, but so were the risks for lenders.) According to some accounts, he was inspired by hearing a storyteller recount the story of St. Alexis and his wife, who on their wedding day agreed to live celibately and to give all their possessions to the poor.

Because he could not read Latin, Waldo could not study the Bible for himself, but he could afford to pay two priests to translate parts of the New Testament into the French of his day. When Waldo had his translations, he read and reread them. Eventually he decided that his prosperous life was incompatible with true Christianity; he gave away his money, and declared that he would become a wandering preacher, following the *vita apostolica* ("apostolic life"), the wandering life of Jesus and his disciples. Waldo's wife, not ready to take so radical a step, complained to the archbishop of Lyons, who forbade Waldo to preach without

authorization. Waldo, however, would not be swayed. He offered his real estate and other property to his wife, rather than selling them and giving the proceeds to the poor; and, abandoning home and family, he gathered followers—people impressed by his simple, vernacular presentation of the Gospels and by his own personal commitment to the "apostolic life."

The people who followed him were primarily poor people—hence the movement's alternate name, the Poor (Men) of Lyons—but Waldo did not turn his preaching into a rebellion against the rich and powerful. He sent his followers out two by two, as Jesus had sent his disciples, with instructions to preach and to beg for food and shelter.

Because Waldensian preachers and *AL-BIGENSIAN* "perfects" often traveled in pairs (both types being persecuted as heretics), the two movements are often confused, but they

Dispersal area of Waldensianism (13th–15th centuries)   Main centres of Waldensianism

Later spread of the Waldensian heresy (thirteenth–fifteenth centuries). (Map by Matthias Weis, reprinted, by permission of the publisher, from Erbstösser, Heretics in the Middle Ages, *Edition Leipzig, 1984.)*

were quite different. The Waldensians were attempting to lead what they saw as more moral, Christian lives; the Albigensians, while nominally Christian, significantly altered Catholic theology to their own ends.

Having been rebuffed by the archbishop, Waldo appealed to Pope Alexander III for authorization to preach, but he was turned down despite the pope's approval of his voluntary poverty. Some of his followers—and perhaps Waldo himself—visited Rome in 1179 during a major church council, seeking recognition and approval of their mission and of their translated Scriptures. A commission was appointed to consider their requests, but its members, church intellectuals, considered the Waldensians to be simple people, unfit to expound Christian doctrine. Walter Mapp, an English-born cleric, headed the commission and scornfully wrote, "Shall pearls, then, be cast before swine? Shall the Word be given to the ignorant, whom we know to be incapable of receiving it, much less of giving in their turn what they have received?" The Waldensians looked harmless, Mapp continued, with their "apostolic" poverty, but in fact, "they are making their first moves now in the humblest manner because they cannot launch an attack [on the church]. If we admit them, we shall be driven out."

Turned away by the pope, whom Catholics viewed as successor of the apostle Peter, Waldo brooded on Peter's words as reported in Acts 5: "We must obey God rather than men." He kept on preaching, and his followers spread throughout southern France, northern Italy, and eventually to countries beyond. If threatened, they disguised themselves as wandering craftsmen— "a cobbler or a barber or a harvester," as one Dominican monk described. Some Waldensians began to teach the same messages as other medieval reformers: that no sinful priest could celebrate the Eucharist or, variously, that any believer could consecrate the bread and wine as well as pronounce the absolution of sins. Unlike the Albigensians, however, Waldo's followers affirmed the humanity and physical suffering of Christ.

Waldo's defiance caused him to be summoned in 1180 by a church synod in Lyons. He affirmed his faith, but he and his followers were determined to continue their evangelizing with or without the approval they sought.

Waldensian preachers crisscrossed France and parts of Germany and northern Italy, reaching as far east as the present-day Czech Republic. Because they defied the ban on their preaching, Pope Lucius III condemned them; in the 1180s the Waldensians were excommunicated. Subsequently, many Waldensians were persecuted by the *INQUISITION,* an organization that grew up in the wake of the Albigensian Crusade.

The Waldensians who survived the persecution withdrew into the isolated alpine valleys of southeastern France and northern Italy. Gradually, a split developed between the Italian Waldensians in Lombardy and those in France, with the Lombards becoming settled in towns and the French Waldensians rejecting organization and maintaining a wandering life style. During the fifteenth century, Waldensians were again victims of the Inquisition. Some were reconverted to Catholicism. Others, after the Protestant Reformation, formed a small "reformed" church, of which a remnant continues to survive in northern Italy. See also entry for *CONRAD OF MARBURG.* For similar popular reform movements see the entries for *LOLLARDS* and *HUSSITES.*

Waldo, Peter   See *WALDENSIANS.*

Weavers   As an occupational group, medieval weavers were often considered to be heretics or potential heretics. Italian *CATHARS* were sometimes referred to as "weavers" in the thirteenth century, while weavers were also implicated in the spread of *WALDENSIAN* doctrines and later forms of Protestantism. The connection between the occupation of weaving and the spread of heresy might be explained in three ways. First, cloth merchants who traveled between Italy and the Byzantine Empire (making the last link of the long Silk Road between China and Western Europe) had been implicated as agents of heresy, carrying Eastern *DUALIST* and *BOGOMIL* doctrines, writings, and missionaries to the West. Such merchants would be in contact with clothiers who in turn retailed the Eastern goods to customers, including local weavers of wool and linen. Second, weavers were often itinerants who went wherever they could find work. While working, they had to sit still but could talk with each other, visitors, and customers over the sound of the hand-powered looms. Third, women, whether weavers or buyers of cloth, were frequently involved in heretical movements. The necessity of visiting weavers and clothiers in order to get the cloth needed for their families gave them opportunities to get together and pass on their heretical doctrines.

Witchcraft   More than any other heresy—for so the Catholic church considered it—medieval and Renaissance witchcraft has provoked a wide variety of incompatible explanations. Unlike the other heresies outlined in this volume, it was not a reinterpretation of Jesus's teaching, a new formulation of church doctrine, or a reform movement within Christianity. That being the case, we might ask why witchcraft was considered a heresy and not (as a few historians and also adherents of the revived "Old Religion" have insisted) a continuation of pre-Christian Pagan religion.

Witchcraft is also unique in that it is the one heresy whose very existence has been seriously questioned. While no one has ever seriously suggested that *MANICHAEANS, CATHARS,* or *ARIANS* did not exist, over the last three centuries many voices have suggested that the entire persecution of witches was based on mass delusion. According to these skeptics, no one ever attended a sabbat and worshiped the devil or tried to ruin a neighbor's crops through magic. The whole era of witchcraft persecution was nothing but a conjunction of religious mania, official greed, and the mental illness of a few confessed "witches."

One such skeptical historian, Rossell Hope Robbins, saw the entire persecution as a makework project for otherwise under-employed inquisitors who were running short of *WALDENSIANS* and *ALBIGENSIANS* to burn. He wrote that "with the work of the notorious inquisitor Bernardus Guidonis [Bernard Gui] from 1308 to 1323, the Albigensians and other heretics had been exterminated. . . . Witchcraft was in fact invented to fill the gap; the first trials for sorcery were held in Provençe [part of the former Albigensian territory]."

He quoted the inquisitor Eymeric de Campo (the same man who had attacked *RAYMOND OF TARREGA* for being too broad-minded about demons) as lamenting in 1375, "In our days,

there are no more rich heretics, so that princes, not seeing much money in prospect, will not put themselves to any expense; it is a pity that so salutary an institution as ours [in other words, the *INQUISITION*] should be so uncertain of its future."

Already inquisitors in the field had sought papal permission to prosecute sorcerers, despite the existence of church law embodied in the earlier *CANON EPISCOPI,* which stated that belief in the reality of witchcraft, not witchcraft itself, was heresy.

The destruction of the *KNIGHTS TEMPLAR,* Robbins added, had represented another attempt to broaden the definition of heresy. The combined attack in 1307 by French royal and inquisitorial power on the powerful military order had been designed not only to capture the Templars' vast wealth but also to erase what was viewed as a rival religious system. "The success of the extermination of the Templars set the pattern for the subsequent persecution of witches." (Other historians, however, do not view the Knights Templar as heretics, but as victims of a political and economic struggle.)

Bound by their view of the reality of the devil and evil spirits and desiring to keep their powerful jobs, greedy and corrupt inquisitors twisted Catholic doctrine to create a new heresy called Witchcraft, argued Robbins and the other skeptics. The Protestant Reformation brought no essential change in this trend—at most, a partial substitution of prosecutors' manuals from the Catholic *MALLEUS MALEFICARUM* to the *Demonologie* of King James I and other works by Protestants. (The *Malleus* remained good enough for many Protestant clergy and magistrates.)

Furthermore, witchcraft trials poisoned society, providing the perfect opportunity for settling private quarrels. Friedrich von Spee, a Jesuit who denounced the persecution of witches in the early 1600s, wrote that "if only the trials be steadily continued, nobody is safe, no matter of what sex, fortune, condition, or dignity, if any enemy or detractor wishes to bring a person under suspicion of witchcraft." In 1592, another disapproving priest, Cornelius Loos, commented on the businesslike atmosphere of witchcraft trials, where everything was itemized down to the cost of firewood: "Wretched creatures are compelled by the severity of the torture to confess things they have never done, and so by cruel butchery innocent lives are taken; and, by a new alchemy, gold and silver are coined from human blood."

Subsequent scholarship has demonstrated that some of the early witchcraft trials cited by Robbins and several others never took place; the records were forged by clever antiquarians in various cities due to a paradoxical desire to embellish local history. Nevertheless, the skeptical position held by him—and by such earlier historians as Henry Charles Lea, George Lincoln Burr, and many other authors in a line that stretches back to the eighteenth-century Enlightenment—remains popular and operates whenever we hear this phenomenon referred to as "the witchcraft delusion." The skeptical reaction to the witch trials is part of a larger reaction to the excesses of centuries of religious warfare, often expressed in a wholesale condemnation of all forms of organized religion except the most pacifist and benign. Burr, for instance, referred to the witchcraft phenomenon as "a shadow, a nightmare: the nightmare of a religion, the shadow of a dogma."

It has been argued that some of the skeptics overestimated human moral progress, having lived before the Nazi Holocaust and other horrors of the twentieth century, but Robbins, at least, published his monumental *Encyclopedia of Witchcraft and Demonology* after World War II.

An inquisitor's portrayal of witches worshiping the devil. (Courtesy of the Bodleian Library, University of Oxford. MS. Rawl. D. 410, fol. 1R.)

The Development of Witchcraft as Heresy

Whether the witchcraft that was persecuted from the late fourteenth through the early eighteenth centuries existed or not, its persecutors believed that it did, and they developed working definitions and procedures with which to attack it. Magic was considered to exist in two forms—"high magic" and "low magic" (in Latin, maleficia, or "evil-doing"). High magic was depicted symbolically in the *TAROT,* and it included the study of astrology, the mysticism of the Qabala, and ceremonial invocations based on the thinking of Neoplatonist mystics like *IAMBLICHUS.* Restricted mainly to educated men, many of them in holy orders, it rarely caused anyone to be sentenced to the stake. (The few exceptions such as GIORDANO BRUNO are thereby noteworthy.) Low magic, however, was equated with sorcery and favored by women. Through its powers one could cause or cure illness, bring lovers together (or keep them apart), change the weather, and so on. During the Roman Empire and also during the early Middle Ages, sorcerers were treated like any other criminals, if they were persecuted at all. Causing injury through magic was analogous with simple physical assault. In its views on low magic in particular the early medieval church maintained two paradoxical positions. It tacitly admitted that all magic involved the aid of demons, but it also held, based on the *Canon Episcopi* and other precedents, that the belief in witches flying through the air, for instance, was heretical.

While witchcraft persecutions were unknown during the early Middle Ages, the components were already being assembled. Even before the Christian era, Roman writers had accused followers of certain mystery cults of cannibalism, infanticide, and sexual orgies in darkened rooms; after Christianity arose, Pagan authors such as *CELSUS* charged them similarly. Christians would make similar accusations against the Gnostic followers of *CARPOCRATES* or *MARCUS*; the very term *BOGOMIL* became to Western Europeans a synonym for sodomist or homosexual (see *HOMOSEXUALITY*). In 1022 the heretics of *ORLÉANS* were accused not only of holding sexual orgies, sacrificing babies, and all the other clichés but also of worshiping the devil, who appeared as a black man or as an angel of light. Similar charges were leveled against the heretical preacher *TANCHELM* in the following century.

What drew all these beliefs together in the late Middle Ages and united them in a new "heresy" was the developing notion of the devil and his powers. Here it is hard to deny the influence of the Albigensians and other dualist heretics lumped together as "Cathars" ("pure ones"), if only at second hand. Before their near-eradication, these dualists had taught not merely that the devil was powerful in the material world but that he had created it. This belief can be contrasted with *AUGUSTINE*'s teaching that the devil was the greatest of the fallen angels, given a limited authority to tempt Christians and a greater power over non-Christians. In medieval people's minds his power grew; he could be anywhere, perceive their thoughts, and send his countless lesser demons to do his work. The Evil Principle had grown to the point where it threatened to equal the Good—in the Cathars' view, it owned the Roman Catholic church. (Hence a key dualist text was entitled *The Book of the Two Principles*.) Humans were spirits imprisoned in bodies created by this "counter-God."

As Jeffrey Burton Russell, a historian of heresy and witchcraft, wrote, "It was from the time the Catharists arrived in Western Europe [the mid–twelfth century] that concern with witchcraft greatly increased." While some would try to defeat the devil through moral perfection, Russell continues, is it unreasonable to suggest that as his perceived realm of influence grew, some people would worship him? If one accepted the Cathar identification of the devil with the God of the Old Testament, he continued, "but had been brought up as a Christian to worship that God, it would actually be consistent to worship the Devil. The mighty struggle between God and Satan impressed itself on many a mind, and some [witches] forgot that Catharism promised the ultimate victory of [the 'true'] God and hoped instead for the triumph of Satan."

So while not denying that the heresy of witchcraft was an intellectual creation of the inquisitors, Russell and those who follow him differ with the skeptics by suggesting that there were indeed some devil-worshipers to prosecute. They do not deny, however, that thousands of innocent persons were persecuted. The whole conflict played itself out in a time of social change—the break-up of the old, settled, feudal world in the wake of the Black Death, the rise of cities, and, finally, the rise of Protestantism, which broke down the categories and hierarchies that had sustained medieval life. Mixed with the persecution of actual diabolists was the arrest, torture, and execution of thousands of others who were merely victims and scapegoats for local animosity or larger-scale social change.

Animosity against the Jews also fed the witch mania. An account of heretics in about 1180 adoring the devil in the form of a black cat "of marvelous size" is the first to use the word *synagogue* for the heretics' meeting place. In the fifteenth century the term *witches' sabbat* became commonplace. (Margaret Murray, discussed below, attempted to argue that the similar word *esbat* had a different origin, but this is unlikely since it has the same etymological foundation as *sabbat*.) Jews were not identified with witches per se, but throughout the Middle Ages some of the same accusations of ritual murder and so forth were made against Jews. These people lived among Christians, but stubbornly and suspiciously refused to accept Christianity. A parallel was drawn between their closed meetings and those said to be held by the witches.

Whether or not an organized cult of witches existed, it was necessary both to define them and to find a way around the church law that, until the late Middle Ages, had defined witchcraft as a non-problem. In brief, the answer was to define thirteenth-century witchcraft as a new heresy. Historians in Russell's camp can support this notion by separating the "old" witchcraft—rags and tags of surviving Paganism and folk religion, such as the *Canon*

Episcopi's description of women who, "deluded by Satan," think they have ridden through the sky with the goddess Diana—from the "new" witchcraft, a more conscious diabolism of persons organized into "synagogues" and making pacts with the devil. To deliberately turn away from Christianity and toward the devil was reasoned to be a conscious choice—a heresy. Summing up his research, Russell suggested that the "chief individual components defined as witchcraft in the Classical period [fourteenth and fifteenth centuries] were: (1) those generally derived from sorcery (approximately 31 percent)—shapeshifting, riding or flying, cannibalism, child murder, the use of salves, familiars, invocations of demons, and the choice of night as the time for witch activities; (2) components generally derived from other folklore traditions (23 percent)—the goddess Diana, wild dances, the 'Good Society,' the wild man and the wild chase, incubi, and passing through closed doors or walls; (3) components deriving mainly from heresy (27 percent)—the definition of witchcraft as a sect, secret meetings, desecration of the Cross or sacraments, formal repudiation of church, synagoga, sex orgies, and feasting; (4) components added for the most part by theologians (19 percent)—pact, Devil's mark, worship of, sacrifice to, or homage to the Devil; the obscene kiss, and the sabbat."

Leapfrogging over the earlier canon law and secular legal codes that mandated mild punishments for witchcraft—such as the old Salic law code of the Franks, which required definite physical proof of an evil act—the witch-hunters could always turn to the Bible. Indeed, Protestant witch-hunters of the sixteenth and seventeenth centuries would not be bound by canon law but would take their guidance from such verses as the frequently mistranslated Exodus 22:18. King James I of England, author of *Demonologie,* preferred the words of the Bible translation he requested: "Thou shalt not suffer a witch to live." Reginald Scot, however, had already pointed out in 1584 in his book *The Discovery of Witchcraft* that the Hebrew word *kashaph* was better translated as "poisoner." Likewise, the "witch of Endor" consulted by King Saul in I Samuel was merely a spirit medium. The one reference to witchcraft in the King James version of the New Testament, Galatians 5:20, occurs where it is listed as a "work of the flesh" along with strife, murder, fornication, and so on. Ironically, the increasing use of vernacular translations of the Bible in Protestant lands made it easier for Protestants to justify their witch-burning scripturally. Both Catholics and later Protestants would follow the path laid down by a series of late medieval inquisitors who wrote manuals of witch-hunting.

In 1258 Pope Alexander IV issued a bull against magical practitioners. His successor, Pope John XXII, a man always worried about magical attacks on his life, ordered the Inquisition in southern France to prosecute sorcerers and magicians as heretics. He ordered inquisitors to "seek out and otherwise proceed against those who sacrifice to devils or worship them, or render homage to them, by giving them a charter or something else signed in their name; those who make an open avowed pact with the devils; those who fashion or cause to be fashioned any waxen image, or anything else to bind the devil, or by invocation of devils to commit any kind of maleficium; those who, by misusing the sacrament of baptism, baptize a figure of wax or one made of something else, or cause it to be baptized, or by invocation of devils make or cause anything similar to be done. . . . " Further bulls of the paranoid pope continued this theme: magic was a heresy and a crime against God; witches were real and were heretics.

The image of inquisitors sending convicted witches to the stake is lodged firmly in modern minds even though many witch trials took place after the Reformation (and hence outside the borders of this book). Historians favoring Catholicism or Protestantism still trade accusations over which branch of Christianity sent more accused witches to the stake or gallows: the Catholics in France, Italy, Spain, Poland, portions of the Netherlands, Switzerland, and Germany, and elsewhere; or the Protestants in their portions of those countries and in Sweden, Denmark, Scotland, England, and the American colonies. Herbert Thurston, a Jesuit historian, wrote that witch-burnings only began in Denmark and Transylvania after the Reformation. He noted that " . . . the Protestant states, which would have nothing to say even to Gregory XIII's urgently needed reform of the calendar, simply because it came from Rome, were foremost in employing torture and fire in the extirpation of witches. . . . the Reformers seem to have been more keen and cruel in the pursuit than the adherents of the ancient faith [Catholicism]" and that secular courts willingly carried on the persecution even in the absence of the Inquisition. On the other hand, Patrick Collinson, an English historian, stated flatly in a recent work that "Catholics burnt more witches than [did] Protestants."

A War against Women

A significant percentage—80 to 85 percent—of the people executed for witchcraft were women. In fact, no historian agrees on what the death toll was, but informed estimates usually range between 200,000 and 300,000 over three centuries. Gerald Gardner (see below) and other followers of the new religion called Witchcraft (or Wicca) have used a figure of 9 million, an exaggeration, considering European populations at the time, that was more likely designed to gain attention by inflating the number of witch-hunt victims to a total larger than that of the Nazi Holocaust, whose death toll is usually rounded off at 6 million.

When one reads, for instance, the denunciation of midwives in the *Malleus Maleficarum,* it comes as no surprise that the persecutions are also viewed as a reaction by a male-dominated church against women, old women in particular. Although some of the victims were pre-teen girls, and artists such as Albrecht Dürer would portray some witches as attractive, young women, the overwhelming image of the witch to this day is the hag—the woman who is no longer sexually desirable, past menopause, and no longer defined by her roles as wife or mother. Indeed, one of the reasons that the sixteenth-century writer Reginald Scot took a skeptical view of witchcraft was that the so-called witches had failed to make themselves young and beautiful through magic or pacts with the devil. He reasoned that since any woman would desire to be beautiful, the whole apparatus of devil-worship must be a sham.

The witch-craze also coincided with a new professional attitude among male doctors, one based more on theoretical training in the university than on bedside practice. (The famous fifteenth-century physician Paracelsus would outrage the university-based medical establishment by inviting herbalists, barber-surgeons, and other non-academic healers to his lectures.) Thus, some historians see the medical establishment as abetting the witch-burnings because they eliminated competition. Historians Barbara Ehrenreich and Deirdre English wrote, "The wise woman, or witch, had a host of remedies which had been tested in years of use. . . . They used ergot for the pain of labor at a time when the church held that pain in labor was the Lord's just punishment for Eve's original sin. . . .

Fifteenth-century portrayal of witches raising a storm. (From Ulrich Molitor, De Lamiis, *1489.)*

Digitalis, still an important drug in treating heart ailments, is said to have been discovered by an English witch." The suppression of female healers by the medical profession was a class struggle aided by the church, they argued; for the *Malleus Maleficarum* was plain: "And if it is asked how it is possible to distinguish whether an illness is caused by witchcraft or by some natural physical defect, we answer that the first [way] is by means of the judgment of doctors."

In addition, the *Malleus* clearly laid out the inquisitors' belief that women should not control the outcome of their sexual activity: on the one hand they excited men's lust, on the other they procured abortions. Indeed, the attitudes of Catholic and Protestant clergy of the time toward sexuality are difficult to disentangle from their attitudes toward what they saw as witchcraft.

Despite the close association in the persecutors' minds of women and witchcraft, to argue only that "witch-hunting was woman-hunting," as some historians have done, ignores the fact that men were seized and executed too. While sexual attitudes undoubtedly played their part in the women's trials, the men's fates may more clearly display the witch-hunt's social and economic aspects since sexuality was not such an important factor when a man was tried.

Witchcraft and Hallucinogens

By the late 1400s, some European writers were beginning to suggest that the tales extracted from witches under torture of flying through the skies to grand convocations, having sexual intercourse with the devil or his representative, and so forth were actually hallucinations produced by psychoactive plants such as belladona, datura (Jimson weed), and others known since Classical times. According to the American anthropologist Michael Harner, who is an authority on the shamanic use of natural plant hallucinogens, the use of mind-altering plants in medieval witchcraft did not fit the traditional anthropological definition of shamanism—contacting the spirit world while in a trance for the benefit of the shaman's community—because the drugs used were too powerful to permit the witch to retain conscious control of the shamanic journey.

The suspicion that many of the activities described in the witch-trial accounts were based on drug experiences was raised as soon as the early fifteenth century. Johannes Nider, a Dominican theologian and author of the *Formicarius* (The Anthill), a book on witchcraft written around 1435, gave a typical second-hand account as follows:

> I heard my teacher give this account: a certain priest of our order entered a vil-

lage where he came upon a woman so out of her senses that she believed herself to be transported through the air during the night with Diana and other women [as described by the earlier *Canon Episcopi*]. When he attempted to remove this heresy from her by means of wholesome discourse, she steadfastly maintained her belief. The priest then asked her: "Allow me to be present when you depart on the next occasion." She answered: "I agree to it, and you will witness my departure in the presence (if you wish) of suitable witnesses." [When the priest arrived that day with two townsmen, they saw her act as follows.] The woman, having placed a large bowl, which was used for kneading dough, on top of a stool, stepped into the bowl and sat herself down. Then, rubbing ointment on herself to the accompaniment of magic incantations, she lay her head back and immediately fell asleep. With the labor of the devil she dreamed of Mistress Venus and other supersitions so vividly that, crying out with a shout and striking her hands about, she jarred the bowl in which she was sitting and, falling down from the stool, seriously injured herself about the head. As she lay there awakened, the priest cried out to her that she had not moved: "For Heaven's sake, where are you? You were not with Diana, and as will be attested by these present, you never left this bowl." Thus, by this act and by thoughtful exhortations he drew out this belief from her abominable soul.

A sixteenth-century physician quoted by Harner described finding a jar of ointment in the home of a couple accused of witchcraft in Lorraine. The jar contained hemlock, nightshade, henbane, and mandrake mixed with grease and had a heavy and offensive odor. As an experiment, the physician, Andrés Laguna, used it to annoint the insomniac wife of the public hangman of Metz. She was insensible for 36 hours, lying with her eyes open, and when Laguna finally awoke her, she said she had been "surrounded by all the pleasures and delights of the world." In particular, she said with a smile to her husband, she had been making love with a man "younger and better than you."

The ointment's original owners confessed their guilt under torture and met the usual fate. Even a dream of "riding with Diana" or attending the witches' sabbat still involved commerce with demons in the prosecutors' eyes.

Such plants as the ointment included, all members of the potato family (Solanaceae), do contain hallucinogenic compounds; indeed, some twentieth-century individuals who have experimented with "flying ointment" recipes have also dreamed of flying, wild dances, and similar subjects. These compounds can be absorbed through the skin, particularly through the mucus membranes or through cuts, insect bites, and other breaks in the skin. Their effects depend on dosage. For example, belladona in low doses can produce excitement and delirium; in larger doses it is deadly. Hemlock can produce similar symptoms; too large a dose causes overall motor paralysis and death from suffocation.

Because most of the traditional European hallucinogens (not forgetting fly agaric mushrooms) could be fatal, some sort of traditional wisdom would have had to have accompanied their preparation. Once made into an ointment, however, they could be used by any individual. Indeed, it seems that their use was widespread. Harner, following Margaret Murray (see below), speculates that European witches must have had two kinds of meetings, one for "business" (Murray's "esbat") and one that occurred only in a drug-assisted dream state (Murray's "sabbat"), the wild festival of dancing, feasting, and sexual encounters with human and demonic lovers described by the trial literature. An intriguing open question is who experimented with these hallucinogenic plants to learn the safe doses, and how was the information passed on?

Witchcraft as Surviving Paganism

The idea that witchcraft had nothing to do with worshiping the Christian devil but represented a surviving Pagan practice libeled by generations of inquisitors is most associated with Margaret Murray (1863–1963), a British archaeologist who wrote three books on this topic between 1921 and 1954. Murray had worked mainly in Egypt until World War I interrupted her and her colleagues' efforts. Back in England she became ill and decided to convalesce in Glastonbury, a town associated with the legend of the Holy Grail:

> One cannot stay in Glastonbury without becoming interested in Joseph of Arimathea and the Holy Grail. As soon as I got back to London I did a careful piece of research, which resulted in a paper on Egyptian Elements in the Grail Romance. . . . Someone, I forget who, had once told me that the Witches obviously had a special form of religion, "for they danced around a black goat." As ancient religion is my pet subject this seemed to be in my line and during all the rest of the war I worked on Witches. . . . I had started with the usual idea that the Witches were all old women suffering from illusions about the Devil and that their persecutors were wickedly prejudiced and perjured. I worked only from contemporary records, and when I suddenly realized that the so-called Devil was simply a disguised man I was startled, almost alarmed, by the way the recorded facts fell into place and showed that the Witches were members of an old and primitive form of religion, and the records had been made by members of a new and persecuting form.

Murray's work, although initially well received, came to be roundly criticized by folklorists and historians. She was asked to write the "Witchcraft" entry for one edition of the *Encyclopaedia Britannica,* but subsequent editions abandoned her ideas of the "Old Religion" struggling against Christianity. Nevertheless, her idea that some sort of fertility cult had survived Christianity has been echoed by scholars studying such varied regions as Rumania and Italy. One example of such a cult that is frequently cited is that of the Benandanti (good walkers), an agricultural brotherhood in Friuli in northeastern Italy whose members claimed that they battled against "the witches" in order to protect the crops. Under decades of interrogation and torture by the Inquisition, whose officials were convinced that the Benandanti were themselves witches, the Benandanti

A 1514 illustration, by the German artist Hans Baldung Grien, depicting the concoction of a hallucinogen, or "flying ointment."

accepted the inquisitors' definition of themselves as "devil-worshipers" and soon began to serve up descriptions of typical Satanic revels.

Concentrating on British, Irish, and northern French materials, Murray decided she had uncovered the worship of a male god, often represented with spreading stag's horns and known as Herne or Cernunnos (from the Latin for "the horned one"), but the witch-hunters, due to their bias, referred to him in their accounts as "the Devil." His image dates back centuries and was even carved in the stone ornamentation of medieval churches, while some contained his phallic image concealed within the main altar.

Murray further developed her hypothesis to claim that the Norman rulers of England from 1066 onward had all been secret Pagans who either died in ritual executions as Divine Victims for the good of the land and people (for instance, William Rufus's mysterious "hunting accident" in 1100) or found substitutes to die in their place, as Henry II selected his old friend, Thomas à Becket, the archbishop of Canterbury, in 1170. Murray even explained the events leading up to the execution of *JOAN OF ARC*—her apparent abandonment by the French prince she had aided so much and her switching between male and female dress—as part of Joan's acceptance of her role as Divine Victim.

While not generally accepted in academia, Murray's version of witchcraft was taken up in the 1930s and 1940s by people who claimed to be inheritors and lineal initiatory "descendents" of her supposed underground Western European Paganism. The most outspoken was Gerald Gardner (1884–1964), a retired British civil servant who claimed to have been initiated into

the Old Religion—also called Wicca—in 1939. Despite the subsequent spread of this avowedly Pagan and polytheistic religion in Europe, North America, and elsewhere, the evidence suggests that Gardner and his associates were more creators than inheritors.

Wycliffe, John   (also Wyclif, Wyclyf, or Wicliff)   An English priest and university professor who lived from about 1330 until 1384, John Wycliffe repudiated papal authority and oversaw the first complete translation of the Bible into English. His followers, who taught from this new English Bible, were known as *LOLLARDS;* the Lollard movement, however, surpassed and outlived Wycliffe. His writings were circulated in various European reformist circles and influenced the Bohemian religious rebel Jan *HUS* and later Martin Luther.

While at Oxford University during the 1370s, Wycliffe wrote a number of treatises suggesting that the king should control both the civil government and the church in England (similar to the doctrine later endorsed by Henry VIII when he broke with the Roman Catholic church). All churchmen, meanwhile, including the pope, should live in "apostolic poverty" with a minimum of money and possessions—here Wycliffe walked the same perilous path as did the more radical Spiritual *FRANCISCANS*.

His important works included *On the Office of the King* (1379) and *On the Power of the Pope* (1379), which said that Christ should be the head of the church and that any pope was, in effect, the Antichrist.

Wycliffe's ideas were endorsed initially by King Edward III and his son, Edward, Prince

John Wycliffe. (Copperplate engraving by Hendrik Hondius the Elder, from Staatliche Kunstsammlungen Dresden, Kupferstichkabinett.)

IOANNES WICLEFVS ANGLVS.

of Wales (known as "the Black Prince"), for the king was disputing whether he should pay a tribute owed to the pope when he would rather have put the money into the royal treasury to finance his interminable wars in France (the "Hundred Years' War"). King Edward appointed Wycliffe to help represent him at a meeting with papal representatives in 1375; nothing came of the conference, but Wycliffe's capable performance earned him considerable respect from the king's party.

He was condemned, however, by William Courtenay, bishop of London, and summoned in 1377 to account for his views before Courtenay and other bishops. This hearing broke up when one of Wycliffe's supporters, John of Gaunt, who was Prince Edward's younger brother and later duke of Lancaster, quarreled with Bishop Courtenay, whereupon Wycliffe and his party walked out.

Later that year Pope Gregory XI issued several bulls condemning Wycliffe as a heretic, but the English bishops refused to endorse the pope's condemnation for a combination of theological and political reasons. Some agreed with Wycliffe's views, while others were cowed by the vocal royal and popular support he received.

As the controversy progressed, Wycliffe repudiated the doctrine of "transubstantiation," or the real, physical presence of Christ in the Eucharistic bread and wine, although he was willing to say that Christ was "sacramentally" present. He accused the Roman Catholic hierarchy of corruption, extending his condemnation to the very Franciscan order that had been founded in an effort to purify Christianity.

While Wycliffe's views drove away some of his royal supporters, he continued to press them. In the late 1370s he began the work for which he is best known, preparing a translation of the Latin Bible into English, for he argued in *On the Truth of Holy Scripture* (1378), as would many later Protestants, that the Bible should be the church's sole authority and therefore all believers should be able to read it in their own languages. He did much of the translation himself, the rest being completed by his colleagues from Oxford University.

Wycliffe's translation was carried forth by the Lollards. He is generally credited with helping to organize this group of wandering preachers, but how much he did himself is not known. Regardless of the degree of his personal involvement, Wycliffe's views helped initiate the movement, and he in turn was blamed when some Lollard preachers advocated radical social changes.

When the archbishop of Canterbury, the head of the Catholic church in England, was murdered during the Peasants' Revolt (Wat Tyler's Rebellion) of 1381, Wycliffe's old enemy William Courtenay was made archbishop. In 1382 he convened an ecclesiastical court to pass judgment on Wycliffe's ideas. The court of bishops and theologians met in London and condemned ten propositions taken from the reformer's works. Courtenay then forced Wycliffe's supporters at Oxford to disavow him.

Wycliffe left the university and retired to Lutterworth, Leicestershire, where he had held a living as parish priest while studying and teaching at Oxford. (For centuries, it was common for an absentee parish priest to collect the post's tax income, keep some of it, and use part to pay a vicar to actually fill the position.) Here he died from a stroke in 1384.

The influence of Wycliffe's writings and Bible translation outlived him and so goaded the church hierarchy that he was again condemned as a heretic in 1415 by the Council of Constance, the same body that condemned Jan Hus in 1414. The council ordered that Wycliffe's body be dug up and ceremoniously burnt. Eventually, at the prodding of Pope Martin V, this action was carried out in 1428.

BIBLIOGRAPHY

Amidon, Philip R., ed. *The Panarion of St. Epiphanius, Bishop of Salamis*. New York: Oxford University Press, 1990.

Anonymous. *A Short History of the Inquisition*. New York: Truth Seeker Co., 1907.

Aston, Margaret. *The Fifteenth Century*. New York: W. W. Norton, 1968.

Augustine. *Confessions*. Harmondsworth, Middlesex: Penguin Books, 1961.

Baigent, Michael, Richard Leigh, and Henry Lincoln. *Holy Blood, Holy Grail*. New York: Delacorte Press, 1983.

Bauer, Walter. *Orthodoxy and Heresy in Earliest Christianity*. Philadelphia: Fortress Press, 1934, 1971.

Bettenson, Henry, ed. *The Early Christian Fathers*. London: Oxford University Press, 1956.

Bigg, C. *Neoplatonism. Chief Ancient Philosophies*. London: Society for Promoting Christian Knowledge, 1895.

Brown, Harold O. J. *Heresies: The Image of Christ in the Mirror of Heresy and Orthodoxy from the Apostles to the Present*. Garden City, New York: Doubleday, 1984.

Burman, Edward. *The Inquisition: The Hammer of Heresy*. Wellingborough, Northamptonshire: Aquarian, 1984.

Chadwick, Henry. *Augustine*. Oxford: Oxford University Press, 1986.

Chuvin, Pierre. *A Chronicle of the Last Pagans*. Cambridge, Massachusetts: Harvard University Press, 1990.

Cohn, Norman. *Europe's Inner Demons: An Enquiry Inspired by the Great Witch-Hunt*. New York: Basic Books, 1975.

Collinson, Patrick. "The Late Medieval Church and Its Reformation: 1400–1600." *The Oxford Illustrated History of Christianity*. Edited by John McManners. Oxford: Oxford University Press, 1990.

Cooper-Oakley, Isabel. *Mason and Medieval Mysticism*. London: Theosophical Publishing House, 1977.

Coulton, G. G., ed. *Life in the Middle Ages*. New York: Macmillan, 1931.

Cristiani, Msgr. León. *Heresies & Heretics. Twentieth Century Encyclopedia of Catholicism*. New York: Hawthorn Books, 1959.

Currer-Briggs, Noel. *The Shroud and the Grail*. New York: St. Martin's Press, 1987.

Dart, John. *The Jesus of Heresy and History*. San Francisco: Harper & Row, 1988.

de Rougemont, Denis. *Love in the Western World*. New York: Harcourt, Brace & Co., 1940.

Ehrenreich, Barbara, and Deirdre English. *Witches, Midwives, and Nurses*. Old Westbury, New York: Feminist Press, 1973.

Eliade, Mircea. *A History of Religious Ideas*. 3 vols. Chicago: University of Chicago Press, 1978, 1982, 1985.

Erbstösser, Martin. *Heretics in the Middle Ages*. Leipzig: Edition Leipzig, 1984.

Fox, Robin Lane. *Pagans and Christians*. New York: Alfred A. Knopf, 1987.

Godwin, Joscelyn. *Mystery Religions in the Ancient World*. San Francisco: Harper & Row, 1981.

Grant, R. M. *Gnosticism and Early Christianity.* New York: Columbia University Press, 1966.

Guillaumont, A., et al., eds. *The Gospel According to Thomas.* New York: Harper & Row, 1959.

Harner, Michael J., ed. *Hallucinogens and Shamanism.* New York: Oxford University Press, 1973.

Heer, Friedrich. *The Medieval World: Europe 1100–1350.* New York: New American Library, 1961.

Hoeller, Stephan A. "Sophia: The Gnostic Archetype of Soul-Wisdom." *The Goddess Re-Awakening.* Edited by Shirley Nicholson. Wheaton, Illinois: Quest Books, 1989.

Hoyt, Charles Alva. *Witchcraft.* 2d ed. Carbondale, Illinois: Southern Illinois University Press, 1989.

Jonas, Hans. *The Gnostic Religion.* 2d ed. Boston: Beacon Press, 1958, 1963.

Jung, Carl G. *Aion: Researches into the Phenomenology of the Self. The Collected Works of C. G. Jung.* 2d ed. Edited by Sir Herbert Read, M. D. Michael Fordham, Gerhard Adler, and William McGuire. Princeton, New Jersey: Princeton University Press, 1968 (originally published 1959).

———. *Memories, Dreams, Reflections.* New York: Random House, 1963.

Kraemer, Ross S., ed. *Maenads, Martyrs, Matrons, and Monastics: A Sourcebook of Women's Religions in the Greco-Roman World.* Philadelphia: Fortress Press, 1988.

Lambert, M. D. *Medieval Heresy: Popular Movements from Bogomil to Hus.* London: Edward Arnold Ltd., 1977.

Leff, Gordon. *Heresy in the Later Middle Ages.* 2 vols. Manchester, England: Manchester University Press, 1967.

Lerner, Robert E. *The Heresy of the Free Spirit in the Later Middle Ages.* Berkeley: University of California Press, 1972.

McDonnell, Ernest W. *The Beguines and Beghards in Medieval Culture.* New York: Octagon Books, 1969.

New English Bible. London: Oxford University Press, Cambridge University Press, 1970.

Nigg, Walter. *The Heretics.* New York: Alfred A. Knopf, 1962.

Oulton, John, and Henry Chadwick, eds. *Alexandrian Christianity.* Philadelphia: Westminster Press, 1954.

Pagels, Elaine. *Adam, Eve, and the Serpent.* New York: Random House, 1988.

———. *The Gnostic Gospels.* New York: Random House, 1979.

Partner, Peter. *The Murdered Magicians: The Templars and Their Myth.* London: Oxford University Press, 1981.

Pike, Frederick. "Latin America." *The Oxford Illustrated History of Christianity.* Edited by John McManners. Oxford: Oxford University Press, 1990.

Raschke, Carl A. *The Interruption of Eternity: Modern Gnosticism and the Origins of the New Religious Consciousness.* Chicago: Nelson-Hall, 1980.

Robbins, Rossell Hope. *Encyclopedia of Witchcraft and Demonology.* New York: Crown Publishers, 1959.

Roberts, Alexander, and James Donaldson, eds. *The Writings of Irenaeus.* Edinburgh: T & T Clark, 1868.

Robinson, James M., ed. *The Nag Hammadi Library in English.* San Francisco: HarperCollins, 1990.

Runciman, Steven. *The Medieval Manichee: A Study of Christian Dualist Heresy.* Cambridge: Cambridge University Press, 1947.

Russell, Jeffrey Burton. *Dissent and Reform in the Early Middle Ages.* Berkeley: University of California Press, 1965.

———. *Witchcraft in the Middle Ages.* Ithaca, New York: Cornell University Press, 1972.

Smith, Morton. *Jesus the Magician.* San Francisco: Harper & Row, 1978.

Sumption, Jonathan. *The Albigensian Crusade.* Boston: Faber, 1978.

Thurston, Herbert, S. J. "The Church and Witchcraft." *Satan.* Edited by Bruno de Jesus-Marie, O.C.D. New York: Sheed & Ward, 1951.

Wakefield, Walter L., and Austin P. Evans. *Heresies of the High Middle Ages.* New York: Columbia University Press, 1969.

Weigle, Marta. *Brothers of Light, Brothers of Blood: The Penitentes of the Southwest.* Albuquerque: University of New Mexico Press, 1976.

Yates, Frances. *Giordano Bruno and the Hermetic Tradition.* London: Routledge and Kegan Paul, 1964.

INDEX

Ptolemy, astronomer (died 160)
Emperor Marcus Aurelius (r.161-180)
Mahayana and Hinayana Buddhism develop

Shapur I, king of Persia (r.241-272)
Emperor Diocletian (r.284-305) stops decline of Rome

Emperor Constantine the Great (r.312-337)
St. Jerome (c.347-419)
Roman Empire split into eastern and western realms (395)

Rome sacked by Visigoths (410)
Huns invade Roman Empire (c.430-440)
St. Patrick (died c.461) founds Celtic church in Ireland
Fall of Western Roman Empire (476)
Theodoric founds Ostrogoth kingdom in Italy (c.489)

"Golden Age" of Justinian I (r.527-565)
St. Benedict (died 547) authors Benedictine Rule
Muhammad (c.570-632)

Hegira (622)
Muslims conquer Mecca (630)
Muslims conquer Persia (637)
Muslims conquer Jerusalem (638)
Muslims conquer Egypt (641)
Koran (652)
T'ang dynasty, China (619-907)

Muslims conquer North Africa (711)
Muslims invade Spain (711)
Muslims defeated at Tours, France (732)

Charlemagne (r.768-814) crowned emperor
of Romans by the pope (800)

A.D. 100   **A.D. 200**   **A.D. 300**   **A.D. 400**   **A.D. 500**   **A.D. 600**   **A.D. 700**   A.D. 8

Basilides
Simon Magus

Mani

Epiphanius

Cerdo   Celsus

Carpocrates

• First Council
  of Nicaea

Marcion   Irenaeus

Porphyry

• Nag Hammadi
  books buried

Tertullian   Iamblichus

Augustine
of Hippo

Montanus

Hippolytus   Arius

Pelagius

Ammonius Saccus

Emperor Julian
reigns

Origen

Emperor
Constantine I
reigns

Donatist controversy

Paul of Samosata

Plotinus

Monophysite controversy

Paulician heresy

Hypatia

Manichaeism

Arian controversy

Novatian Cathars

Early Gnosticism

Mithraism

• Sec
  of

Iconoc
contro